The Genesis of Values

The Genesis of Values

Hans Joas

Translated by Gregory Moore

The University of Chicago Press

The University of Chicago Press, Chicago 60637
Polity Press, Cambridge CB2 1UR, United Kingdom

The publication of this work was subsidized by a grant from Inter Nationes,
Bonn.
Printed in Great Britain

09 08 07 06 05 04 03 02 01 00   1 2 3 4 5

ISBN: 0-226-40039-5 (cloth)
ISBN: 0-226-40040-9 (paperback)

A CIP catalogue record for this book is available from the Library of
Congress.

This book is printed on acid-free paper.

For Heidrun

Properly speaking, there is no certitude;
all there is is men who are certain.

Charles Renouvier

Contents

Preface

Without ever really having been planned, this book had its origin in two sorts of questions, which in recent years were put to me time and time again. One type of question arose out of the debates surrounding liberalism and communitarianism, the other from the discussions of the book on the theory of action which I published in 1992 (and which appeared in English translation in 1996).

In the communitarianism debate, it soon becomes clear that every effort to protect or resuscitate endangered value commitments implies resolving the question as to how value commitments arise in the first place. This question has not been adequately answered by contributions made either in moral philosophy or political science or by the social scientific diagnoses of contemporary society. This is to ignore, of course, a fundamental question concerning the transmission and instilling of values. This is all the more regrettable because by resolving this question we could also open up the possibility of mediating between the quarrelling parties of 'liberalism' and 'communitarianism'.

Though setting out from a different starting-point, several of the critical discussions of my book, *The Creativity of Action*, gestured in the same direction. Time and time again, critics raised the question of the normative dimension of my proposed theory of action. This question partly took the form of the insinuation that in this book I had declared the creativity of action itself to be the highest value. For this I was partly praised, partly censured. Both responses, however, rest on the same misunderstanding, which unambiguous assertions made in the book, and, indeed, even its epigraph with its reference to criticism and self-criticism, should have prevented. But mere repudiation of a misunderstanding is not a satisfactory answer to the question. One reviewer was right to point out that a theory of creativity is too narrowly conceived as long as it thematizes the production of new solutions to problems, but not also that of new standards of evaluation. Hence in this connection, too, it turned out that it was impossible to dodge the question as to what my proposed (pragmatism-inspired) revision of our understanding of action means for our conception of norms and values, of how in particular norms and values themselves arise.

The stimulus to working out my thoughts on this issue I owe to an invitation extended to me by Amitai Etzioni. At this point I feel the need to express my gratitude to a group of North American sociologists and philosophers whose work has been, ever since my student days, a model and incentive for me, and some of whom have personally helped me in various ways with encouragement and support. In alphabetical order they are: Robert Bellah, Richard Bernstein, Amitai Etzioni, Donald Levine, Philip Selznick, Charles Taylor and Edward Tiryakian. Without them, my books would be inconceivable.

In addition, my thanks go to those who took the trouble to read the first draft of the manuscript as a whole or in part, and who gave me valuable suggestions for improvements. Of my friends I must mention above all Axel Honneth and Peter Wagner. I thank the following for making important suggestions regarding specific chapters: Christoph Menke for the chapter on Nietzsche; Donald Levine for the chapter on Simmel; Gunnar Schmidt for the chapter on Dewey; and Hartmut Rosa for the chapter on Taylor. Dieter Rucht made astute comments about several sections. Robert Westbrook's exhaustive criticism of an earlier version of the Dewey chapter led to its being completely revised. I am also grateful to my collaborators Jens Beckert, Berit Bretthauer and Wolfgang Knöbl for their excellent suggestions and criticism. My thanks also go to Matthias Schloßberger not only for his help with the notes and the index, but also, above and beyond this, for making important substantial improvements to the text itself. V. Heinrich Yberg helped me to correct the English proofs. I thank Karin Goihl for always completing the extensive typing promptly, and for doing so without ever losing her good humour. I am also grateful to Greg Moore for his translation.

In his usual way, Friedhelm Herborth, my editor at Suhrkamp, the German publishers, supported this book as well; this time he deserves additional thanks, because, with resolution and wise counsel, he prevented me at the right time from weighing down the present theoretical work with an additional empirical part. This will, therefore, reach the public in another form.

My wife Heidrun supported this book even more than my previous ones by providing me with intensive encouragement. I would like to thank her, who embodies so many values for me, by dedicating this book to her.

Acknowledgements

The author and publishers wish to thank Northwestern University Press for permission to reprint from *Formalism in Ethics and Non-Formal Ethics of Values* by Max Scheler translated by Manfred S. Frings and Roger L. Funk (1973).

1

Formulating the Question

This book asks a clear question: how do values and value commitments arise? And it seeks to supply an equally clear answer to this question: values arise in experiences of self-formation and self-transcendence.

However, the precise meaning of this answer, even that of the question, as well as the urgency of this question, are perhaps not immediately obvious. The concepts employed in both question and answer are not clearly defined – neither in philosophy and the social sciences, nor in the wider public debate about values; they are, in fact, extremely difficult to determine and are often essentially contested. It might be asked: what exactly is a value, for instance, and what is the relationship between values and value commitments? Is the concept of 'value' still an acceptable philosophical concept today at all – or is the public debate about values hopelessly old-fashioned, lagging behind more contemporary issues in philosophy? Can the concept of value remain a key concept in the social sciences once we have recognized the difficulties in operationalizing it for empirical research? Or would it be better simply to replace it with other concepts which better correspond to the methods of various branches of research, concepts such as 'attitude', 'practices' or 'culture'? What actually is the relationship between 'values' and 'norms', categories which are frequently used as if they were interchangeable?

If my initial question can hence be shown to rest upon numerous tacit and possibly problematic assumptions – or to be not as urgent as I presume – then my answer must expect an even rougher ride. The concept of the 'self' used in such formulations as 'self-formation' or 'self-transcendence' belongs without a doubt to the vocabulary of the empirical social sciences, ever since it was introduced at the end of the nineteenth century by American thinkers such as William James, Charles Horton Cooley and George Herbert Mead. This conception of the personality and its development also represents for me personally – as this book will make clear – one of the greatest discoveries in the history of the social sciences, and doubtless marks a real theoretical advance. Nevertheless, it cannot, unfortunately, be claimed that this concept is wholly free from controversy either, and that all contemporary schools of thought are aware of its logical implications or empirical consequences. But while it is still true that the process of self-formation is universally accepted as the object of study in social psychology and pedagogy (usually known in sociology as the study of socialization processes), the other term, 'self-transcendence', unquestionably arouses scepticism in secular and rationalist minds. This is because it sounds religious, mystical or even esoteric as soon as it is taken to mean more than mere altruism and the moral willingness, at least occasionally, to sacrifice individual interests in favour of collective or 'higher' goals.

Intellectual states of affairs in which the meaning of key concepts necessary for the expression of cultural self-understanding is either contested or unstable make hermeneutic efforts, in addition to empirical work, unavoidable. Even if it is our goal to arrive at clear-cut explanations, we cannot presume that the concepts we employ will always be understood in the way we intended. We are therefore forced to move to and fro between competing conceptual frameworks, probing and penetrating each of them, making each reciprocally permeable. We shall have to be on the look-out for old answers. At the same time, we must recall the kinds of questions to which these answers were once given, and reflect anew upon old solutions in the light of new problems. The following discussion is, therefore, a deliberate combination of conceptual analysis, of philosophical and sociological textual interpretation, as well as of efforts to describe empirically the cultural predicament of important Western societies.

The question of the genesis of values is a problem which urgently requires clarification, as much within the wider public debate as within specialized academic theory construction. In all Western societies today, serious discussions are now taking place about the shift in, and loss of, values, the opportunities and dangers which such processes present, and the necessity of either reviving old values or searching for new ones. The results of empirical sociological research leave little doubt that so-called 'postmaterialistic' values have gained ground during the last decades in the highly developed Western societies. Accordingly, non-instrumental value orientations, which

declare as desirable goals aesthetic creativity, individual self-realization and the protection of the environment from human despoliation,
have, at least in the younger generations, increasingly replaced traditional attitudes to work and the attainment of material security.
What was analysed above all by Ronald Inglehart and others in his
wake by means of quantitative methods of empirical social research
has also been corroborated by qualitative investigations.[1] One such
original investigation focused on the children of those surveyed in the
1950s as the basis for a classic study of the psychological make-up of
the 'Organization Man', the employee in large organizations.[2] The
results revealed spectacular differences between both generations of
one and the same family. Whilst the fathers devoted themselves
entirely to their careers, restricting all non-instrumental impulses to
their private lives – where, however, life also had to be lived within
the narrow framework of social conformity to the neighbours' expectations – their sons (and daughters) attempt to find a highly individual
lifestyle, where the line between work and leisure is less sharply
drawn. They desire a career which either permits individual, creative
self-realization within the profession itself or within the pattern of life
as a whole.

Of course, these findings do not themselves furnish a complete
explanation for the change in values. Serious objections have been
raised against the too simplistic linkage of economic well-being with
changing values that is assumed in many accounts.[3] It is by no means
always true that, during times of material scarcity, materialistic and
instrumental value orientations have always and everywhere predom-
inated. Nor does the triumph of postmaterialistic values exclude the
possibility of a swift return to materialistic values in periods when
material comfort is threatened. The thesis of the change in values
refers to a phenomenon of aggregation, and it is quite unclear at the
level of the individual whether any one person actually gives precedence to postmaterialistic values or only assumes that his material
needs are sufficiently and securely satisfied. What is certain, however,
is that this shift in values presupposes a background of economic and
legal stability. Without employment, or without the opportunity of
democratic participation, it is certainly more difficult and less usual to
orient oneself to postmaterialistic values.

Not only the causes but also the effects of this change in values
have yet to be fully explained. Depending on the value-standpoint,
the consequences of a postmaterialistic orientation for behaviour in
the labour market or in politics have been variously assessed. A more
unanimous conclusion is usually reached when a loss of values, rather
than a mere change in values, is at issue. Ever since the French

sociologist Émile Durkheim developed his concept of 'anomie' at the end of the nineteenth century, the social sciences have quite rightly distinguished between a change in values on the one hand, and a loss of values or a weakening of their binding force on the other. Whilst a change in values can be variously interpreted – either optimistically or pessimistically – a loss of values can only be perceived as a symptom of crisis. Certainly, those phenomena which both the public and the social sciences usually explain by the thesis of the loss of values are evaluated as thoroughly negative. These phenomena include the decay of family ties, the neglect or vandalizing of public spaces, addiction, and, in particular, apparently unmotivated acts of violence, especially those committed by juveniles, which go far beyond the logic of ends and means. Here, sociological studies also often suggest taking as a starting-point the corrosive effects of societal processes on values. Once again, though, the identification of these processes is usually already controversial in the extreme. Whilst some place negative emphasis on the effects of the market economy and capitalism, others point to the influence of a liberal upbringing and the loss of both role models and the courage to demand discipline.[4]

Thus, sociological diagnoses often have profound consequences for the intensive public discussions. The parched soil of the public thirstily absorbs the analyses proffered by the social sciences on the subject of the change in and loss of values. But when it comes to dealing with the consequences of this change in or loss of values, the public feels that it has been left in the lurch by science. This disappointment is inevitable if the ethos of value-freedom in the sciences means that they can only diagnose, but not treat the symptoms. This abstinence from value in the social sciences, and often in philosophy as well, nevertheless opens up the space – or rather the gap in the market – for superficial syntheses or even a merely strategic handling of the public's unsatisfied needs. Books written by political and social commentators on the subject of 'values', from *Der Ehrliche ist der Dumme* to *Values Matter Most* and *Petit traité des grandes vertus*, have been published with great success in the leading Western societies.[5] For some time now, conservative politicians in particular have also demanded a 'spiritual and moral change of heart' (Helmut Kohl), a return to 'family values' (Dan Quayle) or a 'back to basics' approach (John Major). In political rhetoric at least, 'values' have assumed a fundamental importance – even if it is often only to call into question the moral qualities of political adversaries and underscore the integrity of one's own leadership. Stage-managed and increasingly frequent scandals have replaced issue-based political debates, including the debate about values. This can instil in the electorate a cynicism *vis-à-*

vis the entire 'political class', and frustration with the politicians leads to political frustration as such. During the three decades which have passed since the great social upheavals of the 1960s, it might have seemed as if the political debate about values was ideological ground occupied entirely by conservatives. This was to change radically in the United States under the influence of the so-called communitarianism debate.[6] In it, leading intellectuals argued that a defence or resuscitation of community-based values was necessary in order to halt the march of individualism in all its forms (utilitarian, obsessed with individual rights or centred on the notion of aesthetic self-realization), and that such 'communitarian' values can also be the prerequisite for political goals like the protection and expansion of the welfare state, goals more commonly associated with the 'Left'. Accordingly, though this discussion did not attempt to declare the Left–Right schema in politics obsolete, it circumvented it in a number of policy areas, or dismantled traditional polarizations. The legacy of the 1960s was evaluated ambivalently here: greater democratization had been achieved, but hedonistic-individualistic tendencies had also been strengthened. The influence of this American discussion on the different camps of European politics has varied from country to country. Here and there, in the politics of the British Labour Party, for example, it has had a significant impact.

Although, therefore, an increasing number of people take seriously and support a politics of values, the answer to the question as to how a stronger commitment to (old or new) values is actually supposed to come about, indeed, how value commitment arises at all, is still wholly lacking in the public debate. Wide-ranging agreement has only been reached in a negative respect: that values cannot be produced rationally or disseminated through indoctrination. Ulrich Wickert has said: 'Values can neither be stolen nor transferred nor bought on credit. A purpose in life and obligations to the community cannot be simply prescribed.'[7] Value commitments clearly do not arise from conscious intentions, and yet we experience the feeling of 'I can do no other' which accompanies a strong value commitment not as a restriction, but as the highest expression of our free will.[8] Without wishing to provide a compendium of tried and tested advice for politicians or educators, this book can be understood itself as a contribution to the fundamental resolution of this question: from what experiences does this apparently paradoxical feeling of an ineligible and yet voluntary, commitment to values result?

Three kinds of objections are regularly raised, though, when this question is introduced into a discussion; without being able to do full justice to these objections right at the beginning of my argument, I shall nevertheless briefly outline them in order to bring the question into sharper focus. There are, first of all, viewpoints from which a debate about values and the genesis of value commitments seems superfluous, because human action *per se* and its value orientations are credited with only a minor influence on the course of socio-historic processes. These include radical materialist approaches as well as extreme functionalist theories. The former are, though, if I am not mistaken, rarely endorsed nowadays. In Marxist-influenced circles there is even a great willingness to concede at least a limited autonomy to the cultural forming of human action and institutions. Sociologically, it seems clear to me that the discourse about values must become more intensive the less it is thought that political attitudes or social movements result quasi-automatically from material interests or resources. If we consider, say, ecological movements or waves of religious revival, we see that these certainly do not take place in a space wholly free of interests and independent of resources. But that does not mean, by any stretch of the imagination, that we may attribute a value-oriented character to them only in the sense that movements can develop, after passing through many stages of escalation, a fundamentally alternative value orientation. A radical shift in value orientation can, rather, be *constitutive* of them. Such a constitutive shift in value orientation certainly does not arise by mere coincidence, either. To explain its genesis, or at least its distribution, we can often cite social structural conditions which first prompted the search for a reinterpretation of the principles justifying a prevailing status hierarchy. But the question of the availability of alternative values, of the affinity of certain belief systems for social structural change and of the conditions for 'ideological' innovation, leads back to the irreducible character of the cultural, even in such materialistically influenced diagnoses.[9]

The other variant of an analysis which deliberately ignores or reduces value orientations is the extreme functionalism represented above all by Niklas Luhmann. Though cultural 'codes' and cultural 'subsystems' very much exist according to this viewpoint, they do so only in the sense that functional principles in law, science, art, education, religion, politics or economics are each governed by their own meaning. With a gentle smile, Luhmann shelves the notion still entertained by his predecessors in the functionalist tradition that it was precisely cultural values which offered the opportunity to step back from the functional principles of the individual subsystems and to represent the whole. He maintains that functional differentiation is the principle of societal organization and historical development so resolutely that every argument which claims for it only limited scope appears nostalgic. This is not the place for a thorough rebuttal of this total affirmation of modernity as functional differentiation. Suffice to say that the basic premise, namely, that societal domains are organized systemically and according to a logic of functional differentiation, is not, by any means, advanced with empirical arguments, or even in a manner that takes account of empirical reality; it is, rather, an a priori postulation. Serious objections, however, can be raised against this and the logic of functional argumentation and explanation as a whole.[10]

The second kind of sceptical objections raised against the whole discussion about values originates in a completely different point of view. The suspicion harboured by some liberal and postmodern critics here is that every discourse about values represents an attempt to impose values on others. Yet within the modern, culturally highly diverse, pluralistic and often increasingly multicultural social order in particular, they claim, any attempt to reduce difference by means of a value discourse is not only condemned to failure, but is also dangerous. Any attempt to make a certain value system obligatory would be more likely to provoke counter-movements than achieve its goal without encountering resistance. But if the various milieux and subcultures of a society insist on their particular values, this would lead to a potentially violent 'Balkanization' of domestic political argument. In contrast, the liberals prefer the orientation of all to value-free procedures of peaceful co-operation and communication; and the postmodernists an ethos of respect for difference and all-inclusive tolerance. But the aforementioned debate about communitarianism, as well as the debate about the ethical implications of the 'postmodern',[11] has made it clear that a simple polarization of the advocates and opponents of a value discourse does not do justice to the matter under discussion. The liberals must ask themselves whether the value of the value-free procedures they favour must not at least be consensually shared and internalized as value; and the postmodernists cannot avoid portraying tolerance of and respect for the Other itself as utterly non-relativizable value-contents. This is not to say that, with a wave of the hand, we can dismiss as invalid the doubts expressed by both the liberal and postmodernist camps. All I wish to stress for the time being is that their scepticism does not offer sufficient grounds for ignoring the question we are pursuing here. I shall propose one possible way of bringing together the 'good' and the 'right' which evades these sceptical objections in the concluding chapter of this book.

At this point, however, I want to move on to discuss and actually to repudiate a third objection. This objection seeks to dispute the significance of the values discussion in an age in which there is complete uncertainty about values. Of prime importance for the assumption that we live in such an age is again the postmodernist thesis that the great framing narratives postulated by the philosophy of history have collapsed.[12] Zygmunt Bauman in particular has earnestly undertaken the (possibly paradoxical) attempt to search for an ethics for the age of complete uncertainty.[13] His 'postmodern ethics' is the ethics for just such an age, an age in which awareness of the uncertainty about the foundations of values has become inevitable. His search leads him to Emmanuel Lévinas's philosophy of the Other as the 'unfounded foundation' of moral impulses, and he guides us from society as a 'factory of morality' to the 'presocietal sources of morality'. With all due respect to this attempt, I would like nevertheless to express some reservations as to whether the initial diagnosis is correct and the solution practicable. The thesis of the end of the metanarratives rightly marks the exhaustion of teleological and evolutionistic philosophies of history and their implausibility in the face of twentieth-century reality. But this thesis itself represents a metanarrative which claims to describe an irreversible, epochal turning-point. If we are willing to follow this reflexive turn, then we see that the abandonment of teleological and evolutionistic interpretations of history does not spare us the effort of placing ourselves in an historically reflective relationship to the origin of our ideals and to the fate of their realization. A limited justification for teleological or evolutionistic ways of thinking then becomes perfectly possible. Then, again, we cannot be certain that we have entered an age of complete uncertainty and that there will never again be traces of new certainty. Even Nietzsche's dictum about the 'death of God' must not be taken then as a positive truth.

Nor should we misconstrue Bauman's diagnosis of the end of all certainty as an empirical thesis concerning the spread of doubt about values among the populations of Western societies. Even the most dedicated advocate of the uncertainty thesis will not dispute that many people continue to feel absolutely secure in their particular values and react to their violation with intense outrage. But this has always been – again since Émile Durkheim – the surest sociological indicator of the actual validity of values. From the viewpoint of this unavowed philosophy of history with its claim that we have reached the end of certainty, however, empirically ascertainable value-security makes it look as if the news that there is no longer any certainty simply has yet to reach everyone. Can we really interpret subjective value-certainty today as a sign of ignorance or as the expression of an historically inadequate consciousness? Would this not be an even worse elitism than that represented by those intellectuals who claimed a privileged insight into the logic of history?

There is also another possible way of dealing with the discrepancy between widespread subjective value-certainty and the modern uncertainty about the foundation of values. In one of the most sensational American books of the 1980s to diagnose contemporary society, the authors report their findings from a number of interviews in which they asked people to justify values that they obviously endorsed. The reactions which they encountered often expressed helplessness, and anger at this very helplessness. Thus, one interviewee replied to the attempts to get him to justify why honesty was good and lying bad in the following way: 'I don't know. It just is. It's just so basic. I don't want to be bothered with challenging that. It's part of me. I don't know where it came from, but it's very important.'[14] Robert Bellah's group of authors interprets the inability to justify value-security contained in this answer as indicative of the loss of a common language which makes such justification easier. Evidently, the interviewee could not appeal to the Ten Commandments of the Judaeo-Christian tradition and assume that both he and his interlocutor were agreed on the validity of such divinely revealed commandments. Nor does he have at his disposal a secular vocabulary of rational moral justification (Kant's moral philosophy, for example) to defend the value of honesty. But if there are no shared tacit assumptions underlying a discourse, then every justification claim only leads to deeper disagreement, or makes necessary complicated intellectual constructions which often overtax the individual. In that case, we would establish not a lack of value-certainty, but a lack of communal, self-evident truths.

But perhaps this too would not be quite the right description of the situation. The group of interviewers obviously does not itself doubt the value of honesty; neither would it like to imply that there is no possibility of justifying this value. Perhaps there are today not only a great many separate individuals who are absolutely certain of their values; perhaps the thesis of the end of all certainty also underestimates the extent to which there is consensus on values in our societies. Individual rights to freedom, conceptions of justice, the rejection of physical violence – all can in any case reckon with widespread approval. Though fundamental conflicts of values – about the right to abortion, for example – do exist, these do not represent a loss of all common vocabulary.[15] If this is true, then this collective certainty even contrasts with the picture painted of supposed uncertainty. Then we must not only seek to understand why individuals, but even entire modern societies, find it so difficult to articulate their values and to justify them in this articulation. The inadequacy of their self-description, which for the Bellah group results from the prevalence of individualistic 'languages', is then not to be corrected by ensuring that everyone receives the news of uncertainty, but by revising the way we reflect on the foundations of our experience of value.

Precisely this is the fundamental goal of this book. It does not aim to propagate particular values and to appeal for their reinforcement – although I am quite prepared to admit that certain of my own value orientations and concerns have motivated me to write this book. My intention is, rather, to look out for those action contexts and types of experience in which the subjective feeling that something is a value has its origin. And I am concerned with making available the appropriate theoretical tools to describe these experiences. I take it we are all familiar with the feeling that something evidently and in an emotionally intense way is to be evaluated as good or bad. Though we may often judge something valuable with our intellect, without at the same time experiencing strong feelings, this does not mean that there are not certain values which are deeply rooted in our emotional life. Though we may believe that we should be able to justify our value orientations – and justifying and discussing may themselves be an important value for us – this does not mean that we actually obtained our values through processes of justification and discussion, and that we would discard them should their justification prove difficult. The expositions contained in this book serve to draw us closer to that centre of human experience in which values originate for us.

These expositions are necessary because neither present-day philosophy nor sociology has ready a convincing proposal with which to answer the question we are addressing here. In this respect, things were once much better. I argue that, between the end of the nineteenth century and the 1930s, a whole series of important thinkers was aware of this question; their answers, even if they may often have been one-sided or misleading, are definitely worth recalling. A large part of this book, therefore, consists first of all in just such a searching recollection, beginning with a brief look back at that thinker who first posed the question of the genesis of values in the sense intended here: Friedrich Nietzsche. In doing so, the reason why this question neither needed to be, nor could be, raised before him must be made clear. While appreciating the intellectual audacity which inspired him to take this step, I take issue with the misleading answer he supplied to his own question. Yet, as misleading, indeed downright mistaken, as the answer he expounded chiefly in *On the Genealogy of Morality* is, it left a deep impression on this aspect of subsequent German and European intellectual history.

In contrast, it went almost unnoticed that one of Nietzsche's contemporaries on the other side of the Atlantic was no less radical in his questioning, but at the same time developed a far more fruitful answer. I shall therefore deal with him extensively – with the American pragmatist William James, and above all with his work *The Varieties of Religious Experience*. James distinguished sharply between 'religion' and 'morality'. For him, religion is not a kind of hypermorality, an intensification of self-control; it is based, rather, on experiences of self-surrender. However, he analyses these experiences with exclusive reference to individuals 'in their solitude'. Both the empirical substance and the theoretical means of James's answer will serve as a foil for the subsequent interpretations. Despite its significance in pointing the way forward, his theory is still, I argue, somewhat one-sided from an empirical point of view and also possesses theoretical inadequacies. After James, therefore, I shall analyse writings by Émile Durkheim, Georg Simmel, Max Scheler and John Dewey mainly on the theory of religion. Although these writings, and thus my subsequent interpretations of them, are mostly concerned with religion, my claims are in each case directed at the problem of value commitment in general – and not only at religious value commitments. In his study of archaic religiosity, Durkheim opposed James's individualism with an equally radical collectivism, deriving the genesis of values from the ecstatic states of collectives. But he lacked the conceptual means necessary to appreciate the interpretation of experience and the possibility of a process of identity formation in which the individual disassociates himself from the collective. In his later metaphysical works, Georg Simmel attempted to grasp the self-transcendence of life using the language of *Lebensphilosophie* and with it to explain the genesis of values. Max Scheler combines a highly suggestive phenomenology of value-sensations with the ambitious and problematic attempt to establish a non-formal ethics of value. John Dewey reflects on intersubjective experiences in which the boundaries of one's self open up in relation to others, to oneself, to nature and to God. We can glean from all these thinkers important empirical suggestions for a rich phenomenology of value-experiences, as well as theoretical means for understanding them. I shall conclude that John Dewey, who was, like James, a representative of American pragmatism, has been the most vigorous in pointing the way towards the possibility of theoretical integration, and thus to a consistent answer to the question of the genesis of values – though with him, too, this accomplishment is distorted by a time-bound and probably untenable message:

a sacralization of democracy. Although these attempts at recollection make no claims to exhaustiveness, an answer to the question I have posed does indeed begin to emerge.

In order to bring the question into still sharper focus, I shall move on to discuss the contemporary thinker who has been the most consistent in dealing with the question of the genesis of values: Charles Taylor. I argue, indeed, that this question was suppressed from the 1930s onwards and to a large extent forgotten. The merits and limits of Taylor's work must therefore be outlined before my own answer – that values and value commitments arise in experiences of self-formation and self-transcendence – can be adequately formulated. To this end, moreover, I discuss in a separate chapter, which deals above all with the work of Richard Rorty, the question whether the concept of the self (or ego-identity) is still tenable at all in the face of its postmodern challenge. If I am successful in proving that it is, then the last stage of my argument will show how this thesis about the genesis of values can be integrated with ideas about a universalistic morality that have a completely different underpinning. This proposal, which I develop primarily from pragmatist suggestions, is then finally confronted with the discourse ethics of Jürgen Habermas. From this confrontation there arises the prospect of mediating between liberalism and communitarianism.

The theoretical contribution presented here of course corresponds to various empirical attempts (including my own) to discover which values in which societies are at present rooted in living traditions, and what the chances are of value-oriented movements going beyond an individualism oriented towards utility, rights or self-realization and articulating a contemporary meaning of the ideals of mutuality, solidarity, fraternity and charity. But the present contribution is itself neither a sociological diagnosis of contemporary society, nor part of an historical sociology of values. Its aim is, rather, to clarify a question which, situated on an anthropological level, is mostly overlooked, rather than answered, by empirical research.

Without furnishing either proof or explanation, I have repeatedly maintained that the question of the genesis of values was neglected during the period after the Second World War. If it should be possible to verify this assertion, its explanation seems to me to lie in the dominance of the belief in progress during the age of the 'brief dream of everlasting prosperity' (Burkart Lutz). If history itself is conceived as a largely automatic process of modernization (as in the academic social sciences) or as a law-bound progression towards socialism (as with the Marxists), then values are so deeply embedded in the postulated historical trends that their separability from this history, their perspectivism and the fragility of their realization become completely inconceivable. We can see quite clearly how important postwar schools of thought grew out of highly value-related impulses of the pre-war period, but then endeavoured to emancipate themselves from their value-related origins and to give the impression of their being a constantly advancing, professionalized solution to purely scientific problems.[16] Thus, for example, the investigation of everyday language use in 'ordinary language philosophy' sprang from the profoundly ethical ideas of Ludwig Wittgenstein; or, in sociology and political science, a mechanistic systems theory expressing quasi-behaviourist assumptions about human action issued from Talcott Parsons's critique of utilitarianism. Even so, a social science endorsing a value-free procedure may seem less surprising than a philosophy which has little interest in the realm of values and which endeavours to find a neutral metaposition even when dealing with ethical questions.

I do not wish at this point to provide further proof of philosophy's neglect of the question of the genesis of values; what is lacking here will to some extent be made good in the chapter on Charles Taylor, who represents the most significant exception to this rule. What I shall do here, however, is set forth in more detail the inadequacy of the contributions of rival sociological theories to this issue. In doing so, the non-specialist reader cannot be spared a few difficulties; but this effort may be rewarded in so far as this critical discussion simultaneously pursues the goal of circumscribing the concept of value in its surrounding conceptual field before the properly constructive discussion begins.

For one hundred years, and thus since the birth of the academic discipline of sociology, a permanent gulf has divided those who, mainly influenced by economics, view human action as the pursuit of self-advantage or clear interests, or at the very least stable and largely context-independent preferences, and those who emphasize the irreducible character of the normative dimension of human action. The controversy between 'utilitarians' and 'normativists' runs through the entire theoretical development of this discipline, although that does not mean that there have been no attempts to synthesize the rival directions or to find a third way. It is my thesis that both sides on the front-line between utilitarianism and normativism – at least in their previous and present forms – have the greatest difficulties in analysing the genesis of values (and norms). To consider these difficulties is instructive for understanding the problem we are dealing with here, as well as showing that this book is justified in not starting from either of these two positions, but rather from old and new contributions which rise above this controversy.

For a long time those approaches which I have labelled utilitarian did *not* attempt at all to explain the origin of values and norms. Values were either assumed to be simply self-evident – in the sense, for example, that all action could be conceived as a striving for private and instrumental goods – or they were conceived as completely exogenous, as lying outside the area of interests, so that economic theory and also – if obviously with less justification – sociological and psychological theories could simply abstract from their genesis, or view them as conditioned by nature or varying by chance. Today, this time is clearly past, and the calls urging an examination of the distinctive features and the genesis of values and norms echo everywhere – not only amongst the critics of the utilitarian approaches, but also amongst their champions. But all their attempts suffer, as I shall demonstrate, from the restrictive character of their initial premises. Admittedly, advocates of utilitarianism no longer declare the plurality of values to be illusory as opposed to the harsh reality of the universal orientation to utility or rationality; nor do they declare the question of the genesis of values to be irrelevant. They are forced, however, to explain the genesis of values with a theory whose unifying core consists precisely of certain restrictive assumptions about the role of values in human action. How can a theory which emphasizes the individual (or collective) optimization of utility calculations explain not only the behaviour of persons in accordance with given rules, but also the genesis of such rules, and of values which go beyond mere rules?

As examples let us take two respected and discriminating representatives of the 'utilitarian' approach: James Coleman and his attempt to explain the 'emergence of norms',[17] and Michael Hechter and his survey of explanations of the genesis of values.[18] Coleman first of all cleverly divides the problem into two subproblems. On the one hand, he wants to explain the origin of a demand for norms and, on the other, the satisfaction of this demand by the realization of effective norms. In his account of the need for norms he shows that an 'action that has externalities generates interests in the action among those actors who experience the externalities', and that these externalities frequently 'cannot be overcome by simple transactions that would put control of the action in the hands of those experiencing the externalities'. Many of Coleman's predecessors have been more or less satisfied with inferring the genesis of norms from a situation that requires normative regulation[19] – but this is self-evidently inadmissible, since the demand for regulation is by no means satisfied everywhere it arises, and since norms by no means exist only where a normative demand for regulation prevails in the manner described. Coleman, however, does not succumb to this error.

He goes one step further and turns directly to specifying the conditions under which the need is actually satisfied – namely, when (in his terminology) 'beneficiaries of a norm, acting rationally, either will be able to share appropriately the costs of sanctioning the target actors or will be able to generate second-order sanctions among the set of beneficiaries that are sufficient to induce effective sanctions of the target actors by one or more of the beneficiaries.' In my opinion, we have here an admirably clear demonstration of the fact that norms *can* arise even when we operate with the premise of exclusively rational action. This demonstration represents an advance in so far as this fact was questioned by normativist critics of utilitarianism. What Coleman's argument does not establish, however, is that this is indeed the most plausible explanation of the genesis of norms in general. The proof that a need for normative regulation and its satisfaction can be explained, even with a model of action that initially turns a blind eye to the normative, does not permit us to rule out the possibility that further plausible hypotheses about the genesis of norms, and ones which are more frequently accurate from an empirical point of view, could be constructed using a model of action that takes the normative dimension more fully into account from the very beginning.

There is a further difficulty. Coleman restricts himself to the thematics of the genesis of norms; he does not comment on the genesis of 'values'. This would be unproblematic only if we were able to use both of these terms interchangeably, or if the explanation of the one entailed the other. But this is anything but self-evident, as becomes immediately clear in the terminology used by the other representative of utilitarian thought we shall discuss here.

Michael Hechter addresses the problem of values directly. He defines values as 'relatively general and durable internal criteria for evaluation' and distinguishes them from preferences, which he describes as 'labile rather than durable, and particular rather than general'. He distinguishes norms from values *and* preferences, because they are said to be external – and not internal – to the actor and require sanctioning for their effectiveness. He lists the bewilderingly large number of ways in which values can apparently arise, and includes among these biological conditions, processes of institutionalization and personal experiences. Ultimately, he concludes that all of these factors somehow combine together: 'All told, for any individual, some values are selected biologically . . ., some are the by-product of the physical and institutional environments, and the rest are the by-product of personal history.'[20] Presumably, this explanation does not sound like a particularly convincing theory.

But another point is of greater interest here. When Hechter cites natural selection as one of the sources of value-genesis and explicitly applies the concept of value to animals as well, it becomes immediately clear that he employs this concept in a specific and not unproblematic way. Though values are for him more durable and more general than preferences, they do not reside on an entirely different logical level from them.

At this point, it might be asked why we require two separate terms if the distinction between values and preferences is, so to speak, only a quantitative, rather than a qualitative, one. However, what is important is that this terminology seems to me to conflict with ordinary language use. We are all familiar with the discrepancy between 'values' and 'preferences', not only in the sense of a difference between short-term and long-term goals, but in the deeper sense that we do not experience some of our desires as good or, conversely, that we do not succeed in making something we evaluate as good into a vital desire in our lives. 'Values' evaluate our 'preferences'. In the dimension of values, we take up a position towards ourselves as well. Of course Hechter is right when he ascribes long-term and stable orientations to animals as well as to humans, but do we really want to accept that animals – like humans – have the ability to relate reflectively and evaluatively to their preferences? This would in any case require a more sophisticated argument than the one he offers us. If a fundamental anthropological difference should exist, however, it would then be crucial to separate the question of the genesis of values clearly from that of the genesis of our desires and preferences. At issue would then be the question of how reflective standards according to which we evaluate the evaluations embodied in our desires can actually arise.

A preliminary result of these considerations is, then, that the question of the genesis of values ought to be clearly separated from that of the genesis of norms and that of the genesis of preferences and desires. The contributions of the leading 'utilitarian' theorists, however, overlook these distinctions in one way or another. They are, therefore, irrespective of how persuasive their accounts of the genesis of norms or desires are, unsatisfactory for the question of the genesis of values.

It would not conform to this book's methodology if at this point I were to determine my own alternative definitions in advance. Problems are not going to be solved by acts of definition at this stage of the argument; the determination of the concepts does not lie at the beginning, but rather at the end, of the path of reflection which lies before us. All I want to do here is draw attention to some points where distinctions could be important.

Perhaps, however, these problems resolve themselves if we turn to the 'normativist' alternative to utilitarianism. Indisputably, its most important representative in the sociology of the last few decades was Talcott Parsons. In his work – in his critique of utilitarianism, as well as in his constructive work – the concept of 'value' was always one of the key categories, perhaps even the central category itself. I do not want to furnish detailed proof of this here.[21] Parsons and his school certainly had a clear notion that values do not express desires, but instead imply what is worth desiring – and this difference they describe as a customary view in the history of ideas. 'A value is not just a preference but is a preference which is felt and/or considered to be justified.'[22] Parsons also clearly distinguishes values and norms. Whereas Hechter describes norms as something external to the actor, Parsons, under the influence of Émile Durkheim, Sigmund Freud and George Herbert Mead, is especially interested in their internalization – in the processes through which initially external expectations of conduct become components of a person's inner life. For this reason, Parsons could never define the distinction between norms and values as one between external and internal points of orientation. Norms are for him specifications of general cultural values in response to particular action situations. The action orientations of concrete actors result from internalized values.

Although values, norms and desires are thereby distinguished from one another with acceptable clarity, this now gives rise to the impression that the three levels are related to one another like the levels of a hierarchy. According to this theory, the general cultural value system forms the moral and legal norms through processes of institutionalization; through processes of internalization, it also forms the structures of persons by shaping vague and plastic biological dispositions into object-oriented drive structures. Although a possible failure of these processes is certainly taken into account, tensions between the levels appear to be ruled out in principle. A whole lot of Parsons's critics from various camps have focused on this point. Thus, within the Parsons school it soon became obvious that the theory – despite all the emphasis which it places on the role of values in human action – actually contributes nothing to the question of how values are actually 'applied' in concrete action situations. The question arose as to whether actors are really only the puppets of cultural values[23] – or whether, in the dynamics of everyday situations, it is not rather the case that vague values must always first be translated by individual effort into concrete orientations, balanced with other considerations and possibly revised on the basis of the consequences of actions. A further objection stems from the influence cultural anthropologists and historians have had on sociology.[24] To be sure, Parsons does not in his work ascertain 'values' through deep hermeneutic penetration into cultures, nor does he represent them in terms of a 'thick description' of their nature (Clifford Geertz); they are analytic constructs abstracted from a culture as a whole and then designated as responsible for concrete actions. This objection not only argues that it is necessary to work with better empirical methods than those employed by Parsons if we are to discover the values which really orient action, thereby dispelling the scepticism resulting from the difficulties in making the central theoretical concept of 'value' productive in empirical work. The objection also denies, from a theoretical point of view, that values have a separate mode of existence, completely detached from the other ways in which we relate to the world, like our cognitive relation to objects or our self-reflection. The concept of 'value' itself is said to encourage a thinning out of the symbolic patterns and their detachment from the practices in which they become operative.[25] A third objection, finally, might state that Parsons simply never addressed the problem of the genesis of values.[26] Admittedly, he speaks from the perspective of universal history of the fundamental innovations in values during, say, the Reformation; likewise, generalization belongs to the most important dimensions of the social change he assumes to take place in modernity. But value generalization is of course not innovation, and those innovations which Parsons analyses are in his theory stages in an evolutionistic, historical process which admits no openness in principle.

For this reason, even this brief journey around the normativist position raises more questions than it provides answers. Self-critical representatives of this school endeavour to eliminate the recognized shortcomings, as do empirical cultural sociologists. But hitherto this has no more given rise to an actual synthesis than those writings which cannot be described either as utilitarian or normativist.[27] Without actually having proved this here, the foregoing arguments may nevertheless have made plausible the idea that the answer to the question of the genesis of values is bound up with a revision in our understanding of human action. It is my conviction that only an appreciation of the creativity of human action can explain the genesis of values over and against the restricted utilitarian and normativist understanding of action. The distinction between values, norms and desires; the clarification of their respective role in the dynamics of human action; the elucidation of the relationship of our evaluative orientation to the world to other ways in which we understand the world and ourselves – these are tasks which lie before us on this path. The following discussions attempt to take a few steps down this path. The first step involves turning back to that point in the history of ideas when the question of genesis of values was first posed in all its radicalness.

2

The Genesis of Values as Genealogy of Morality?

(Friedrich Nietzsche)

The question of the genesis of values was first raised towards the end of the nineteenth century. Even the use of the concept 'value' outside economic (and certain mathematical) contexts first became current around this time. The concept's modern meaning in the public discussion does not, then, derive from colloquial language; rather, this international usage has its origin in nineteenth-century German philosophy. Understanding this fact can help us to recognize the tacit historical presuppositions involved in this question.

The existing studies on the history of the concept of 'value'[1] agree in locating its genesis first in the economic life and then in the science of economics of the eighteenth century, and trace its subsequent development in nineteenth-century philosophy through to the cultural and social sciences and the public usage of the twentieth century. A key figure in this development is the philosopher Hermann Lotze, from the fabric of whose work and teachings the various threads of the value theories of neo-Kantianism, phenomenology and *Lebensphilosophie* are derived. Even more than Lotze, Friedrich Nietzsche's dramatic use of the concept of value had a decisive influence on *Lebensphilosophie* and especially on the public discussion. A reference point behind all these debates is Kant's philosophy. Kant had himself already occasionally spoken,[2] in the context of the critique of contemporary utilitarianism, of the 'absolute value' of rational beings, of their status as ends in themselves, which eluded a valuation according to their usefulness for achieving ends. But the terminology of the philosophy of value did not issue from Kant's language, which was, rather, rediscovered in retrospect, after the new usage had evolved. It evolved because basic assumptions underlying post-Kantian German philosophy had lost credibility during the nineteenth century and, at the same time, boundaries which Kant had drawn no longer commanded respect. 'The realm of values is formulated in opposition to Kant, who denied the moral world all empirical character and derealized the phenomenal world; and in opposition to Hegel, who subjected the moral world to the dictates of the logic of the historical process.'[3] In a culture as strongly imbued with historical consciousness and marked by the development of the historical humanities and political science as was German university life in the nineteenth century, Kant's pure postulate of moral freedom could no longer be felt to be satisfactory. Conversely, Hegel's speculative philosophy of history and especially that of classical positivism did not carry much conviction in such a culture either, since the meticulous examination of historical and cultural diversity, as well as the prevailing mood of the time, no longer permitted a resolute faith in the meaningfulness or progressiveness of history. The philosophy of value has its genesis at precisely that point where faith is lost in the historicizing variants of a way of thinking that asserts the identity of the true and the good.

The genesis of the concept of value is certainly no innocuous conceptual innovation; this has been clearly recognized above all by those who cling to the belief that it is still possible to defend the metaphysical unity of the true and the good.[4] The concept of 'value' takes the place once occupied by the concept of the 'good' in the philosophical tradition. However, whereas the 'good' could, according to this tradition, be accorded a status ascertainable either by rational contemplation of the cosmos or through divine revelation, and thus had a 'being' – even a higher being than other existents – there is attached to the concept of 'value' an ineradicable reference to the valuing subject. The metaphysical unity of the true and the good is replaced in the philosophy of value by a dualism between 'facticity' and 'validity', between a realm of verifiable facts and, opposed to this, another, peculiar mode of being, in which values and valuations are given. The philosophy of value does not fix this dualism, but is instead concerned, in its various forms, to bridge it. It is for this reason that the path from the merely subjective value-sensations to value judgements claiming an objective validity is for it so significant, as is the relation between value-sensations and value judgements on the one hand to factual claims on the other. To retreat behind valuation's reference to subjectivity, however, strikes all representatives of the philosophy of value as a relapse into bad old metaphysics, or what is for science an unacceptable mixture of science and 'academic prophecy' (Max Weber).

For as long as the good was construed as the highest being, the question of its genesis could only have seemed perfectly meaningless. It was quite possible to question the genesis of every individual existent, but not that of the being towards which all others strive and which is the object of human knowledge. For this reason, the question of the genesis of values presupposes the *shift towards subjectivity* in the philosophy of value. But this is only a necessary, not a sufficient, condition for the emergence of the question. Indeed, on its own it could just as easily lead to a reformulation of the postulate of objective value. Although values could no longer be conceived as existing independently of the subject, one could now try to find in the subjectivity of valuation the conditions for its universal validity. This was the path trodden by neo-Kantian philosophies of value in particular, the way having been paved by Kant himself. Central to a way of thinking such as this was the issue of the ontological status of the validity of values, and that of the relationship between their objective validity and the subjective value-cognition or value commitment. The gulf between it and pre-critical, that is to say, pre-Kantian, metaphysics was just as great as the distance separating it and a teleological or evolutionistic philosophy of history. But this did not lead to a second, more radical step: the recognition of the *historical contingency of values* themselves. On the contrary, it could be claimed, rather, that the whole enterprise of the philosophy of value was aimed at averting this menacing insight and confronting the concomitant cultural dangers with the tools of academic philosophy. Neo-Kantian philosophers of value like Wilhelm Windelband and Heinrich Rickert were filled with a sense of mission, believing that the only thing that could prevent the fall into bottomless value relativism was their project of a philosophy of value and their conception of philosophy in general as a theory of valuation. For them, too, the ideal realm of valid values could not *originate* in human action or experience; rather, this realm belonged to another mode of being and, for this reason, subjects could only embody and discover values, not produce them. It is not, therefore, this variant of the philosophy of value, but rather only those ways of thinking that are prepared to contemplate the subjectivity *and* contingency of valuation, which are of interest for our question of the genesis of values. Only in such thought is the question of the genesis of values not restricted to the participation of contingent subjects in a realm of ideal validity, but also extended to encompass the genesis of this ideal validity out of contingent subjectivity.

Friedrich Nietzsche was the first to take this step. He was also fully aware, perhaps excessively so, of the novelty and daring of his undertaking. He delivered what he had to say with the grand gestures of one who has wandered through a 'vast and dangerous land',[5] and who knows that only the courage of a few can be measured against his, whilst the narrow-minded and unfree spirits will turn a deaf ear to his teaching. The 'problem of the origin of evil'[6] exercised Nietzsche from earliest childhood, as he himself tells us, and this problem gradually matured during the course of his intellectual development, in particular through his historical and philological training, into the question: 'under what conditions did man invent the value judgments good and evil? *and what value do they themselves have?*'[7] He seems to accept as his only precursors in this question the British utilitarian and evolutionist psychologists who, like their German imitators, endeavoured to construct a history of the origins of morality. But the way in which he proceeds makes it readily apparent that his answer has nothing to do with the one which they arrive at, and that he is only using them – as he later confesses[8] – to mislead the reader and to give the impression that he is undertaking a sober scientific work. By no means, though, does Nietzsche want merely – if at all – to furnish a scientific explanation of the genesis of values. Instead, he intends to use this question of genesis to clear the way for us to call into question those values themselves. Repelled by the morality of pity, the 'Euro-Buddhism'[9] of his early philosophical role model, Schopenhauer, he sees himself driven to the question of 'the value of pity and of the morality of pity', and thence to the programme of a 'critique of moral values'.[10] This critique certainly does not shy away from questioning the value of the prevailing Judaeo-Christian moral tradition – on the contrary, Nietzsche is attracted by the prospect that 'good' is not more beneficial to man than 'evil', so 'that morality itself were to blame if man, as species, never reached his highest potential power and splendour? So that morality itself was the danger of dangers?'[11] Nietzsche himself was profoundly aware of the unsettling nature of his questioning, as palpable today as it was then. But frequently it was the liberating effect of his ruthlessness and the prospect of freedom from intolerable moral pressure that weighed more heavily for him and his readers.

To be sure, I cannot do justice in what follows to Nietzsche's work as a whole – contradictory, ambiguous and controversial as it is. In our context, it must suffice to focus on the work in which he developed his solution to the problem of the genesis of values most succinctly: the 'polemic' from the year 1887, *On the Genealogy of Morality*, and especially the first essay of that volume. I shall not, therefore, trace the gradual development of this aspect of Nietzsche's thought until it found its provisional expression in the aphorisms of *Human, All Too Human* and in sections of *Beyond Good and Evil*; nor do I consider how Nietzsche, after the *Genealogy*, extended his supposed insight ever further, transferring it from moral values to embrace all values. The only thing we should not lose sight of is that he intensified his critique of values to propose a 'revaluation of all values', as proclaims the final sentence of *The Antichrist*, that work which curses Christianity and borders on madness.[12]

The British positivist-utilitarian moral psychology constitutes, as I have said, the point of departure for Nietzsche's thought. For this reason, he begins with arguments intended to refute Herbert Spencer's equation of the good with the useful and, with even more vehemence, his claim that non-egoistic actions were originally designated as good by those for whom they were useful, before the causal link between utility and goodness was then forgotten through habit – so that ultimately the good was no longer experienced as 'good' because it was useful, but instead as good in itself. Nietzsche has nothing but scorn and contempt for the psychological implausibility and historical naïveté of this account. Yet he initially develops his own account by simply turning the very claim he is attacking on its head: the origin of the predicate 'good' lies not in the identification of something as useful by other people, but in the self-affirmation of a superior caste.

> Instead it has been 'the good' themselves, meaning the noble, the mighty, the high-placed and the high-minded, who saw and judged themselves and their actions as good, I mean first-rate, in contrast to everything lowly, low-minded, common and plebeian. It was from this *pathos of distance* that they first claimed the right to create values and give these value names: usefulness was none of their concern![13]

It has been so difficult to gain this simple insight and for it to meet with acceptance, Nietzsche says, because it presupposes that one restrains the obstructing influence 'which the democratic bias within the modern world exercises over all questions of descent'.[14] Nietzsche only comes to the real crux of his thesis, however, when he again turns his attention from the superior individuals to the inferior members of the herd. The latter, he argues, cannot affirm themselves as the naturally weaker in the face of those who are stronger; instead, they project feelings of hatred and vengefulness onto the noble caste, feelings which, however, they cannot actually act upon, precisely because of their inferiority, and therefore take refuge in imaginary revenge. These revenge fantasies harden into *ressentiment* – into jealousy of the superior individuals' qualities and suspicion of everything that makes their superiority manifest. Such *ressentiment* would remain poisonous, yet ultimately impotent, if there had not appeared those who sought to articulate and systematize *ressentiment* in terms of a value system according to which precisely everything that is noble and strong is devalued and, conversely, everything that is impotent and weak is valued more highly. As the carriers of such a devaluation of chivalric-aristocratic values, Nietzsche identifies first of all the priestly castes of ancient civilizations, in which, at the very least, the value 'purity' is held to be inimical to that of 'strength'. The priestly way of life, which Nietzsche ambivalently describes as 'essentially dangerous'[15] – because it undermines the integrity of noble self-affirmation and opens the door to all kinds of morbidity, but also to the cure for these morbidities – thereby becomes the precondition for the genesis of ideals born out of *ressentiment*. The whole of the third essay of *On the Genealogy of Morality* is consequently devoted to the genesis of ascetic ideals from the priestly way of life. Even more fateful than the priestly castes is, Nietzsche maintains, a people which at the same time best exemplifies the historical consequences of *ressentiment* born out of impotence: 'the Jews, that priestly people, which in the last resort was able to gain satisfaction from its enemies and conquerors only through a radical revaluation of their values, that is, through an act of the most deliberate revenge'.[16] With the Jews begins the 'slaves' revolt in morality' – as the famous formula has it, which Nietzsche had already coined in *Beyond Good and Evil*. Jesus Christ's gospel of love is understood by Nietzsche as the quintessence of Judaic values and ideals; his crucifixion is for him the bait that lured the enemies of Israel, and through which they then fell victim to the slaves' revolt. Once this devaluation of the noble ideals has become established, the innocent self-enjoyment of the strong is at an end; they are then seized by bad conscience and guilt – and the masters succumb to the contagion passed on by the slaves. Judaea has triumphed over Rome, and the subsequent history of the West has confirmed this victory again and again, further reinforcing the domination of the ideals born out of *ressentiment*. The flame of the 'noble method of valuing' briefly flared up once more during the Renaissance, but was again soon extinguished 'thanks to that basically proletarian (German and English) *ressentiment*-movement which people call the Reformation'.[17] The French Revolution in particular represents for Nietzsche one of these victories of 'Judaea' – and the later democratic and socialist movements of the nineteenth century are anathema to him and harbingers of an age of cultural mediocrity and de-individualization.

Despite the cult which began to surround Nietzsche's personality and work at the end of the nineteenth century, criticism of this adventurous construction left very little of it intact. Ferdinand Tönnies, one of the classic figures of the nascent German sociology, reproached

Nietzsche as early as 1897 for the 'most profound ignorance of the social sciences'.[18] On the one hand, Max Scheler takes Nietzsche's psychology of *ressentiment* very seriously and refines it further. He calls Nietzsche's theory of *ressentiment* as the source of moral feelings 'the most profound' among 'the scanty discoveries which have been made in recent times about the origin of moral judgments . . . This remains true even if his specific characterization of Christian love as the most delicate "flower of *ressentiment*" should turn out to be mistaken.'[19] On the other hand, however, Scheler's study *Ressentiment* (*Das Ressentiment im Aufbau der Moralen*) aims to show Nietzsche's thesis to be false, thereby refuting his devaluation of the Judaeo-Christian tradition. Scheler's argument turns on his contrast of the Christian idea of love with ancient Greek thought. The former is characterized by what he calls the 'reversal in the movement of love'.

> The Christian view boldly denies the Greek axiom that love is an aspiration of the lower towards the higher. On the contrary, now the criterion is that the nobler stoops to the vulgar, the healthy to the sick, the rich to the poor, the handsome to the ugly, the good and saintly to the bad and common, the Messiah to the sinners and publicans. The Christian is not afraid, like the ancient, that he might lose something by doing so, that he might impair his own nobility. He acts in the peculiarly pious conviction that through this 'condescension', through this self-abasement and 'self-renunciation', he gains the highest good and becomes equal to God.[20]

This idea of love is constitutive of Christianity and from it issues a concept of God at odds with that of classical antiquity. God becomes a loving God; there is no longer any conception of the good that might take precedence over divine love. This means that for human action there are 'no longer any rational principles, any rules or justice, higher than love, independent of it and preceding it, which should guide its action and its distribution among men according to their value'.[21] Nietzsche, however, Scheler claims, did not grasp at all this essence of the Christian idea of love.[22]

Scheler not only disputes the connection between *ressentiment* and the Christian morality of love from the standpoint of the history of ideas; he also employs a psychological argument. To this end he distinguishes two ways in which the strong might bow to the weak. On the one hand, this approach can be grounded in a primary self-hatred and, because it constitutes a kind of self-flight, represents more a turning away from oneself than a turning towards the Other. If this is the case, Nietzsche's claim that the superior caste was infected by the *ressentiment* of the weak would presumably be correct. On the other hand, though, this care for the needs of the many might also result from an abundance of the capacity for love. Seen in this way, the truly powerful person is someone whose love knows no bounds – and the egoist is a person in whom the creative life-forces are inhibited and restricted to self-preservation and self-assertion at the expense of others. Love in all its forms, from simple charity right up to self-effacement, is then, as the Christian ethic suggests, an expression of strong character and not impotent *ressentiment*. Scheler denies that Jesus Christ's promise of salvation to the weak, the sick and the disenfranchised represents a simple reversal of values, as the *ressentiment* thesis would have it. Rather, Jesus created through the idea of love a reference point of value which lies beyond the prevailing classifications and implies their ultimate nullity.

> The world had become accustomed to considering the social hierarchy, based on status, wealth, vital strength, and power, as an exact image of the ultimate values of morality and personality. The only way to disclose the discovery of a new and higher *sphere* of being and life, of the 'kingdom of God' whose order is independent of that worldly and vital hierarchy, was to stress the vanity of the old values in this higher order.[23]

Thus, the Christian idea of love does not originate in a simple inversion of a pseudo-natural ethics of nobility; nor can overflowing love be a consequence of the affective charge of *ressentiment*.

Despite the radicality of this repudiation, Scheler is nevertheless willing to concede to Nietzsche that there have been cases in history where Christian ethics have been distorted and that the idea of love is psychologically susceptible to serving as a convenient camouflage for *ressentiment*-guided falsifications of the basic conviction of love. If one frees the Christian idea of love from these misleading forms, however, then the gulf between it and a plebeian social movement born of *ressentiment* becomes obvious. Nietzsche, like a good many advocates of the democratic and socialist ideas he loathed, made the mistake of projecting backwards into history and failed to appreciate the truly religious core of Christianity.

As comprehensively as Scheler refutes the psychological and historical aspects of Nietzsche's account, he nevertheless touches only briefly on its sociological dimension. Here Max Weber is the decisive voice in the critique and qualification of Nietzsche's thesis. A long passage from the introduction to his comparative studies on the 'economic ethics of world religions' is more or less explicitly dedicated to this task; it may also have informed his discussion of important issues in the studies themselves.[24] Weber describes Nietzsche's thesis as one of the attempts to interpret the connection between religious ethics and the world reductively; that is to say, in such a way that ethics is traced back to the level of interests that actually determines it. In this regard, Nietzsche's 'brilliant essay' is for him a counterpart of the historico-materialist critique of religion. Just as he rejects the latter, so he also advises caution when reading Nietzsche.

> As is known, this theory regards the moral glorification of mercy and brotherliness as a 'slave revolt in morals' among those who are disadvantaged, either in their natural endowments or in their opportunities as determined by life-fate. The ethic of 'duty' is thus considered a product of 'repressed' sentiments for vengeance on the part of banausic men who 'displace' their sentiments because they are powerless, and condemned to work and to money-making. They resent the way of life of the lordly stratum who live free of duties. A very simple solution of the most important problems in the typology of religious ethics would obviously result if this were the case.[25]

But the social and economic ethics of the world religions cannot be reduced to a common denominator as easily as Nietzsche suggests. In Weber's hands, Nietzsche's sweeping, but ingenious, generalization is transformed into a programme of empirical historico-sociological research, the objective of which is to investigate the role interests and *ressentiment* play in the genesis and transformation of religious ethics.[26] The results of this colossal research, which Weber carried out by himself, are to a large extent negative with respect to Nietzsche's thesis. He rejects out of hand the Nietzsche-inspired account of that other great world religion besides the Judaeo-Christian tradition which prizes the values of compassion, namely Buddhism. The Hindu doctrine of reincarnation had already made the correlation between individual pain and individual guilt, and Buddhism clearly emerged from privileged circles and could not be further removed from a teaching born of resentment.[27] To explain the religiously induced ethical 'rationalization' of life conduct, a dimension so fundamental to his theory, Weber cites completely different causes which have 'nothing whatsoever to do with resentment'.[28] Only where the development of the valuation of suffering in religious ethics is concerned is he prepared to concede to Nietzsche's thesis a limited validity. But here too it seems to me that Weber's point of departure is from the very outset a different one from Nietzsche's. Whereas Nietzsche assumes the self-enjoyment of the strong to be primordial and unproblematic, and attributes all justification of it to the pressure exerted by the weak, Weber assumes a deep-seated psychological ('pharisaical') human need to interpret and to justify the fact of this happiness as well. 'The fortunate is seldom satisfied with the fact of being fortunate. Beyond this, he needs to know that he has a *right* to his good fortune. He wants to be convinced that he "deserves" it . . . Good fortune thus wants to be "legitimate" fortune.'[29] According to Weber, then, religions have from the very beginning furnished a 'theodicy of good fortune'. This train of thought might at first sight seem similar to Nietzsche's, but in my view it differs in one essential respect. For Nietzsche, values lie, before their reversal through *ressentiment*, to a certain extent outside the sphere of the requirements of justification. They are the unbroken expression of the self-confidence of the superior individuals, a feeling that collapses under the weight of *ressentiment*, which compels the justification of values. He sees the 'aristocratic' values not as the expression of an attempt at self-justification, but as self-expression before the compulsion to justify arose. Weber, in contrast, assumes from the start that all experiences must be interpreted and that even the self-experience of strength can never occur without an awareness of the inequality in the distribution of earthly goods. Regardless of whether Weber himself was at all conscious of his disagreement with Nietzsche at this point, the shift from the primordiality of aristocratic values to a theodicy of good fortune seems here more plausible from a psychological and historical point of view.

Yet it is not here that the truly Nietzschean theme lies, but rather where these values of good fortune – however they may be proclaimed – metamorphose into a religious transfiguration of suffering. But here, too, Weber proceeds in a manner at odds with Nietzsche. For the latter, it was solely the experience of a less plentiful endowment of earthly goods which set in motion the dynamics of *ressentiment*-laden value-formation. For Weber, on the other hand, the interpretation of suffering was from the outset embedded in the entirely different notion 'that certain kinds of suffering and abnormal states provoked through chastisement are avenues to the attainment of superhuman, that is magical, powers'. Thus, Weber admits what Nietzsche rules out: that suffering and privation might represent a positive force not through a *ressentiment*-laden reversal of their evaluation, but rather through their inspiring of 'ecstatic, visionary, hysterical . . . states'.[30] Avoidance of the taboo and abstinence from the unclean are also for Weber already indissolubly linked with the archaic belief in demons, and function along the same lines. A pivotal new stage in religious development was reached when cults of redemption, which emerged from magical rituals existing alongside the primeval community cults, promised the overcoming of individual suffering and, to this end, undertook to determine who or what was to blame for this suffering. But whom has individual suffering never befallen? Even Nietzsche's strong and superior individuals may perhaps fall sick – at least they will certainly grow old or lose a loved one. The need for redemption, according to Weber, drew many to these cults of redemption, which in turn became themselves the breeding-ground for redeemer myths, a popular belief in a saviour, a figure bringing salvation. As a rule, this saviour bore 'an individual and universal character at the same time', guaranteeing 'salvation for the individual and to every individual who would turn to him'.[31] What is special about the Jewish people for Weber is that 'with this people, and in this clear-cut fashion only among them and under other very particular conditions, the suffering of a people's community, rather than the suffering of an individual, became the object of hope for religious salvation.'[32] Weber investigates the precise character of these conditions in his study on ancient Judaism.[33] He is not only free of the enmity towards Jews which Nietzsche exhibits;[34] he also delivers a substantive alternative explanation of the outstanding role that Jewish religious history has played in the development of the 'theodicy of suffering'.

It is when Weber goes on to develop the notion that a prophetically heralded saviour-religiosity was everywhere able to attract followers, above all from among the lower social strata, and that in such a religiosity the explanation of suffering was increasingly predicated on violations of the codes of conduct promulgated by the prophets, that he comes closest to Nietzsche's thesis – even though his starting-point is a different one. The 'theodicy of suffering' does indeed frequently involve a positive evaluation of suffering; it is indeed repeatedly coloured by a *ressentiment*-laden devaluation of happiness. But here too it soon becomes apparent how much Weber qualifies Nietzsche's thesis. Even Nietzsche's assumption that the distribution of goods was entirely unproblematic for the 'masters' is in his view implausible. For them too, and according to their own criteria, the question arises as to whether the best are always the most successful and whether every failure is deserved. Weber sees great systems of thought like the doctrine of predestination or the transmigration of souls as rooted in a metaphysical need for the interpretation of meaning, and considers the question of justice to be an unavoidable dimension of our position in the world, by no means exclusively fuelled by a desire for vengeance or raised by socially oppressed classes. Though the idea of a compensation for earthly woes, as well as the ideal of justice, can for this reason bear traces of *ressentiment*, they in fact develop from separate roots. Weber does not really analyse these roots of experience and the dynamics of their interpretation, but instead investigates above all the transformation manifested by those ethics and religious conceptions of the world which developed from such roots, a transformation influenced by interests and institutional constraints. He leaves no doubt, though, that he does not reduce ideas to interests as he believes Nietzsche's *Genealogy of Morality* to have done.

For Nietzsche's *Genealogy* does indeed share with the rationalist (and historico-materialist) critique of religion the idea that the analysis of religion frees us from faith by laying bare a more fundamental process and permitting us a glimpse into the workshop and the procedures governing 'how *ideals are fabricated* on this earth'.[35] But unlike Feuerbach and Marx, Nietzsche even appears to revert to the eighteenth-century Enlightenment critique of religion when he describes the process of the genesis of ideals in intentionalist images which emphasize the deliberate nature of the deception. Malice and falsehood, counterfeiting and necromancy – these are the attributes which he finds appropriate, and not only as part of a stylistic strategy of exaggeration, but as actually descriptive of the process itself. Even for the genesis of chivalric-aristocratic ideals from the self-love of the strong and superior individuals, he had thought it plausible 'to conceive of the origin of language itself as a manifestation of the power of the rulers'.[36] Although this might be a salutary reminder of the dimension of power inherent in our systems of classification, it is grossly overstated. The conceit that language emanates from one-sided acts of designation and that sociality is constituted through mastery also falls back on eighteenth-century conceptions prevalent before Herder's epochal critique of them.[37] Although only a few critical voices have been heard here, the arguments they have articulated have surely been sufficient to undermine the persuasiveness of Nietzsche's thesis as an account of value-genesis.

But what are the moral consequences of Nietzsche's critique of morality? Its reception shows to good effect all the ambiguity of his argument. Does he condemn all morality as inimical to life and life-denying – or does he envisage a higher morality in the synthesis of morality with the 'motivating forces of life'? Does he derive all values from *ressentiment* – or does he hold out the prospect of a sovereign self-positing of values, and thereby admit a second possibility for their genesis? If one surveys his work as a whole without dwelling on individual statements, which are often distorted by an unrelenting hatred of all that is Christian, then there can be no doubt that his critique of morality is motivated by a strong ethical impulse. Accordingly, many expositors have attempted a more sympathetic interpretation of Nietzsche, aiming to resolve the paradox of a moral message promulgated by the most radical of all critics of morality.[38] Nietzsche's plea for a Dionysian affirmation of the world can then be reformulated as an exhortation to become more willing to admit freely to one's own desires, regardless of their moral value. This willingness makes the person more spontaneous, more decisive, more able to experience pleasure. The concern for others, for the evaluation of one's own actions and their consequences, diminishes. A person can thus become more diversified within himself, experiencing morality as one aspect of himself amongst others, and not as his totality. This curbs the compulsion towards hypocrisy and dissimulation. Read in this way, Nietzsche's critique of morality does not abolish morality; rather, it dramatically alters the way it is anchored in the person. He thus rejects every merely conventional morality, but also rejects a universalistic morality which, at the cost of forgetting one's own desires and inclinations, reigns supreme over a person's inner life. One might even say – and Nietzsche himself does so repeatedly – that it is the critique of morality, even the denial of God (as he understands it), through which the individual achieves redemption and is set free to embrace an authentic morality. It transforms morality into 'the *virtue of singular self-legislation*, the *ethics of sovereign uniqueness*'.[39] According to this interpretation, when Nietzsche speaks of aristocratic values he has in mind not high-handedness and hedonism, but rather the dignity and nobility of the individual. The critique of *ressentiment* is thus at the same time a plea for the release of the individual to himself.

In contrast, a less sympathetic interpretation elaborates the idea that Nietzsche's undoubted ethical impulse is thwarted from the outset by a viewpoint according to which domination on the basis of natural differences appears absolutely necessary. The majority of men can only achieve dignity by supporting great individuals in the process of their development. If valuation, even linguistic designation, is nothing other than the positing of superior individuals, then this immediately raises the question as to who then succeeds in asserting his valuations over and against other valuations. What might still retain the semblance of the playful in the solitary, creative individual immediately takes on in Nietzsche the appearance of arbitrariness – which can escalate to brutality – as soon as he considers the relationship between individuals. It was even Nietzsche himself who had proclaimed the imperative of obedience to contingent authorities and held out for all, save for those exceptional individuals who are either capable of the sovereign positing of values or of voluntarily submitting themselves to the evaluators, the prospect of the need for great wars and social upheaval as the remedy for nihilism. The German ideologists of war during the First World War were able to appropriate motifs from Nietzsche's work just as easily as were fascist thinkers in their attempts consciously to produce new myths.[40] In Germany in particular, metaphysical needs were, under Nietzsche's influence, charged again and again with antidemocratic affects.[41] Democracy and prosperity for all could be felt to be 'nihilism in practice' (Gottfried Benn), in contrast to which war or the National Socialist movement meant the positing of new ethical realities. This is not to make Nietzsche responsible for political and intellectual developments which took place long after his death, even if one sees this thread of his reception history as rooted in his critique of morality. Just as evident as the negative impact of his critique is the aporetic character of his attempts to capture the overcoming of morality in an image somewhere between the 'innocent amorality' of children and the 'superhuman' self-denial of moral impulses by the amorally acting Caesar. The only thing that unites these, however, is their distance from the ideal image of the moral individual which had provoked Nietzsche's fury. His fury at this ideal image is so great that it seems that any alternative is more attractive to him. But he thereby remains fixated on the premises of the morality and moral philosophy he is combating. He attempts only to reverse it – not to overcome it with a philosophy that truly marks a new beginning.

It has often been remarked how much Nietzsche's critique of morality remains ensnared in the dichotomies of Kant's moral philosophy.[42] Just as Kant tears duty and inclination apart and situates morality in the dimension of duty, so that happiness, because it remains excluded from morality, can only appear in a moral context as moral happiness, as happiness achieved through morality – so Nietzsche wants to obliterate the 'original sin of reason' by crediting the 'well-constituted human being'[43] with an instinctive certainty of his actions, which rules out the conflict of duty and inclination by making inclination and virtue identical. But this reversal is just as one-sided as its counterpart. Max Scheler had already recognized that Nietzsche's image of Christianity is distorted from the outset because he interprets it 'as a mere "morality" with a religious "justification", not primarily as a "religion"'.[44] In this distortion, too, Kant's influence continues to be felt.

Just as Nietzsche's image of morality is shaped by a simple inversion of a Kantian dichotomy, so he develops its envisaged counter-image from a reversal of Schopenhauerian thought.[45] Whereas for Schopenhauer the absence of an absolute value sphere means that life appears to be no more than the manifestation of a cosmic Will striving eternally and without meaning for unattainable satisfaction, Nietzsche postulates a 'will to power' governing all faculties of consciousness which allows 'free spirits' to be creative and rise above all existing intellectual constructs. Consequently, whereas for Schopenhauer only renunciation of the Will promises redemption, Nietzsche sees deliverance in the maximum intensification of the 'will to power'. Although he does not construe this 'will to power' as the will of concrete subjects, but rather as a nexus of suprasubjective events, it is still possible to see the consummation of the metaphysics of subjectivity in the notion of the intensification of life as the source of values.[46] Nietzsche's constantly renewed attempts to come to terms with the origin of values and the obvious contradictions between his various writings make it likely that he was thoroughly aware of the aporetic character of his answers – despite the thunderous tones in which he portrayed himself.

The epochal boldness of Nietzsche's attempt to investigate the genesis of values, and through the answer to this question to usher in a revaluation of values, therefore leaves us rather helpless. Nietzsche's account is implausible to the point of absurdity; his revaluation of values deeply aporetic. We must therefore be no less bold in our questioning – and yet seek a more circumspect answer.

3

The Varieties of Religious Experience
(William James)

On the European continent, and especially in Germany, a rich literature followed in the wake of the radicality of Friedrich Nietzsche's
questioning and the destructiveness of his answers. During the cultural crisis which preceded the First World War, but also during and
after the war itself, a younger generation found its own motifs
brilliantly anticipated and prefigured in his work. The verdict of
irrationalism passed by neo-Kantian academic philosophy could not
really prevent the spread of Nietzsche's influence: even his opponents
respected his courage and utter lack of illusions in seeking the truth.
   A school of thought which emerged on the other side of the Atlantic
was no less radical than Nietzsche in its questioning, and yet suffered
an entirely different fate. I am referring to American pragmatism,
which, apart from a few exceptions here and there, unleashed a real
storm of protest in Germany. The reactions were often so prejudiced
and distorting that in most cases we can hardly speak of a serious
appreciation and well-founded refutation of the claims involved. I
hold this moment in the history of ideas to be one of the decisive
crossroads in German intellectual life in the twentieth century.
Momentously, an opportunity was missed here to articulate motifs
critical of modernity in a democratic way – or in a way that was at
least compatible with democracy. Only after the Second World War,
in the aftermath of the catastrophe of the Third Reich and its crimes,
and in a new political order in West Germany installed largely by the
United States, could the balance be redressed.[1]
   During the period before the First World War, two cultural stereotypes in particular hindered an adequate understanding of pragmatism in Europe, and to some extent even in the United States itself.

There were those who maintained that all American thought was only able to express the American spirit – a spirit condemned in advance as being in essence nothing but crass commercialism and ruthless utilitarianism. For others, it was improbable, even impossible, that a new and original contribution to philosophy could come from 'cultureless' America, and they therefore expected American thinkers to produce only shallow and misunderstood versions of the more profound ideas articulated by European philosophers. Without looking very hard, we can find both stereotypes present in the attitudes displayed towards pragmatism as the American philosophy. Those who understood pragmatism as vulgar utilitarianism based this assumption on the belief that its representatives had simply replaced the ideal of truth with the notion of practical utility; such a conviction anyway no longer merited the name 'philosophy'.[2] On the basis of such premises, pragmatism could not accommodate a philosophy of value, an ethics or a philosophy of religion at all. Those who viewed pragmatism as merely an imitation of European originals, took these originals to be Ernst Mach's empirio-criticism, Hans Vaihinger's fictionalism and the *Lebensphilosophie* of Friedrich Nietzsche. Georg Simmel is credited with the presumptuous and misleading remark that pragmatism is 'what the Americans have understood of Nietzsche'.[3] This formulation is misleading because it attributes a surmised correspondence between the ideas expressed by both Nietzsche and pragmatism to an American reception of the German thinker, without being able to prove its constitutive significance for this school of thought. Simmel's remark is presumptuous, moreover, because it imputes those discrepancies in this correlation, which he recognizes only too well, to the limited American understanding of Nietzsche. If one thinks along these lines, then Nietzsche's thought can appear as the profound interrogation of all ideals; pragmatism, on the other hand, only as the naïve abandonment of them.

This bulwark of misunderstandings and distortions must first be dismantled if we are to open our eyes to pragmatism's modernity and the fruitfulness of the solutions it proposes.[4] The question of the genesis of values represents, of course, only one side of a far larger structure. At issue here is the thesis that William James's work as a whole, and his theory of religious experience in particular, provides a key to unlock the answer to this question, the significance of which extends far beyond the more narrow area of religion. In Europe, there does not appear to have been the same animosity towards James's book on religion as that directed at the (misunderstood) theory of truth set out in his lectures on pragmatism.[5] His theory of religious experience is the mature fruit of a decade-long intellectual development, set in motion by a profound personal crisis. This personal crisis had a suprapersonal meaning, and a closer examination of it shows that James's interest in religion did not spring from a naïve, unshakeable religious faith, but from an insight into the contingency of the world comparable to that of Nietzsche.

James's autobiographical accounts and the biographical literature on him[6] leave no doubt that the deep, personality-threatening depression from which he suffered between 1867 and 1872 had a philosophical dimension. He felt, more clearly than any of his contemporaries, the tension that exists between a deterministic world-view supposedly authenticated by the natural sciences and the values expressed in a Christian conception of man. In Germany, speculative idealism had thrust itself between religion and science ever since the late eighteenth century, but in American culture, apart from exceptions like Emerson's Transcendentalism, it seemed possible for religion and science to coexist peacefully. James understood at an early stage that the foundations of this coexistence had lost their stability. If everything is determined, what significance does free will have? Is it then only an illusion of the agent? If, though, free will is more than mere self-delusion, is the scientific world-view defensible?

The problem which paralysed his will-power and robbed the world of its action-motivating meaning first presented itself to the young James in what is, philosophically speaking, a rather conventional antinomy. The first idea to bring a little light to the blackness of depression James took from the work of the French neo-Kantian Charles Bernard Renouvier.[7] The latter had attempted to prove the possibility of free will by appealing to the experience of deliberately sustaining a thought against the upsurge of other thoughts. Concentrated thinking and deliberate attentiveness thus became the first examples of the possibility of freely willed decisions. James immediately gave Renouvier's argument a more radical, voluntaristic twist: 'My first act of free will shall be to believe in free will.'[8] By this he no longer simply means all acts of intellectual concentration as such, but rather the substantive idea of free will. In other words, James is expressing his voluntary decision to believe in the possibility of volition. He was able to experience this intellectual decision as redemptive because previously suicide had seemed the only possible deliberate act:

Hitherto, when I have felt like taking a free initiative, like daring to act originally, without carefully waiting for contemplation of the external world to determine all for me, suicide seemed the only manly form to put my daring into; now, I will go a step further with my will, not only act with it, but believe as well; believe in my individual reality and creative power. My belief, to be sure, can't be optimistic – but I will posit life (the real, the good) in the self-governing *resistance* of the ego to the world. Life shall be . . . doing and suffering and creating.[9]

A statement like this one undermines the image of James as a naïve American, whose historical optimism was left untouched by the deep cultural crisis in Europe and which for that very reason remained superficial. But the impression may now arise that he was a kind of proto-existentialist, making an ungrounded decision to be free. There are indeed similarities with existentialism here, and this idea of James fits in with his lifelong discourse of heroism with responsibility. A closer look, however, shows that he did not leave this decision ungrounded, but actually endeavoured to provide it with a foundation – not, of course, by seeking to restore old metaphysical foundations, but, on the contrary, by developing a new understanding not only of science, but of religion as well. He does not attempt to supply an irrefutable basis for free will, so that it must appear as logically compelling, accessible even without the act of his own decision. Rather, he investigates the conditions that make his decision possible.

His attempt to prove that the natural sciences themselves by no means give rise to a deterministic world-view is a significant step, and many of James's themes can be understood within this context. He recognized with particular acuity the difference between the spectacular scientific revolution instigated by Darwin and the popular evolutionism of Herbert Spencer. Darwin, he claimed, had taught us to see that the genesis and evolution of species takes place in a universe characterized by chance, change and historical open-endedness. Spencer, by contrast, constructed from these insights a new, self-confident theory of history, in which a particular path of progress appeared absolutely necessary.[10]

James is far closer to Darwin than Spencer when he attempts to understand all mental faculties in terms of their function in the organism's active struggle with its environment. Free will also helps human beings to survive in their environment, and thus does not contradict Darwin's discoveries. James's *Principles of Psychology*, published in 1890, represents the impressive synthesis of his efforts in this direction. Even science itself could thus be understood as an active attempt to adapt to the environment. According to this viewpoint, the scientistic ideologies did not account for how science was actually practised. Certainly, James argues, science does not supply any ultimate certainties; but when it produces plausible explanations it makes successful action possible. Pragmatist epistemology and philosophy of science provide an appropriate understanding of science which, without ever creating firm foundations, still permits successful action under conditions of uncertainty. Ultimately, in his late work, James develops the idea of a 'pluralistic' universe – a universe that should not be understood in deterministic terms, but rather as a domain of possibilities in which new phenomena can also arise through human activity.[11]

But the question as to whether science and true knowledge are possible under conditions of uncertainty was only one aspect of James's endeavours. The other aspect with which, to my mind, he was even more deeply preoccupied was the question of whether religious belief was possible under these very same conditions – that is to say, in an age in which institutions no longer imparted dogmatic certainty and the dream of a sound philosophical proof of the existence of God was shattered; in which, rather, fundamental cognitive claims of the Christian tradition, such as the doctrine of Creation, could be regarded as having been definitively refuted by science – by Darwinism, in this case. It is here, in his attitude towards religion in general and Christianity in particular, that the differences between James and Nietzsche become especially clear, differences which led many readers to underestimate James's modernity. Whereas James experienced the decision to believe in his own free will as redemption from the hopelessness of a deterministic universe, the 'error of the free will' is for Nietzsche the occasion for a new diatribe against Christianity. For Nietzsche, the concept 'free will' is the 'most infamous of all the arts of the theologian for making mankind "accountable" in his sense of the word, that is to say for *making mankind dependent on him*'.[12] 'Free will' – to him that reeks of punishing and judging, of the attempt 'to infect the innocence of becoming with "punishment" and "guilt" . . . Christianity is a hangman's metaphysics . . .'[13] Nietzsche yearns for an 'innocence of becoming' liberated from the categories of accountability and guilt – and this leads him to recognize the falsity of the notion that actions issue from a prior and conscious decision. However, he does not attempt to develop a more adequate account of the connection between will and action with anything like the same consistency that James demonstrates; instead, he is more inclined to eliminate the will from the dynamics of action, resulting in his postulating an hypostatized 'will to power' behind the 'innocence of becoming'.[14]

The question of whether the erosion of dogmatic religious certainty has also made the values of Christianity untenable, that is, whether the 'death of God' also means the end of Christian morality, shows up an even more drastic difference between James and Nietzsche. For Nietzsche, there is on closer examination no question about it.

Scornfully, he tears into the 'English shallowpates' and the 'little blue-stockings *à la* [George] Eliot', who believe they can defend morality even without a religious guarantee. He self-confidently proclaims the futility of such attempts:

> When one gives up Christian belief one thereby deprives oneself of the *right* to Christian morality. For the latter is absolutely *not* self-evident . . . Christianity is a system, a consistently thought out and *complete* view of things. If one breaks out of it a fundamental idea, the belief in God, one thereby breaks the whole thing to pieces: one has nothing of any consequence left in one's hands. Christianity presupposes that man does not know, *cannot* know what is good for him and what evil: he believes in God, who alone knows. Christian morality is a command: its origin is transcendental; it is beyond all criticism, all right to criticize; it possesses truth only if God is truth – it stands or falls with the belief in God.[15]

For James, much of what Nietzsche claimed to be unambiguous and certain was indeed ambiguous and uncertain. In this respect, too, Nietzsche is more ensnared in that which he opposes – i.e. in dogmatic Christianity and a morality understood as a command – than he seems to realize. If one compares the world religions and the various Christian denominations with one another, what grounds are there to view Christianity as a self-contained system to the extent that its values can only be justified within a single framework? Why should other foundations of morality besides the religious rule themselves out from the very beginning? And why, finally, should morality even be understood as a command of transcendental origin at all?

Those who are not dead set on abolishing Christian values will ask such questions and proceed in a more moderate manner than Nietzsche. The difference between James and Nietzsche does not lie in the radicalness of their questioning, but in the varying degrees to which they are prepared to admit different answers. For James, it is neither a foregone conclusion that everything is permitted if God does not exist; nor is the 'death of God' an incontrovertible fact. He approaches religion neither as an apologist, nor with a positivistic or Nietzschean conviction of its historical obsolescence, but rather with the intention of investigating whether religious belief is possible in a postmetaphysical, scientifically determined age.

The first important indication of the form James's answer will take is given in the essay 'The Will to Believe', even the title of which gave rise to misunderstandings.[16] For it was all too easy to see in his plea for the will to believe a hypervoluntaristic defence of autosuggestive self-deception,[17] or even the cynical approval of the deception of others, or the construction of a mythology staged for the purposes of the pursuit or preservation of power.[18] Although James himself later regretted his choice of title for the essay, and believed that he should have spoken of the right, rather than the will, to believe, it was no coincidence that he selected this title.[19] The 'will to believe' was a more sophisticated version of that idea which had helped him out of his depression. The argument of this essay contains his provisional answer to the question of the genesis of values.

James makes clear at the very beginning of his text that he is not exhorting us to believe in something that our intellect bars us from believing in, or which we have even recognized as untrue. He even expressly anticipates the misunderstandings which he would nevertheless fall victim to when he writes that the idea of a deliberate belief must of course seem either simply silly or irrationally vile. What James has in mind is something entirely different. He wants to give us the courage to believe when we feel the inclination to believe and there is no logically compelling reason that speaks against that belief. We can, James argues, only believe in that which presents itself to us as a living option. A living option, however, is defined as something towards which there is a tendency of our will. Belief, or the willingness to believe, is already germinating in this tendency of our will. To interpret the will to believe as if a mind simply resolved upon a belief-content independently of all practical contexts is to misconstrue James's concept of will. What he has in mind, rather, is our already existing, pre-reflective volitions, and he inquires how our reflection deals and should deal with these. His thinking is therefore completely different from that behind Pascal's famous wager.[20] Pascal proposed a cost–benefit analysis on the question of religious belief. If belief in divine judgement, say, simply remains without consequence if it should turn out that there is no such thing; but, if this reckoning does actually take place, has a mitigating effect because belief in it deters the sinner from committing misdeeds which God will later punish – then faith is rational. But James makes clear that the outcome of such calculation is not faith; it does not have the same intensity as our spiritual powers, and in a remark aimed at Pascal he adds, with a smile: 'and if we were ourselves in the place of the Deity, we should probably take particular pleasure in cutting off believers of this pattern from this infinite reward.'[21] God is not, as it were, taken in by such rational calculations.

But what stands in the way of the reflective affirmation of a pre-reflective readiness to believe? For James, it is the ethos of the scientific method that seems to oblige us to believe only in what can be confirmed by rational means. Now, he does not have the slightest intention of attacking the scientific ethos; rather, he sees it as indubitably legitimate for solving cognitive problems. But he asks here, as he does in his other works, whether we understand the scientific method correctly if we view it as the accumulation of verified cognitions. The picture changes, however, if – 'fallibilistically' – we assume that it is possible for all cognitions to be revised and, conversely, if we think ourselves indeed capable of true knowledge, yet lacking ultimate certainty on the point when we have attained true knowledge. To believe in truth and to shun error – these are not, for James, two different ways of formulating the same commandment; they are, rather, two different commandments whose priority is open to dispute. It is not self-evident that we should give precedence to the avoidance of error if this limits our access to the truth or even prevents us from answering questions. If that were the case, preference for the second maxim would impoverish us. Preference for the first maxim, on the other hand, makes us ready to attempt answers, even where certain verification does not yet seem possible.

James concedes that it may be salutary for the sciences to proceed according to the second maxim – although he immediately qualifies this concession: it is valid only for the assessment of cognitions, not for the creative processes of discovery, where the researchers' intuition and their passionate interest in confirming their intuitions are indispensable. In moral questions in particular, the situation is usually such that the agent is unable to wait for all the evidence to be presented; instead, he or she must act without being able to attain the certainty which is possible in principle. The dilemma here is that the decision to wait for verification rather than to act is, according to the logic of the moral situation, always itself a decision which is by no means morally neutral. However, the tension between the two maxims of action becomes even greater in those situations where trust arises or is necessary. James cites the example of falling in love. He who waits, cold and aloof, to obtain from the beloved a sure sign of love will usually wait in vain. To enter into the intersubjective process of mutual confidence-building, I must meet the other half-way and guarantee him or her an advance in faith and at the same time be convinced that I am in principle worthy of the other's love. In order for love to arise, I must consider myself to be worthy of love and the other to be capable of love. Without this belief in the possibility of love, a belief that lacks all ultimate security, love does not arise. 'There are, then, cases where a fact cannot come at all unless a preliminary faith exists in its coming. *And where faith in a fact can help create the fact . . .'*[22] To give precedence here to the maxim of waiting would be destructive. The opposite procedure is not only legitimate, it is the only constructive one: 'In truths dependent on our personal action, then, faith based on desire is certainly a lawful and possibly an indispensable thing.'[23]

What holds true in the sphere of interpersonal faith does so too, James argues, in the sphere of religion. If a readiness to believe is a precondition for religion, then every rule which would proscribe all possibility of 'making the gods' acquaintance' would be irrational.[24] The injunction to believe only what we encounter in ordinary experience would thus cut us off from extra-ordinary experiences – but why should we cut ourselves off in this way, why should we give precedence to fear over hope? If our attitude to the world alters its expression, then there is no compelling reason to confront the world without faith. Of course, this is not also a compelling reason to adopt a religious – or even a particular religious – position. James expressly demands respect for the opinions of others and tolerance between believers and non-believers. The right to believe – even in a scientifically determined age disconnected from metaphysical certainty – does not seem to have been itself refuted. Against the constraints of scientism, he attempts to keep at least the possibility of faith open. And to the question of whether morality is even conceivable without religion, James also supplies, in 'The Moral Philosopher and the Moral Life', an essay published in 1891, a considered, not a dogmatic, answer.[25] For him, morality can be many things, ranging from the avoidance of bad deeds to high-flying attempts to change the world He does not dispute in any way that morality is possible even without religiosity, and that an ethics can be anchored perfectly well in a universe in which there is no higher consciousness than the human – only for the more demanding and passionate variants of morality does previous human history offer no other examples of motivation than those pervaded by religious feeling. Religious belief increases the probability that an individual will outgrow a morality of prudence and summon up the strength and stamina to change the world. James says this as a psychologist and as a defender of religious belief; he does not thereby proclaim certainty, but appeals only to his observations which are supported by experience.

All of these remarks on religion are written from the defensive position into which it has been forced by science and the spirit of the age. But with his *magnum opus*, *The Varieties of Religious Experience*, James goes on the offensive. In it, he not only defends the idea that religious belief is possible even today; he also asks what actually is that thing which we simply call 'religion', as if this were itself unproblematic. The manner in which he poses this question and attempts an answer to it is widely regarded as a revolutionary innovation in the history of the study of religion. James's fundamental methodological idea consists in making *religious experiences* the starting-point of a theory of religion. In an age of trivialized psychology it is all too easily forgotten to what extent his work marked a significant break with older approaches. James's book is not only the classic text of the early psychology of religion and a barely outdated example of a phenomenology of religious experience.[26] It also opens up a new pathway to a 'postmetaphysical religiosity', if one can put it like that.[27] As such, this work provides the first element of a constructive answer to the question of the genesis of values.

To understand what is so special about James's analysis of religion, we should first of all be clear what it is *not*. It is not concerned with either theological doctrines or ecclesiastical institutions. In stark contrast to such a science of religion, James proposed 'to ignore the institutional branch entirely, to say nothing of the ecclesiastical organization, to consider as little as possible the systematic theology and the ideas of the gods themselves', and resolved to confine himself to 'personal religion pure and simple'.[28] Thus, personal religion is, in his view, the 'primordial thing' and it is therefore consistent of him to base his study on the following definition of religion: 'Religion, therefore, . . . shall mean for us *the feelings, acts, and experiences of individual men in their solitude, so far as they apprehend themselves to stand in relation to whatever they may consider the divine.*'[29] James thus defines religion as any relation of the *solitary* individual to whatever he or she may understand as the divine. What exactly this 'divine' might be is circumscribed in only the vaguest terms at the beginning of his investigation: it is supposed to be 'such a primal reality as the individual feels impelled to respond to solemnly and gravely, and neither by a curse or a jest'[30] – it is by no means, then, always construed as a personal God. Of course, theological systems and institutions also grow out of this seed that is the individual experience of the divine; but these always remain secondary phenomena, as opposed to the primary phenomenon of individual religious experience. Anticipating obvious objections to such radical individualism, James adds: 'In one sense at least the personal religion will prove itself more fundamental than either theology or ecclesiasticism. Churches, when once established, live at second-hand upon tradition; but the *founders* of every church owed their power originally to the fact of their direct personal communion with the divine.'[31] James therefore seeks to draw on material which expresses this kind of direct individual experience of the divine.

What is more, James's investigation of such experience is clearly differentiated from all 'nothing but' explanations of religion[32] – that is, from all attempts to view the religious as merely the displaced expression of what are really other, more effective, needs. The public consciousness has often been dominated in the twentieth century by Marxist and psychoanalytical interpretations, according to which, for example, religiosity can be traced back either to the postponement until a hereafter of hopes for justice and prosperity, or to the projection of a father figure or erotic desires of fusion onto imaginary personages. In James's own time and culture, his emphatic protest was provoked not so much by these ways of thinking as by a vulgar medical materialism and by an anthropology which claimed that religion was the relic of primitive ages. The most important objection raised by James against both these ways of thinking was the typically pragmatist maxim that we should judge faith just as we would scientific propositions: not in the light of its origins, but in terms of its consequences. In the natural sciences and in engineering we would never dream of attempting to refute an hypothesis by pointing to the neurotic character of those who advance it. This should, however, also apply to 'religious opinions'. Referring directly to the contemporary German philosophy of value, James distinguishes between 'existential judgments' and 'propositions of value', and resists the idea that the former can be derived from the latter, and vice versa. He wants to open up the space for an investigation of religion that can take into account the empirical variety of religious phenomena, and which does not construe these as either deviations from the one true belief or as the mere delusions of unenlightened people. It should be possible to reflect on what 'religious experience' and 'faith' are without the origin of either being taken as a dogmatic truth-claim or as clear evidence of untruth. This does not mean, though, that James thought that the question of origins could be ignored altogether – on the contrary! Although the answer to this question does not decide the value of a belief, we only correctly understand this belief when we can see how it is rooted in experience. In his study, then, James does not want to evaluate, but to describe – however, he is not seeking to describe the rationalized forms of expressing experience, but rather the experiences themselves, which are nevertheless only accessible through such forms of expression.

This objective also distinguishes the meaning of James's inquiry into the origin and genesis of belief from all historical or evolutionistic forms of reductionism. James declares his unequivocal opposition to the suggestion that religion represents merely the survival of anachronistic ideas from past epochs[33] – as if it were better for science to answer the questions that interest individuals when they reflect on their personal destiny or for these questions to be proscribed because science cannot answer them. For James, by contrast, the religious is always experienced anew by living individuals. It should not be traced back to historically older forms which, he also claims, cannot necessarily reveal more to us about a subject than more highly evolved forms.[34] However, more highly evolved means for him not the historically more recent, but the more succinctly formed, phenomena. Guided by such 'exaggerations and perversions', he hopes to be able to map structures which also underlie the more obscure cases, and wants to ascertain the nature of these structures using empirical and inductive methods. It is for this reason that he also defines the key concept of religious experience only in vague terms, because he fears that any more precise circumscription of the subject would only prevent us from observing it in all its diversity. He posits no essence underlying all religion, or even a specifically religious need, sentiment or organ as the origin of religious experience. For him, 'religion' is, rather, an umbrella term describing a phenomenon of human life which cannot be easily delimited; as soon as we are prepared to accept this, we also recognize that all religious emotions are nothing other than our natural emotions directed towards religious objects.[35] Perhaps there is also no common essence shared by all religious objects and acts – but all this does not mean that there is no religious experience *per se*, only that it cannot be isolated from the totality of our experience. To study religious experience is, therefore, to study human experience in one of its most intense and universal manifestations.

With insatiable curiosity and palpable fascination, James collects together a wealth of documents relating to religious experience in order to put his programme into effect. He draws mainly on material of two kinds. First, he uses writings, diaries and self-portraits of religious virtuosi: saints, the founders of sects and other geniuses of faith from all ages and from all world religions. Second, he employs a collection of autobiographical accounts relating primarily to conversion experiences, which were compiled by early American psychologists of religion and made available to him. His book contains long verbatim passages from both kinds of testimony and it is for this very reason, quite apart from James's own gifts as a writer, that it has become so gripping and deeply moving for so many people.

For our purposes, it is neither necessary nor possible to give an impression of the richness of this investigation. From his descriptions and analyses of religious phenomena such as conversion and prayer, mystical experience and personal 'rebirth', I shall isolate those elements which are of significance for the question of the genesis of values. If I see things aright, there are essentially three such elements at issue.

I should point out, first of all, that from the outset James distinguishes the question of religious experience from that of moral experience. In the Victorian age, religion was regarded as nothing more than, as Matthew Arnold famously put it, 'morality touched by emotion'. The character of morality seemed clear, and so did the fact that all religion contained a moral code; but James's contemporaries became increasingly uncertain of what religion was in a positive sense, that is, besides morality and largely problematic 'unscientific' assumptions about the world. The way in which James delimits the subject of his inquiry already points to the different emphasis he puts on the question. For him, religion is not merely an ornament embellishing morality; it is, rather, distinguished from it in principle.

> Morality pure and simple accepts the law of the whole which it finds reigning, so far as to acknowledge and obey it, but it may obey it with the heaviest heart, and never cease to feel it as a yoke. But for religion, in its strong and fully developed manifestations, the service of the highest is never felt as a yoke. Dull submission is left far behind, and a mood of welcome, which may fill any place on the scale between cheerful serenity and enthusiastic gladness, has taken its place.[36]

Although religion and morality may often be linked with one another in practice, James argues that they exercise their forces in opposite directions. Whereas morality restricts the possibilities for our action, proscribing certain goals and means, religion increases those possibilities. Whereas the moral person might be likened to a top-level athlete, having to concentrate on his will in order to act morally, the religious person lives his life, James claims, with passion and excitement, with an 'added dimension of emotion ... in regions where morality strictly so called can at best but bow its head and acquiesce'.[37] In so far as we can say that religion is something particular at all, then this fervour displayed by the religious person is an integral part of it.

James's clear distinction between religion and morality is certainly not the product of the puritanical background of American culture. Rather, its origins lie in his break with this background, a break which he especially, of course, did not have to make – for his father, Henry James Sr., had in his own writings already attempted a 'humanization of Calvinism' (Giles Gunn). Non-Protestant Christianity had never reduced religion to morality in such drastic fashion, and Protestant Christianity had again and again produced religious revivalist movements or aesthetic rebellions which opposed the narrowness of mere morality. From James's point of view, given his appreciation of the passion experienced by the religious person, Marx's slogan that religion is the opium of the people must seem erroneous, because it implies that religion always has a soothing and deferring effect, although it might be just as possible, perhaps even more plausible, to interpret religion as something that invigorates and empowers the individual.

A whole range of empirical religious phenomena attracts James's attention precisely because they show up the difference between religiosity and morality with particular clarity. The analysis of mystical experiences demonstrates that such experiences are not a precondition for moral action, nor are they demanded by morality; it demonstrates, furthermore, that the individual does not have to aspire to these experiences in order to undergo them. Likewise, the significance of his long discussion of the various trends towards a religion of 'healthy-mindedness', trends which were so important in late nineteenth-century America, as they are again today (that is, an attitude of exclusively 'positive' thinking propelled by a compulsive reaction to Calvinist pessimism focusing on human sinfulness), lies in the fact that James saw in such trends a popular movement against the dominance of morality over religiosity – although he regarded with hostility and concern its superficial ignoring of evil and guilt. Furthermore, he turns back from these contemporary trends to scrutinize Martin Luther's doctrine of justification by faith alone, John Wesley's teaching that one must learn to accept God's grace, and to Methodist conversions. In all of them he sees at work the liberating, empowering and morality-transcending dynamics of the religious. The common denominator here is the impulse to give 'your little private convulsive self a rest, and finding that a greater Self is there'.[38] Plainly fascinated, he speaks again and again of the marvellous or repulsive, heroic or ascetic achievements which religiosity has made possible in all ages and in all cultures.

Now, the demarcation of religious experiences from moral ones is not only the prerequisite for the study of exceptional states in human life, but also for the analysis of a permanent attitude which characterizes the religious person's entire relationship to the world. James calls this state of religiosity the 'faith-state'.[39] This state has both a cognitive and an affective side; in order to avoid ambiguity, he proposes to designate the affective side as a 'state of assurance'.[40] Of course, James does not really think of these sides as wholly distinct from one another, nor does he hold the cognitive side to be the really decisive one; that would signal a relapse into Cartesian dualism, to overcome which pragmatism had first joined battle. James lists the following as characteristics of the 'state of assurance': the central one is 'the loss of all worry, the sense that all is ultimately well with one, the peace, the harmony, the *willingness to be*, even though the outer conditions should remain the same . . . A passion of willingness, of acquiescence, of admiration, is the glowing centre of this state of mind.'[41] Secondly, this state is bound up with the sense of perceiving truths hitherto unknown, which are difficult, even impossible, to express in language. Thirdly, the objective appearance of the world is altered in this state, confronting the believer with beautiful and everlasting newness. Finally, a stream of bliss, even ecstasy, flows through the believer.

This characterization of the affective side already hints at some of the cognitive features of the faith-state. It should by now be clear that faith is not simply a cognitive holding-to-be-true that can be undermined by argumentative discourse. Though assumptions about a reality that is not accessible to the senses (a 'reality of the unseen')[42] are also an integral part of faith, they do not take the form of intellectual hypotheses. James finds an appropriate expression for the idea he has in mind here when he compares the ontological imagination of the religious person with the vital attitude of the lover: 'A lover has notoriously this sense of the continuous being of his idol, even when his attention is addressed to other matters and he no longer represents her features. He cannot forget her; she uninterruptedly affects him through and through.'[43] Faith is, then, an attitude towards reality sustained by a conviction that a stronger power is present. It is for this reason that James cites so many examples of this sense that the objects of faith are present. Experience shows that arguments for or against do not have the same force as this certainty that emanates from a sense of presence. Faith cannot be instilled by proofs, but neither can it be refuted by them.

> If you have intuitions at all, they come from a deeper level of your nature than the loquacious level rationalism inhabits. Your whole subconscious life, your impulses, your faiths, your needs, your divinations, have prepared the premises, of which your consciousness now feels the weight of the result; and something in you absolutely *knows* that that result must be truer than any logic-chopping rationalistic talk, however clever, that may contradict it.[44]

Thus, the second element of faith stressed by James, in addition to the way in which the 'religious' expands the possibilities for acting, is the feeling of certainty that is grounded in a sense of presence and to a large extent immune to reason. It is in his analysis of mystical experiences in particular that he develops the notion of the 'noetic quality' of such feelings.[45] They are experienced by the subject not only as emotional states, but as sudden illuminations, insights and revelations, whose translation into words may indeed be difficult, but which yet radiate an intense authority. James does not sacrifice rational argument, as one might fear, to the irrational authority of such experiences of conviction. 'Mystical truth exists for the individual who has the transport, but for no one else.'[46] One can argue with such a feeling of conviction just as little as one can dispute the certainty we achieve through our senses, but this does not mean that the former is not a component of human experience and that to understand this aspect of our experience cannot be of fundamental importance.

James constantly contrasts the affective and cognitive characteristics of faith with descriptions of a melancholy and depressive state. This is of interest not only because we can recognize in this the memory of the depression which was so decisive for the development of his thought, and which lingers as the dark backdrop to his inspired descriptions of the cheerful serenity of the faithful. What is more important is that, by making this contrast, James invites us to participate in a thought experiment which demonstrates the vital impossibility of abstracting from the value-contents that bestow meaning in our experience of the world. Anyone who sees faith as a merely irrational addition to the world of facts has not grasped that we could not act, we could not live, in a world of mere facts.

> Conceive yourself, if possible, suddenly stripped of all the emotion with which your world now inspires you, and try to imagine it *as it exists*, purely by itself, without your favourable or unfavourable, hopeful or apprehensive comment. It will be almost impossible for you to realize such a condition of negativity and deadness. No one portion of the universe would then have importance beyond another; and the whole collection of its things and series of events would be without significance, character, expression, or perspective.[47]

The world of pure facts is for us not simply neutral, but dead. Although it is our organic (and spiritual) needs which first invest the world with interest and meaning, we do not experience these as something superadded to the world, but as the world itself. James returns to the example of the lover, for whom the beloved, and the whole world around him or her, appears in a different light than for a person who is not in love. For James, love and faith are cases of the 'sense of value in general'[48] – and he is concerned not so much with the question of the genesis of this or that value, as with the genesis of the world of value in general.

Although James wants to describe, with the concept of faith, a permanent attitude towards the world, he is particularly interested in how such an attitude arises in experience. This is the reason why mystical and conversion experiences occupy more space in his account and are given priority over what is probably the principal expression of individual religiosity: prayer. Although he refers to prayer as the 'very soul and essence of religion' and as 'real religion',[49] James only comes to discuss it towards the end of his book. His analysis of prayer provides a third component which we can use to answer our question.

James describes prayer not simply as the repetition of sacred formulae or petitions directed at a higher being, but, in a wider sense, as every kind of inward communion with the divine. Prayer represents the attempt to enter into communication with those forces whose presence is sensed with certainty in faith, and, by this means, to maintain contact with the power from which the life-force of the individual flows. Prayer in this sense constitutes religion. Anyone who can pray is religious – even if he or she does not bother with religious teachings or has no access to them. Prayer is a transaction in which we open ourselves up to this supraindividual source of power.[50] Already in his *Principles of Psychology*, written in 1890, James had derived the impulse to pray from the inner sociality of the human being.[51] Because we relate to ourselves as if to an interlocutor, we need an ideal '*Socius*' – and this we find in prayer. This aspect of self-opening, as well as the relation to the ideal, is elaborated more clearly in his magisterial study of religious experience.

The opposition of religious and moral experience already contained the idea that moral discipline corresponds, in religion, to a capacity for 'self-surrender', to abandoning oneself to the forces of attraction. In his analysis of conversion experiences, James distinguishes first of all the volitional type of conversion from self-surrender, and notes that the former gradually builds up the new moral and spiritual habits, while the latter only removes the obstacles to the new faith and is swept away by it.[52] Immediately after introducing this distinction, however, James qualifies it again, declaring that a moment of self-surrender is also indispensable for the volitional type of conversion. The old self strains beyond itself towards a new one; but while its will still belongs to the old self, it experiences the forces which lead it to the new self as a liberation from the constraints of the old. With this strong emphasis on the involuntary character of religious experience, James finds it prudent to qualify his old formula, the 'will to believe', even more than he had done when he was faced with the misunderstandings this concept had given rise to. Now he stresses that we 'can make ourselves more faithful to a belief of which we have the rudiments, but we cannot create a belief out of whole cloth when our perception actively assures us of its opposite'.[53] There is no longer any suggestion that we decide to believe through a speculative cognitive act. James now thinks in a fashion more similar to the Christian tradition before him: that faith is itself a state of grace; we can aspire to it, but we cannot coerce it.

The idea of the involuntary character of faith is elaborated above all in the middle chapters of the work. To begin with, James counters the superficial positivity of the 'healthy mind' with a phenomenology of the 'sick soul' and the 'divided self' in order then to show how the inner dividedness within individuals can be overcome through experiences of conversion and being born again.[54] James was already a decisive inaugurator of the conception of the 'self' in the aforementioned *Principles of Psychology*.[55] However we regard the conception developed there, in *The Varieties of Religious Experience* he posits no crisis-free process of self-formation; on the contrary, the person's inner being is imagined as the battleground 'for what he feels to be two deadly hostile selves':[56] the actual self and the ideal self. With a passage from St Augustine's *Confessions*, he illustrates the tension within the person between the old and new will, the carnal and spiritual will, as a real conflict which tears the personality apart. Here valuations are not just set against valuations; the whole person is at stake when he is forced to decide which valuations he wants to make his own. James does not dispute that our decisions are often not quite so dramatic and that our character can also change gradually – but again he is more interested in the more succinct form of conflict within the individual striving towards a new self in which the old disunity no longer exists. This he calls the 'transformations' of the self.[57] Conversion is a 'unification' of the self because it overcomes the now intolerable dividedness by forming a higher unity. And prayer is for James the everyday repetition of such a radical experience of transformation: it constantly releases energy from that source which is constitutive of the self.

There are three ways in which the thought of William James, especially his vivid and penetrating phenomenology of religious experience, brings the question of the genesis of values into sharper focus. There are, evidently, experiences of attraction and captivation distinct from moral experience, and these can assume a subjective character of certainty independent of cognitive arguments. What is more, they are achieved not by exercising the will, but through self-surrender; to be precise, when, through this self-surrender, ideal powers empower and sustain the individual. But no matter how vivid

James's descriptions of phenomena might be, his conceptualization is often hard to grasp. In addition, he himself remained very cautious about the conclusions to be drawn from his account. Though his respect for the unreduced subjectivity of individual experience does itself imply a certain value-standpoint, which James also knew very well how to articulate,[58] in no sense did he use the phenomenology of religious experience to construct a positive philosophy of value. Originally, James had intended his book to comprise two equal parts: one part was to deal with the psychology, the other the philosophy, of religion.[59] But ultimately, he only hinted, towards the end of *Varieties*, as to what the second part was supposed to contain, and he never did write a separate volume addressing this topic. So, we can only garner allusions to James's pluralistic pantheism. But to do this would divert us from the task in hand. Here we are seeking to understand better and qualify critically James's account of the genesis of values by contrasting it with other approaches. Can, then, the concept of experience really be employed in the manner in which it is here? What is the connection between experience and the feeling of certainty? Must values be grounded in religion? These are just some of the questions which the following chapters attempt to answer.

4

Collective Ecstasy
(Émile Durkheim)

The decision between Nietzsche and James – between, on the one hand, a genealogy of morality which is radically hostile to Christianity and reduces moral value to expressions of power and, on the other, a phenomenology of individual religious experience which defends the right to believe and respects the endless varieties of subjectivity – is a decision all readers, depending on their prior attitude towards religion and faith, will want to make for themselves. Anyone who poses the more abstract question of the genesis of values, however, should not regard the choice between Nietzsche and James as the only alternative offered by the history of ideas. While Nietzsche was, and remains, a significant figure, especially in German thought, and while James exercised a lasting influence in America, academic sociology can proffer its own solution which cannot be reduced to either Nietzsche or James, although its author was certainly familiar with the work of both. I am referring to the theory of religion advanced by Émile Durkheim, the classic exponent of French sociology who towers above all his rivals. Examining it will help us to expand and qualify our answer, which thus far rests upon the insights provided by James.

Durkheim's theory of religion is elaborated in the work he completed in 1912, *The Elementary Forms of Religious Life*.[1] The main empirical sections of this work comprise a study of totemism, the (supposed) religion of the Australian aborigines – at least as far as it could be reconstructed from contemporary travel accounts and research reports. This choice of subject, which at first glance appears outlandish and might deter potential readers outside specialist circles, is justified by an underlying 'evolutionist' premise of Durkheim's. He believes, namely, that

whenever we set out to explain something human at a specific moment
in time – be it a religious belief, a moral rule, a legal principle, an
aesthetic technique, or an economic system – we must begin by going
back to its simplest and most primitive form. We must seek to account
for the features that define it at that period of its existence and then show
how it has gradually developed, gained in complexity, and become what
it is at the moment under consideration.[2]

Durkheim assumes, therefore, that to explain present-day social
phenomena we must return to their oldest forms, and that these are
more simple, that is, less complex, than their later manifestations. As
far as his interest in the origin and effects of religious life is concerned,
this meant going back to the most 'primitive' extant form of religion –
and this is precisely what Australian totemism seemed to him to be.

This rabbi's son had been fascinated by religion all his life. His
magnum opus on religion is the culmination of decades of research in
this field, which he had undertaken since at least the middle of the
1890s. Yet even his early work[3] contains criticisms of research undertaken in the science of religion. In these writings, Durkheim had
already viewed religion as an eminently social affair, and had even
seen in it the embodiment of those beliefs and practices which unite a
community. If for a time he assumed that such communal beliefs and
practices must decline with the progressive division of labour, then it
was only logical for him, as for typical representatives of positivist
thought, to assume that religion was doomed to extinction. The early
works are hesitant and unclear on the question of what is in the
process of replacing, and what should replace, this declining religion,
or whether it might in fact be meaningless to talk of its extinction in
view of the emergence of functional equivalents for religion. One can
see as the driving force behind the changes in Durkheim's theoretical
position his ongoing search for a new morality[4] – a morality which
would ensure social cohesiveness in the French Republic and modern
society *per se*, and at the same time protect the values of individualism
against a Catholic critique seeking to restore the old order.[5] As a
committed laicized republican, Durkheim had regarded institutionalized religion as his political and moral opponent from the very
beginning of his career. His actual theoretical interest in it, however,
could only develop once his historical optimism about the quasi-
automatic emergence of the sought-after new morality through the
progressive division of labour had begun to disintegrate. In his major
work of 1893, *The Division of Labour*, Durkheim still treated the dangers
accompanying the loss of values, like 'anomie', as problems arising
during the *transition* to modern society, not as problems inherent in

modern society itself.[6] His position had already changed by the time
he came to write his pioneering empirical study *Suicide* in 1895.[7] As
his hopes for the self-generation of the new morality diminished, so
his search for the possibilities of creating, grounding and consolidat-
ing such a morality intensified. For morality to have a transcendental
ground seemed to Durkheim both questionable and impossible. The
question therefore had to be: how is a this-worldly substitute for such
a transcendental ground possible? In my view, this constellation of
intellectual developments excited the passionate interest in religion
characteristic of the militant atheist Durkheim and informed the
nature of his concern with it.

This is not the place to document with philological precision the
gradual development of Durkheim's mature theory of religion. All I
wish to emphasize here is that his mature theory makes a decisive
contribution to the question of the genesis of values.[8] The best way of
determining the specific nature of this contribution is to consider first
the definition of religion on which Durkheim bases his account.

'A religion is a unified system of beliefs and practices relative to
sacred things, that is to say, things set apart and forbidden – beliefs
and practices which unite into one single moral community called a
Church, all those who adhere to them.'[9] Three aspects of this definition
are worth highlighting. Firstly, by defining religion as a 'system of
beliefs and practices', Durkheim differentiates himself from the strong
tendency to regard religion chiefly as a system of beliefs and to
interpret ritual practices, say, as merely expressions of this belief. In
his early writings, Durkheim had already argued against seeing
mainly metaphysical speculations at work in religion. In his mature
theory, he emphasizes that all religions contain a cosmology – but this
does not mean that he sees as the essence of religion the supplement-
ing of thought with impressions of some supersensory realm of the
'unknowable'. Rather, the cognitive classification of the world is
originally prompted and informed by religious ideas; religion is thus
constitutive of the human capacity for thought itself.[10] Secondly, his
definition of religion in terms of the 'sacred' can only be fully
understood when we take into account the way in which it differs
from other possible definitions. Based on sound reasons deriving from
his studies in the history and ethnology of religion, Durkheim resists
defining religions in terms of their relation to the 'supernatural' or to
a belief in a God or gods. The 'supernatural' already presupposes a
concept of the 'natural', and we should be aware that 'there are rites
without gods, and indeed rites from which gods derive. Not all
religious virtues emanate from divine personalities . . . Thus, religion
is broader than the idea of gods or spirits and so cannot be defined

exclusively in those terms.'[11] Instead, Durkheim declares the dichoto-
mous division of the world into the sacred and the profane, that is,
the setting apart of certain objects, beliefs and practices as incommen-
surable with all others, to be a universal characteristic shared by all
cultures. The third aspect of Durkheim's definition of religion that I
want to emphasize here is its unambiguous commitment to the social
character of religion. 'Religious representations are collective representations that express collective realities; rites are ways of acting that
are born only in the midst of assembled groups and whose purpose is
to evoke, maintain, or recreate certain mental states of those groups.'[12]
All individual relations to the sacred are derived – as individual cults
– from the collective or, as forms of magic, are opposed to actual
religion.

A collective, cognitive as well as practical relation to the sacred – it
is here, then, that the essence of religion lies for Durkheim. Of course,
an abstract definition alone can only delimit, not illuminate, the
phenomenon of the religious. Accordingly, the main body of Durkheim's work is devoted to the rebuttal of erroneous views about the
elementary forms of the religious life, as well as to describing and
analysing the beliefs and rituals of the Australian aborigines. In this
connection, Durkheim elaborates an idea about a suprapersonal force
or power being the actual essence of totemism: 'In other words,
totemism is not the religion of certain animals, certain men, or certain
images; it is the religion of a kind of anonymous and impersonal force
that is identifiable in each of these beings but identical to none of
them.'[13] Religious thought, then, emanates not from a belief in mythical personalities, gods or spirits, but from 'indefinite powers, anonymous forces. They are more or less numerous in different societies
(sometimes, indeed, they are only one force)'.[14] Accordingly, the
sacredness of sacred objects or practices is not grounded in their
essence, but stems from the fact that they are construed as the
embodiments of this principle of sacredness, of a force that is operative and experienceable in them.

Durkheim approaches the climax of his investigation when he
reflects on how the idea of this sacred power might have originated.
In order to answer the question of the origin of totemism, he reminds
us of the well-known fact that a gathering of people, particularly
when it lasts for a lengthy period of time and certain, more fully
describable conditions obtain, diminishes the self-control of all participants and exerts a powerful, stimulating influence upon them. This
effect is the more intense the weaker the usual self-control of the
participants. Durkheim employs a number of naturalistic metaphors
in order to describe what he has in mind: he talks of a growing heat

between the participants, an increasing electrical tension, an echo or avalanche effect. He recalls the 'demon of oratorical inspiration' which takes hold of a speaker who succeeds in communicating with his listeners:

> His language becomes high-flown in a way that would be ridiculous in ordinary circumstances; his gestures take on an overbearing quality; his very thought becomes impatient of limits and slips easily into every kind of extreme. This is because he feels filled to overflowing, as though with a phenomenal oversupply of forces that spill over and tend to spread around him. Sometimes he even feels possessed by a moral force greater than he, of which he is only the interpreter.[15]

However, the effect of this excitement is by no means always, as in this example, an experience of empowerment. Durkheim claims that from a certain threshold onwards it becomes, rather, an experience of being overwhelmed, and can extend as far as loss of self.

> It is not difficult to imagine that a man in such a state of exaltation should no longer know himself. Feeling possessed and led on by some sort of external power that makes him think and act differently than he normally does, he naturally feels he is no longer himself. It seems to him that he has become a new being. The decorations with which he is decked out, and the masklike decorations that cover his face, represent this inward transformation even more than they help bring it about. And because his companions feel transformed in the same way at the same moment, and express this feeling by their shouts, movements, and bearing, it is as if he was in reality transported into a special world entirely different from the one in which he ordinarily lives, a special world inhabited by exceptionally intense forces that invade and transform him.[16]

These descriptions alternating between totemism and modernity serve to clarify Durkheim's basic idea. The experience of self-loss in the ecstasy of the collective – Durkheim himself speaks of a 'collective effervescence'[17] – is at the same time the experience of a force – an extra-ordinary power which holds the individual in its sway and transports him to another world. This force is indubitably efficacious; it is highly real. For Durkheim, it is nothing more than the effect of the individuals uniting to form a collective. In his analysis of the totem, he had already made constant efforts to portray it as the embodiment of sacred power, as well as 'the symbol of a particular society that is called the clan'.[18] After establishing this dual function of the totem, he is led to pose a further question: 'Thus, if the totem is the symbol of both the god and the society, is this not because the god and the society are one and the same? How could the emblem of the group have taken the form of that quasi-divinity if the group and the divinity were two distinct realities?' And he concludes: 'Thus the god of the clan, the totemic principle, can be none other than the clan itself, but the clan transfigured and imagined in the physical form of the plant or animal that serves as totem.'[19]

For Durkheim, therefore, the investigation of collective ecstasy is an attempt to explain the origin of this 'deification'. He assumes that the immense experiences of self-loss and of a force which causes the everyday to vanish are not, as a rule, interpreted with cool-headed reason by those involved as the mere product of their interaction. These experiences, however, especially when they are at an end and ordinary life begins once more, urgently require integration into familiar frames of reference. According to Durkheim, this happens with the participants ascribing their experience to pre-existent powers with which they only came into contact at the time and place of their assembly. Consequently, they do not interpret the anonymous force as the force of their own collectivity. Their affective certainty that higher powers are at work, which results with compelling force from the experience of self-loss, is, therefore, transformed into a pre-reflective attachment to the attributes of the situation in which this experience was undergone. This is the source of the classification of the world into two separate domains: according to the criterion whether an object or action is connected or unconnected with this extra-ordinary experience. Thus, everything that does not manifest such a connection is profane; sacred is that which corresponds to this experience – in however mediated a form. The moment of self-loss, which Durkheim describes metaphorically but none the less vividly, thus does not usually represent hopeless loss, but rather a surpassing of the delimited self in the direction of those forces of sociality which are interpreted as sacred.

Durkheim does not restrict this experience to such 'passing and intermittent states'.[20] He believes that some historical periods are similarly characterized by intensified social interaction, by a collective overactivity and a resultant stimulation of individual forces, which find their expression in heroic and barbaric acts beyond the pale of the everyday. This explains the intensity of revolutionary periods. But Durkheim sees the stimulating influence of collective existence at work even within normal everyday life, in so far as the recognition or respect of our fellow beings always motivates us anew.

> There is virtually no instant of our lives in which a certain rush of energy fails to come to us from outside ourselves. In all kinds of acts that express

the understanding, esteem, and affection of his neighbor, there is a lift that the man who does his duty feels, usually without being aware of it. But that lift sustains him; the feeling society has for him uplifts the feeling he has for himself.[21]

Returning to the elementary case of totemism, Durkheim is ultimately able also to explain the particular form of collective actions and their effects in aboriginal societies as arising from this tension between the experience which constitutes the sacred, and the force sustaining us in everyday life. He sees the life of these societies following a temporal rhythm alternating between their dispersal into small groups and their gathering together for large ceremonies. The individuals undergo the extra-ordinary experiences which Durkheim described in these gatherings – but the force which originates in these experiences sustains the individuals in the periods when they are dispersed over a wide geographical area and makes their ordinary life possible. Collective ecstasy imparts vitality to individuals; its repetition constantly renews their powers.

We need not concern ourselves here with the question as to how far Durkheim was correct in his analysis of the religious life of the Australian aborigines.[22] The subsequent chapters of his book are chiefly devoted to an attempt to derive the concepts of soul, spirit and God from these theoretical foundations, and to an examination of various kinds of ritual. In a concluding summary, Durkheim then makes clear that he believes the theses he has arrived at through his inquiry into totemism have a more general significance. He believes he has demonstrated that the formation of ideals can be accounted for scientifically. The ideal is, he explains,

> a natural product of social life. If society is to be able to become conscious of itself and keep the sense it has of itself at the required intensity, it must assemble and concentrate. This concentration brings about an uplifting of moral life that is expressed by a set of ideal conceptions in which the new life thus awakened is depicted. These ideal conceptions correspond to the onrush of psychic forces added at that moment to those we have at our disposal for the everyday tasks of life. A society can neither create nor recreate itself without creating some kind of ideal at the same stroke. This creation is not a sort of optional extra step by which society, being already made, merely adds finishing touches; it is the act by which society makes itself, and remakes itself, periodically.[23]

Durkheim believes, then, that he has discovered in the elementary forms of religion the secret of religion *per se*: the dynamic formation of ideals in the experience of collective ecstasy. However, his explanation, areligious though it is, should not therefore be confused with the theory of religion advanced by historical materialism. Durkheim himself sets great store by this distinction.[24] Although both regard religion as a social phenomenon, Durkheim does not view religion (and the formation of ideals in general) in reductionist terms, as the mere translation of material interests into illusory forms. In collective ecstasy, social life, he argues, gives birth to *sui generis* phenomena which obey their own laws and can be attributed neither to the individual nor to an 'ideal-free' material reality. Durkheim proposes, therefore, in contradistinction to Nietzsche[25] and Marx, a non-reductive, areligious theory of religion and the formation of values. But how does this account relate to the one put forward by William James?

To answer this question it is helpful to refer first of all to Durkheim's direct criticism of James. Without any doubt, Émile Durkheim was well acquainted with the work of James in general and with his theory of religion in particular. In *The Elementary Forms* he mentions James's *Psychology* twice and his *Varieties* once. He expressly agrees with James that religious convictions cannot be viewed merely as the delusions of the faithful, but as products of specific *experiences*; of experiences which, though distinct from those which can become the basis for scientific claims, are still no less fruitful or significant for those who have them. Even so, after initially agreeing with James, he objects that it does not follow from the fact of such religious experience that 'the reality which grounds it should conform objectively with the idea that the believers have of it'.[26] But James had not claimed that all interpretations of religious experiences made by believers are true statements about reality; they refer for him only to something that undeniably requires interpretation. When Durkheim polemicizes here against James's alleged interpretation of religious experiences as privileged, objective intuitions, he is opposing the religious interpretation of religious experiences in general. Every interpretation of religious experiences which leaves scope for their religious interpretation obviously conflicts with Durkheim's conclusion, supposedly reached by empirical observation, that 'the objective, universal, and eternal cause'[27] of these experiences is nothing other than society in its state of excitement.

Durkheim deals more thoroughly with James's theory of religion in the lectures on pragmatism he delivered in 1913/14.[28] The twelfth of these lectures is devoted entirely to the subject of 'Pragmatism and Religion', and Durkheim provides here a fair and accurate summary of James's theory of religion, emphasizing in particular the fact that

James focuses not on religious institutions or belief systems, but on the religious experiences of individuals. Also worth emphasizing, in Durkheim's view, are James's analyses of the experience of the presence of superior powers which transcend the individual; his thesis of the unconscious sources of this idea; and his profound interpretations of saintliness, mysticism, conversion and prayer. Here, too, he voices his scepticism about a religious interpretation of such experiences and adds, albeit only in a cautious and restrained manner within the context of a general evaluation of pragmatism, the critical remark that James reduces all religious phenomena to the dimension of *individual* experience. This objection certainly deserved to be developed more fully, even though it is from the outset some way off-target – for Durkheim here sees James's radical individualism as rooted in the general orientation of pragmatism, whereas James was the only pragmatist who did not view religion as primarily a social phenomenon.[29]

But the differences between Durkheim and James at this juncture are less interesting than their agreement on one essential point. Namely, Durkheim quite evidently accepts James's fundamental methodological insight, which consists in *making religious experiences the point of departure for a theory of religion*. This agreement between the classic French sociologist of religion and the most famous representative of the theory of religion in American pragmatism might not strike the modern reader as particularly spectacular. The reason for this is that it is easy to forget how revolutionary this methodology was for the study of religion. William James was the first author to apply such a method consistently in a science of religious experience, and one of the main aims of his lectures on the theory of religion was to prove its value.

The priority for this methodological innovation thus clearly lies with James. Yet it is well known that this had been a central theme in Durkheim's work ever since he first encountered Robertson Smith's writings in 1895. It is also true that Durkheim was already endeavouring, in the most important of his relevant works written after the turning-point in his theory of religion, that is, in his 1899 essay 'De la définition des phénomènes religieux',[30] to go beyond the contemporary approaches in theology and the psychology of religion and to place, as Robertson Smith had before him, religious acts of worship, i.e. practices, at the centre of his work. But in this essay, as well as in the other writings of this same period, Durkheim, like his mentor, was still utterly uncertain of the relationship between cult and belief, between practices and experiences. Even though scattered remarks on mass psychology appear from a very early point onwards in Durkheim's work, and foreshadow the idea of collective effervescence, they have, to begin with, no systematic place in the construction of his theory. Neither the consideration of religious practices, nor the attention paid to collective effervescence alone, therefore, can have led Durkheim to the idea that the investigation of the genesis of ultimate values should begin with the analysis of the *religious experience of collectives*. Further evidence to support this claim lies in the fact that the essay on primitive systems of classification, which Durkheim published with Marcel Mauss in 1903, did not yet contain this insight.[31] It must, then, have first been developed after this point – and that means around the time that Durkheim and Mauss read James's book. Although Durkheim's references to James are not especially spectacular with regard to the theory of religion, this does not mean that James did not exert a considerable influence on Durkheim's decision to base his own theory of religion on the analysis of religious experience.

Fortunately, there is another text from which we can infer the provocative role that James's work played for the two French thinkers. In 1904, Mauss published a lengthy discussion of James's book in *L'année sociologique*, the journal of the Durkheim school.[32] The tone of this review is extremely critical, almost schoolmasterly and quite pedantic. Mauss includes the following points in his long list of complaints: the lack in James of a clear definition of the concepts of 'experience' and 'religious experience'; the influence of liberal Protestantism on his views on religion; the overemphasis on pathological types of religious experience; his use of metaphysical concepts and the way he generalizes modern individualism and projects it back into history. Mauss goes so far in his flight of didacticism as to suggest to James another title for his book in order to indicate the limited scope of its validity, namely: 'A Study of Several Psychological Forms of Religious Feeling' or, even more narrowly, 'On Several Strictly Individual Feelings with Reference to Strictly Individualized Religious Phenomena in our Societies'. It would have been a simple thing for James to reply to Mauss's criticisms point by point. James deliberately avoided rigid definitions at the beginning of his account because he thought it foolish 'to set up an abstract definition of religion's essence, and then to proceed to defend that definition against all comers'.[33] For James, rather, the advancement towards an understanding of the divine consisted precisely in analysing the varieties of religious experience without any reservations. Likewise, his concept of 'experience' cannot be grasped in a ready definition, but only when his philosophy of 'radical empiricism' or pragmatism as a whole is taken into account. James would not have described his proximity to liberal Protestantism as any more detrimental to a general theory of religion than proximity to Catholic or Jewish religious traditions. He had already taken precautions in his book to defend himself against the charge that he was too heavily reliant on psychopathological material, and put forward two compelling reasons for doing so. Firstly, he was simply tolerant of so-called pathologies, and thought the designation of a phenomenon as pathological to be a culturally highly variable fact, not a fixed attribute of its nature. Secondly, he attempted, as we have seen, to maintain the distinction between genesis and validity even in the case of religious experience. James used metaphysical concepts because he did not share Durkheim's and Mauss's positivistic confidence in the ultimate triumph of science over metaphysics. And finally, he certainly did not think that his allegedly exclusive concentration on modern phenomena of highly individual experiences represented any greater restriction of the class of phenomena under investigation than Durkheim's and Mauss's almost exclusive concentration on archaic cultures in their sociology of religion.

Irrespective of which party should ultimately be proved right in this imaginary dispute, we should again be careful – as we were in evaluating Durkheim's direct references to James – not to be misled by Mauss's demonstrative declarations that real differences exist between his own position and that of the American psychologist of religion. In an important passage of his discussion, Mauss explains his motives for rejecting James's use of the concept 'experience'. He refuses to apply the term 'experience', or even the term 'state of consciousness' ('état de conscience'), to those mental states in which the autonomy of the personality, and even the capacity to have consciousness, is called into question. Buddhist or similar attempts to reach a 'Nirvana', a state in which consciousness retreats from all bonds with the world, but also mystical and ecstatic states, represent for Mauss the impoverishment or even the destruction of 'experience'. They are for him anything but experience, for the simple reason that he wishes to reserve the concept of 'experience' for well-ordered and reality-related learning processes.

This might sound like a mere quibble about terms, but Mauss's conspicuous reluctance to accept James's terminology conceals a fundamental question. Mauss certainly did not want to dispute the fact that mysticism, ecstasy or trance-states represent changes in the form and content of human consciousness. His remarks must be construed, rather, as a kind of rearguard action. Both Durkheim and Mauss were constantly trying to defend a Cartesian conception of the human mind against the ever stronger influence of pragmatism and Bergsonism. However, it was the very subject of religion which eventually forced them to acknowledge that there are at least certain 'psychological states' which cannot be described in Cartesian-mentalistic terms, since such states are characterized by the fact that individuals do not remain imprisoned within the confines of their discrete consciousnesses; rather, the boundaries of their selves are opened, they transcend themselves and alter their fundamental relations both to the world and to themselves. In 1904 Mauss was still struggling to shunt psychological states into a sphere which could not be encompassed by the concept of 'experience' – whereas later, in the mature version of Durkheim's theory of religion, these phenomena were to be regarded very much as experiences, and the key role was even assigned to the analysis of collective experience.

The differences between James and Durkheim can, then, be summarized in three points. First of all, James's individualist approach differs radically from the collectivist one favoured by Durkheim. Secondly, Durkheim represents an evolutionist way of thinking and James, in contrast, a modernist one. Finally, Durkheim understands his theory of religion as helping to make possible the continuation of those functions which religion performs *without* still clinging to religious belief, whereas James's main concern was to defend the right to personal faith against modern constraints on thought. Yet over and above these divergences, there is quite clearly common ground between them. We have already seen that they agree on methodology: for both, the science of religion is to be constructed upon the analysis of personal experience. A further correspondence consists in their distinguishing between two components which James describes as the difference between religion and morality, and Durkheim as the two characteristic features of morality. Clarifying this point of agreement will serve to connect the analysis of the sacred more closely with issues in moral philosophy.

William James had separated religion and morality from one another because he saw morality as having a restrictive character, while religion actually opened up possibilities for action. In his theory of religion, Durkheim emphasizes the double character of 'moral authority' and, in essays on moral theory dating from the period during which he was writing *The Elementary Forms*, he elaborates this conception above all in opposition to Kant's moral philosophy.[34] He agrees without reservation with Kant's arguments against utilitarianism: that duty constitutes a necessary factor in the definition of moral rules. In opposition to Kant, however, he insists that we are unable to perform actions solely from a sense of duty. Accordingly, he also makes a 'certain degree of desirability' characteristic of morality.[35] 'It is this *sui generis* desirability which is commonly called *good*.'[36] The 'good' and

'duty' are present in all moral actions in complex and varying proportions. Durkheim sees here a direct parallel with the empirically
observable character of the sacred which is simultaneously both
adored and feared. He resists all attempts to accord primacy to either
one of the two components of morality. There are in his view neither
historical nor logical grounds for doing so. If the sacred already
manifests the same duality, then this duality does not seem to have
first arisen with the emergence of a morality distinct from religion. If
the good is accorded priority, all obligatoriness would then vanish
from morality because duty itself must then be declared desirable.
Durkheim is concerned, then, with maintaining the tension between
duty and the good, even if he is prepared to concede that both
components need not in reality be separated, but can reciprocally
permeate one another. 'We feel a *sui generis* pleasure in performing
our duty simply because it is our duty. The notion of the good enters
into those of duty and obligation, just as they in turn enter into the
notion of the good.'[37] Thus, Durkheim builds into morality itself the
same tension which James describes as obtaining between religion
and morality. Neither thinker defines morality, as Nietzsche does,
exclusively in terms of the imperative, so that religion can only be
construed as the metaphysical justification of the imperative. The
proximity between Durkheim and James is even greater in this respect
than the differences in their conceptualization would at first lead one
to suspect. However much Durkheim emphasizes the perpetually
sacred character of morality,[38] thereby extending his concept of the
sacred far beyond the ambit of traditional religions, he also insists on
the fact that the imperative is not 'in fact, the religious element in
morality. However, one could demonstrate that the more sacred a
moral rule becomes, the more the element of obligation tends to
recede.'[39] For Durkheim, as for James, the truly religious is not
imperative, obligatory and restrictive, but rather attractive, empowering and motivating.[40]

This imaginary dialogue between Durkheim and James no doubt
leaves us feeling somewhat confused. It ought to have become clear
by now that both thinkers take the view that to explain the genesis of
values would require us to investigate those actions and experiences
in which the self opens up and a temporary loss of self leads to
contact with powers that can invigorate it. However, neither Durkheim's evolutionist and collectivist, nor James's modernist and individualist approach are, presumably, wholly convincing. In my own
view, at least three points need further clarification.

First of all, Durkheim's analysis of totemism leaves to a large extent
open the question as to what conclusions we are to draw from it for

modern societies. He makes it clear that he thinks collective ecstasies are possible in modern societies too. The memory of mass movements during the French Revolution exerted an unmistakable influence on Durkheim.[41] For him, such events are not primitive or irrational marginal phenomena of sociality, but the constitutive precondition for all emotionally charged social ties to collectives and values. Consequently, the sacred does not vanish in the ongoing process of functional differentiation either, since for Durkheim individuals and social structures cannot survive without a sacred core. He makes clear, especially in his essay on the Dreyfus affair, that the sacredness of a modern, differentiated and individualized society lies for him in the very principle of inalienable rights and the dignity of the individual.[42] This modern sacralization of the individual constitutes for him the affective mainstay of the new morality. For this reason, critics after Durkheim's death were completely wrong to describe his emphasis on collective ecstasy as an apologia for fascist rallies and other mass rituals of National Socialism or communism.[43] These were as far removed as possible from Durkheim's actual political and moral intentions. Nevertheless, this misunderstanding could arise because Durkheim had not really explained how a commitment to the values of individualism can come about in modern societies. Which collective enthusiasm can lead to the commitment to individualism? Are other experiences decisive for it? Or does modern individualism have no future because it cannot itself produce the binding forces on which it remains dependent? However brilliant Durkheim's combination of an evolutionist-collectivist account with modern individualism appears to be, it ultimately fails to answer these questions.

We could, however, apply the reverse argument to William James. His exclusive emphasis on individual experience may better correspond to the conditions of modern societies than Durkheim's analysis of totemism, but it leads him merely to touch on those 'excited assemblies'[44] which are mentioned in his source material, and to project an isolation in prayer and ritual back into history. We therefore certainly need to clarify the relationship between individual and collective experience above and beyond the accounts provided by James and Durkheim.

This problem immediately points to another. In James, as well as in Durkheim, the interpretation of an experience seems to grow out of the experience itself. Durkheim may accuse James of failing to distinguish between the unquestionable reality of individual experience and the individual's eminently questionable interpretation of this experience.[45] But in his own account even the collective interpretation of collective experience evolves from the latter without the individuals who participate in the collective experience having developed differing interpretations of this experience, which they only then refine into a collective interpretation through a process of discussion and argument (a process that is pervaded with power). Both thinkers thus neglect the role played by the interpretation of experience. Together with the unexplained relationship between individual and collective experience, this neglect has important consequences. In James's theory it is difficult to see how the individual continues to depend on a shared language and a cultural repertoire of components necessary for interpreting even his or her most intense personal experiences. Durkheim, in turn, sheds no light on the fact that individuals do not really become one entity, even in the fusion of collective ecstasy; the integration of their experience in everyday life must therefore necessarily manifest individual variations. Even the bond with, and understanding of, the collectively constituted sacred is not the same for all individuals. His theory of religion contains no discussion whatsoever of the way in which an individual might develop by differentiating himself or herself from the collective.

Durkheim has absolutely no theoretical category at his disposal to take account of the individual's interpretative self-reflexivity. Metaphorical language conceals the lack of such a category only with great difficulty in what is otherwise such a conceptually clear work. In contrast, James is one of the pioneers of a theory of the self. Whereas both he and other authors following his lead mainly enlisted this theory in order to investigate self-formation in processes of everyday communication, in his theory of religious experience, James concentrates on self-formation in solitary interaction with the divine. Like Durkheim, James also leaves the problem of the relationship between ordinary communication and extra-ordinary experience unresolved. In what follows, therefore, we must investigate whether other thinkers succeeded in illuminating the interplay of individual and collective experience, as well as the relationship between ordinary and extra-ordinary experience.

5

The Immanence of Transcendence
(Georg Simmel)

If the emphasis on the dynamics of human experience is not yet sufficient to furnish a satisfactory answer to the question of the genesis of values, because the relationship between individual and collective, as well as the relationship between ordinary and extra-ordinary experience, has yet to be clarified, then it makes sense to turn to another thinker, who, familiar as he was with the authors we have discussed so far, promises to contribute ideas which can take us further down the road towards a resolution of our problem. Certainly, we expect Georg Simmel's work to evince a profound comprehension of individual experience, of the cultural preconditions for its differentiation, and of the problems raised by the interpretation of experience and the understanding of cultural forms. What is more, his book *Schopenhauer and Nietzsche* was of decisive importance for the interpretation of Nietzsche's philosophy; he also criticized James's work and pragmatism, and his exchange of ideas with his contemporary Émile Durkheim even led some in France to suppose that Durkheim's theory of religion had been inspired by Simmel.[1] We can assume, therefore, that the thinkers discussed hitherto pursued the question concerning us here in a complex discursive skein.

Admittedly, Georg Simmel is a thinker who as a rule does not reveal his sources, and whose brilliant remarks are usually difficult to pin down to unequivocal statements and conclusions. It is true of Simmel, even more than of the other thinkers we have discussed so far, that to isolate a clearly defined answer to the question guiding our inquiry, even if it is elaborated by considering his entire life's work, means neglecting other aspects of his work and not doing full justice to the complexity of his intellectual development. To chart this development, a tripartite periodization has, ever since an early recognition of Simmel's importance,[2] become established, according to which he progressed from a positivistic-evolutionist early phase to a middle, neo-Kantian phase, before ending up as an exponent of *Lebensphilosophie*. Admittedly, it is confusing that Simmel habitually incorporated revised older texts from earlier phases into new writings, and that, conversely, earlier works frequently foreshadow motifs that would later become fundamental to his thought. With a mind as receptive as Simmel's, any such schema is therefore artificial; it would be more accurate to say that he articulated the ideas preoccupying him in different ways according to the different trends prevailing at the time.

Simmel was interested in the philosophy and sociology of religion and of morality – that is to say, in the areas in which an answer to the question of the genesis of values can most likely be found – during all three phases of his intellectual development. He had already endeavoured to distinguish morality and religion in his early *Einleitung in die Moralwissenschaft*, where he was concerned with the historical and psychological derivation of central categories of moral judgement, as well as their logical structures and psychological consequences.[3] In his middle period, he wrote several essays on the sociology of religion which formed the basis of *Die Religion* (1906), a book he republished in 1912 after revising it according to motifs constitutive of his third phase.[4] Finally, the 'four metaphysical chapters' brought together in *Lebensanschauung* (1918) were composed towards the end of his life.[5] But, as we shall see, in contrast to our analysis of James and Durkheim, we must go beyond the subject of religion if we are to discuss and understand Simmel's answer to our question. It is only by also considering his writings on war and the profound late works on metaphysical questions that we shall arrive at Simmel's most important ideas.

An appropriate first step is to situate Simmel's views on religion within the context of James's and Durkheim's theories.[6] Simmel's early works, with their positivistic-evolutionist impetus, have far more in common with those of Durkheim than with James's thought. Like Durkheim, Simmel also regards the investigation of objects of culture like religion in their 'undeveloped states' as indispensable for comprehending them 'in their highest and independent forms'.[7] But he does not combine this evolutionism with the hope that he will be able to identify positively the one problem to which religion provides an answer. On the contrary, he thinks that the very assumption that there is such a clear-cut origin is misleading. Like Durkheim, but unlike the radical positivism of the nineteenth century, Simmel disputes, further-more, that analysing religion in this way in terms of its diverse origins is itself sufficient to dissolve religion into a mere tissue of illusions:

> In addition, we must insist that no matter how mundanely and how empirically the origin of ideas about the supramundane and the tran-scendent is explained, neither the subjective, emotional value of these ideas nor their objective values as matters of fact is at all in question. Both these values lie beyond the limits that our merely causal, psycho-logical inquiry aims to reach.[8]

The abrupt separation of genesis and validity is clearly reminiscent of neo-Kantian philosophy of value, although Simmel does not conform to its style. He is evidently more interested in genesis than in validity, and a systematization of values never had much appeal for him. Though Durkheim likewise rejects positivistic reductionism *vis-à-vis* religion, he nevertheless believes that his analysis of its elementary forms will enable him to bring to light its fundamental secret; in contrast, Simmel's early linkage of evolutionism and the philosophy of value fails to illuminate the relationship between genesis and validity.

Simmel is also closer to Durkheim than to James on the question of whether religion has a predominantly individual or collective charac-ter: he too has no doubt that the religious is principally social in nature. Unlike Durkheim, however, he does not go so far as to construe the divine as the symbolic transfiguration of society. Instead, he only suggests that parallels might be drawn between the transfor-mation of the divine and that of the social, an idea that, in contrast to Durkheim's approach, at the same time admits the historical possi-bility of individualized religiosity in the face of modern individuali-zation. However, Simmel's understanding of the social differs from Durkheim's, and therefore the way in which he links the religious with the social is also distinct. The basic idea underlying Simmel's sociology is that of social interaction – and thus a conception of the social lying half-way between pure individualism and complete collec-tivism. Accordingly, the religious is for Simmel *a quality of social relationships*: 'human contact, in the purely psychological aspect of its interaction, develops that definite tone which, when heightened to an independent substance, is known as religion.'[9] The religious is thus not only not confined to institutional forms; it can also be expressly encountered in everyday relationships: as examples Simmel cites the relationship of the child to its parents, of the patriot to his country, and similar instances. Religiosity obtains everywhere where social

relationships manifest a certain emotional tone; this Simmel describes
more precisely as

> a peculiar admixture of unselfish surrender and fervent desire, of humil-
> ity and exaltation, of sensual concreteness and spiritual abstraction; this
> occasions a certain degree of emotional tension, a specific ardor and
> certainty of the subjective conditions, an inclusion of the subject in a
> higher order – an order which, at the same time, is felt to be something
> inward and personal. This religious quality is contained, it seems to me,
> in many other relationships, and gives them a tone that distinguishes
> them from relationships based on pure egoism, pure influence, or even
> purely moral forces.[10]

For our purposes, it should be stressed that the religious is thereby
clearly distinguished from the moral, and that a mixture of inclination
(*Wollen*) and obligation (*Sollen*) appears possible in it.

In a third respect which is relevant here, Simmel differs from both
Durkheim and James – on the question, namely, whether the theory
of religion should itself follow a religious or an areligous line of
attack. His position on the question of validity already intimated that
he separates it completely from the scope of a genetic investigation.
He defends the right to such an investigation, but clearly delimits its
consequences, thereby leaving unclear his own position *vis-à-vis*
religion. It is entirely consistent with the general style of his thought
for him to defend simultaneously, and with the same eloquence, both
a thesis and its antithesis – not out of carelessness or indifference, but
because he possesses a broad understanding and keen insight into the
diversity of the possible perspectives.

Contextualizing Simmel in this way shows that his point of departure is not identical with that of either Durkheim or James. But what
conclusions can we draw from this for our question? Our first
impression when sifting through Simmel's contributions to the theory
of religion is that they will yield little in the way of answers. Though
Simmel shows himself to be aware of the relationship between experience, interpretation and social interaction, in so far as he views
cultural forms as objectifications and in his analyses identifies their
genesis in the stream of action, he does not seem to have at his
disposal the proper conceptual means necessary for unravelling this
relationship.[11] Though Simmel's emphasis on social interaction seems
to offer a way of escaping the dualism of individual and collective
experience, the more precise outlines of this path remain quite unclear
in his writings on the theory of religion. Greater caution, however, is
called for here. The full import of Simmel's remarks on religion only
becomes clear when they are related to his sociological diagnosis of

his time.[12] Simmel saw modernity as characterized not only by a rationalist undermining of naïve value-security, but above all by a change in the conditions required for the genesis of new value-security. The variety of attitudes, all directly influencing one another, in, say, the modern metropolis; the speed with which they change; the impossibility of digesting the multiplicity of impressions; the opacity of the means–end chains extended ever further by money – all this, Simmel believes, doubtless makes the formation of new values more difficult. As a result, his interest in religion – or rather the free floating 'religious' – is aroused chiefly because he can explore through it the possibility of value-formation. The definition of the emotional quality of the religious had already signalled the fact that Simmel saw in it a unique balance of conflicting feelings. In his essay 'On the Salvation of the Soul' (1903), Simmel generalized this basic idea, declaring that religion's great achievement was the formation of a new, synthesizing and vital unity. 'One of the great intellectual achievements of religion is that it draws together the vast spectrum of human ideas and concerns and concentrates them into single, unified concepts; unlike those of philosophy, these concepts are not abstract but rather possess the full vitality of being themselves in their immediacy and inner tangibility.'[13] 'God', 'saintliness' and 'eternal life' are for him concepts expressing just such an uplifting reference to some more universal thing: 'that which is most common to all and yet the unique and most personal possession of every soul'.[14] In this spirit, he explains the 'salvation of the soul' as a universal demand made on every individual to wrest from himself precisely 'the most personal and unique elements of his being, real in conception but not yet pure in form'.[15] What is more, in his short monograph on religion, Simmel also applies this idea to the domain of social relationships. Just as the self strives for a 'synthesis of restraint and expansion . . ., of spontaneous will and dependence, of giving and receiving', so the individual's outward search aims at a synthesis of freedom and commitment in social life.[16] The goal is here a 'structure of the whole that is oriented toward the independence and the stable unity of its elements, a structure indeed that such independence and unity make possible'.[17] Religion thus becomes the utopian articulation of a form of social integration under conditions of the highest individuation – a utopia, though, which does not necessarily remain impotent, with no influence on reality, but which instead radiates its attractive force towards social life, thus contributing to its transformation.

A provisional appraisal of these reflections might therefore suggest that, despite its novel point of departure, Simmel's theory of religion

does not take us very far beyond James and Durkheim – and this for
the simple reason alone that it is not as elaborate as their efforts and
perhaps barely merits the description of a theory of religion. Nevertheless, by being embedded in a sophisticated sociological diagnosis
of the difficulties facing the formation of new values in modernity,
these pointers to a theory of religion have an electrifying effect. But
here, too, it is unclear where Simmel's hints are actually leading. His
inspired description of the psychological effects of the religious orientation and of the foreshadowing of utopia in society's relation to the
transcendent should on no account be misconstrued as religious
propaganda. Though he is thus able, say, to appreciate the awakening
interest in mysticism in the early years of the new century, his own
attitude towards mysticism is characterized by a desire to understand
this phenomenon through quiet contemplation, and not by any active
commitment to it or even by an intention to offer a courageous
prognosis of the future of the 'religious'. The strong emphasis on the
claim that the religious is rooted in social relationships sensitized him
not only to the first signs of the rise of a new religiosity, but also
paved the way for the idea that something new could take the place
of religion in the modern age, something which, though having no
relation to the transcendent, would claim for itself the qualities of the
religious.

For the mood of perplexity which had hung over Simmel's remarks
abruptly vanished as the Great War that was to shape the entire
twentieth century broke out in the summer of 1914.[18] Simmel immediately began to interpret the war along the lines of the diagnoses of his
time he had written during the pre-war period. The war seemed to
him the great break – or at least the great opportunity to effect such a
break – with the trends dominating modern culture. While the means–
end chains become ever more incalculable in a culture shaped by
money, in war deprivation, and in particular the experience of being
a soldier, forces us to focus again on the basic ends necessary for our
survival and to renounce our blasé attitude towards everyday needs.
While in the society based on the division of labour we lose sight of
the repercussions of individual actions in the ocean of interactions, in
war we can experience the dramatic consequences of individual
courage and commitment, which enable us to recover a sense of
fulfilled temporality. While the individual under conditions of social
differentiation experiences himself mainly in terms of his difference
from others, in war he is drawn into ecstatic communal experiences,
thereby becoming aware of the soil out of which he has grown and
regaining his plasticity. In all these experiences, war increases life's
intensity to a level of which the culture-critical currents of the pre-war

period could only have dreamt. Hence, if one is searching for value-forming experiences there is no need at all to fall back on premodern history or to determine the potential of religion in the modern age.[19] With one stroke, war solves the puzzle which had seemed insoluble to the intellectual search for the origin of values:

> I venture to say that the majority of us have only now experienced what one might call an absolute situation. All the circumstances in which we otherwise lived have something relative about them; they are decided by considerations of more or less; they are conditioned from this side or that. All this is now out of the question: with the deployment of our forces, the perils and the willingness to sacrifice ourselves, we stand before an absolute decision which no longer knows a balancing of sacrifice and profit, no longer knows ifs and buts, compromise, or the viewpoint of quantity. With this monstrousness, which could never have brought us a war with France alone, but only a war like the one we are now prosecuting, we are ensnared in an *idea*. For the question 'is Germany to be or not to be?' cannot be answered by the intellect of the rationalistic, the deliberations of which always remain relative; nor, of course, can it be answered by the naïveté of children. Only that highest authority of our being which Kant calls the 'faculty of ideas' – that is, the faculty to comprehend an Absolute – is decisive here – even for those who have never read or understood the word 'idea'. For everything particular and contingent that normally determines us now lies beneath us: we stand   something that life usually only permits or demands of a few – on the ground of an Absolute ... to hell with all 'objective' justifications of this willing ... As soon as I fall back on justifications of this kind I run not only the risk of de-objectifying these objective values, but also the risk facing anyone who attempts to prove something: to be refuted. Only what cannot be proved is irrefutable – our will to Germany, which lies beyond all proofs.[20]

The 'absolute situation' and the individual faculty 'to comprehend an Absolute': this was what Simmel, and, he thought, both his generation and the younger ones, had been searching for. Simmel did not only see the war as a possibility, to exploit which he had to appeal to his contemporaries; in the willingness to make sacrifices on a massive scale he saw the practical consummation of the experience of value.[21] What everyone had been searching for had always been there; they had simply been looking in the wrong places. His description of the experience of war opposes the affective experience of a value's unconditional validity to the insights achieved by rational deliberation. Whereas James and Durkheim attempt to bring the experience of values into a constructive relationship with the obligatory character of morality, in Simmel's interpretation of war the experience of value overwhelms the individual so completely that he, the individual, can only curse any objections and doubts his intellect might have. Because it had seemed impossible that the path leading to the experience of value could originate in a culture of rationality, Simmel now denies reason any say in the redemptive feeling of experienced value. The voice of reason should either fall silent or it will be brought to silence.

During the course of the war, Simmel's tone becomes more muted. Little remains of the initial euphoria with which he proclaimed the transformative effects of the experience of war. He now expresses in a more plaintive tone the hope that so momentous an event will not remain wholly without effect. Towards the end of the war, he fully retracts the hopes he invested in it; only the prospect of the younger generation's idealistic, revolutionary convictions (Dionysian or ascetic in character) still seems to him to be reason for holding out for the 'German hope'[22] – that is, the opportunity of creating a modern society radically distinct from Western culture. From the beginning to the end, Simmel had scant interest in the empirical reality of the experience of war. Yet his mature answer to the question of the genesis of values develops out of this whole process: motifs characteristic of his pre-war theory of religion and critique of contemporary culture run through his description of the experience of war and his resigned repudiation of it, before evolving into the answer to our question which he formulated within the framework of *Lebensphilosophie*.[23]

It is by no means self-evident that *Lebensphilosophie* can furnish an answer to our question at all. If we take as the basic impulse of *Lebensphilosophie* the dissolution of all fixed forms in the stream of life and the recovery of experience from ossified conventions, then we would more likely expect it to dismiss the claims of the validity of value, rather than to deduce and describe the genesis of the character of its validity. Or, if it does indeed attempt such a derivation, then it would seem more obvious for it to adopt a reductive approach, as was the case in Nietzsche's *Genealogy of Morality*. But Simmel does not simply continue the Nietzschean line of argument: he is trying to steer a course between Nietzsche's reduction of ethical values to expressions of power and a neo-Kantian philosophy of value indifferent to the question of genesis. While this course had long remained unclear, during which time Simmel had seemed indecisive, oscillating helplessly between Nietzsche and Kant, its outlines can be more clearly discerned in his late work. He formulates an answer which has spectacular consequences for ethics.

In order to enable *Lebensphilosophie* to solve the question of values,

Simmel must first remove the concept of life from its dualistic opposition to the concept of form. He does this by ascribing a transcendental character to life itself. Life does not simply flow through
individuals, Simmel claims; rather, life creates individuals from out of
itself. 'That life is a continuous flowing and at the same time something contained in its carriers and contents, something formed around
centres, individuated, and, for this reason, as seen from the opposite
point of view, a forming that is always limited yet which continually
surpasses its limitedness – that is what constitutes its essence.'[24] Using
the examples of organic and mental life, he vividly demonstrates how
the drawing and transgression of boundaries are interlinked. In
reflecting on the limits of its knowledge, the cognizing consciousness
has already transcended them. In overcoming itself, the moral self is
simultaneously both that which has been overcome and that which
overcomes. A self that drew no boundaries would not be anything
determinate at all; a self, on the other hand, which no longer recalled
the character of its boundaries would be imprisoned within them and
cut off from the stream of life. 'And, for this reason, [life's] self-
transcendence is manifested as the unified act of constructing and
breaking through its barriers, its Other; it is manifested as the character of its absoluteness – which makes life's dismantling of itself into
independent and opposing entities perfectly conceivable.'[25] For Simmel, transcendence thus no longer refers to an other-wordly realm;
still less is it construed in terms of, or devalued by, a loss of faith in
such a realm – it is immanent, so that *this very immanence of transcendence* is proclaimed as life's true essence. Whenever we believe we
have seized an absolute, life puts us right and once more relativizes
this absolute. In this way, however, 'the transcendence of life shows
itself to be the true absoluteness, in which the conflict between
the absolute and the relative is sublated'.[26] In these formulations,
Simmel is no longer searching for something valuable that encompasses competing conceptions of value; instead, he elevates life itself,
in so far as it is always more than mere life, to the status of the
valuable.

In order not to misunderstand Simmel here, we must take utterly
seriously what he says about the distinctive feature of mental life.

Just as the transcending of life beyond its current limiting form within
its own level is the more-life (*Mehr-Leben*), which is, however, the
immediate, ineluctable essence of life itself, so its transcending towards
the level of its objective contents, of logically autonomous, no longer
vital meaning, is the more-than-life (*Mehr-als-Leben*); this is completely
inseparable from it and the essence of mental life itself.[27]

After Simmel has modified the concept of life so that it is not simply opposed to fixed forms, but also encompasses the production of individuated forms, he now attempts to prove that the 'ideal worlds' of Kantian and neo-Kantian philosophy have their origin in this 'life'. By this he means neither the dissolving of the ideality of these worlds through a recovery of the merely vital, nor merely adding genetic analyses to the ideals, whose validity is ultimately untouched by the history of their genesis – instead, far more radically, and also more productively, he proposes to solve the question of how life itself can produce 'ideal worlds' at all.

Just as the concept of self-transcendence characterizes the peculiarity of Simmel's concept of life, so the concept of 'axial rotation' (*Achsendrehung*)[28] characterizes the basic idea underlying his account of the genesis of ideal validities. He sharply contrasts the genesis of ideal validities with the process whereby a means becomes an end, something that is common in extended means–end chains. This reversal remains enmeshed in the structure of teleological action. 'If someone, instead of procuring pleasures with a sum of money, declared himself satisfied with possessing the money itself, like the miser – this only makes a difference to the material, but not to the essential form of the valuation'.[29] In contrast, Simmel's 'axial rotation' does not signal a reversal of end and means in a means–end chain, but rather a break with the means–end category as a whole.[30] In order to be able to contemplate such a break and not misinterpret it as a mere failed orientation to an end, Simmel endeavours first of all to relativize the category of ends or purposes in general. He describes the human being in anthropological terms as the only life-form capable of consciously acting in a purposive manner; yet he or she is also a 'non-purposive being',[31] because he or she can elevate himself or herself above end-oriented action. The realm of purposiveness is thus an intermediate zone located between pure impulsiveness and the liberation from teleology. The 'axial rotation' even takes place at the level of our impulses when – in love, for example – the original compelling desire leads to an intense personal relationship, which then contains not only its own satisfactions, but also demands and norms. Simmel rejects any (Kantian, for example) talk of 'ends in themselves', seeing it as a doomed attempt to express with an inadequate vocabulary the emancipation from purposiveness. However, particularly in all creative action, structures emerge which, though in every respect the product of vital conations, assume *qua* structures an independent existence and then react upon life. 'Culture in general arises where the categories that have been produced in and for the sake of life become independent moulders of intrinsically valuable formations which are objective *vis-à-vis* life.'[32] Citing the examples of art and science, he explains how these objectifications of life become autonomous, how their conformity to an inner law develops and how, as standards and models, they have a retroactive effect upon the processes of life. He sees in religion the most perfect rotation around the forms

> which life produces in itself in order immediately to give its contents coherence and warmth, depth and value. Now, however, they have become strong enough not to be determined by these contents, and instead determine life wholly of their own accord; the object which they themselves have formed and which corresponds to their now unlimited scope can now assume command of life.[33]

In his sociological diagnosis of his time, Simmel had isolated the problematic of a culture against whose structures life also 'often chafes, unable to gain access to them, failing in its subjective form to meet the demands it makes in their form'.[34] Now this problematic becomes for him fresh proof of the objectivity of the forms produced by the creative life. Simmel is nevertheless deeply ambivalent *vis-à-vis* the objectifications of the religious life. He wavers between, on the one hand, the notion 'that the fixed content of religious belief tends to dissolve into modes of religious *life*, into religiosity as the purely *functional* tuning of the inner process of life'[35] and, on the other, the assumption that trends towards dissolution discernible in his time are in fact the prelude to the development of new 'forms'.

The concepts of the 'self-transcendence of life' and the 'axial rotation' towards objectivity serve to prepare the ground for the actual value-theoretical nub of Simmel's argument. He arrives at this by focusing on that process of life which produces from itself the structure 'that one can call the self'.[36] In his reflections on the self-transcendence of life, Simmel had already, in order to depict the dialectical process of the drawing and transgression of boundaries, repeatedly referred not to the structure of the organism, but to the constitution of the self. In the third of his 'metaphysical chapters', he addresses the themes of 'death and immortality' and thus brings into sharper focus the self of an organism whose life is temporally limited.

An organism's boundaries are of course not only spatial, but also temporal. Every organism must die; only human beings, however, are aware of the fact that, as organisms, they must die. Simmel maintains that we do not understand our mortality until we have ceased to think of death as the Grim Reaper approaching us from a point outside life, or as the severing of our life-thread by the Fates,[37] and until we realize that death is actually part of life and shapes its entire course. He utilizes both biological and psychological data to lend plausibility to this metaphysical statement. This recognition of our finitude becomes for Simmel the necessary precondition for the genesis of values.

> If we lived for ever, life would probably remain undifferentiated, fused together with its values and contents; there would be no real motivation at all to construe them outside of the only form in which we can know and often experience them. But we die, and thus experience life as something contingent and transient; as something which can also, so to speak, be other than it is.[38]

The theme of contingency, which had formed the point of departure for the question of the genesis of values, thus resurfaces in a completely unexpected fashion. The recognition of the contingency of our existence does not mean for Simmel that all value evaporates into mere contingency; rather, this insight creates, in contrast to itself, the idea of a value existing beyond the temporal. The self's awareness of its own finitude is thus the indispensable co-ordinating point in the genesis of ideal validities.

For Simmel, the category of the self thrusts itself between the poles of facticity and validity. 'This self exists in its own peculiar category, . . . a third category lying beyond the self's merely present reality and the unreal, merely demanded idea of value.'[39] The self as such emerges from the same process which also produces the conception of ideal validity. The will, Simmel argues, can only be experienced as will because our desires are not always completely fulfilled. The self would have, as it were, no cause to detach itself from reality if it existed in perfect harmony with its environment. It is another matter entirely, however, 'when the will persists after its contact with reality because it has not been satisfied, when the willing self is still there where reality no longer is'.[40] The self, like value, is a category produced by the process of life. This is no mere analogy; rather, the self is itself permeated by the ideal validities. This becomes clear when Simmel elucidates his concept of the will, which should be confused neither with Schopenhauer's will to life nor Nietzsche's will to power. For Simmel, will and life do not reside on the same level at all, in so far as the ideal contents produced by the axial rotation have entered into the will. For this reason, Simmel must view the prayer which Jesus uttered in Gethsemane before his betrayal and arrest, 'Lord, not what I will but what thou wilt', not as a logical paradox, but rather as the pure expression of a will which knows itself to be at its strongest when obeying the will of an ideal authority.[41] Simmel describes not only this pure expression of a higher willing, but also the conflict of the volitions and the feeling of unease when we wish to impose upon them a higher will in which we do not quite recognize ourselves.

By introducing the category of the self into the zone of tension between radical contingency and ideal validity, Simmel arrives, first of all, at a new interpretation of the immortality of the soul. He sees in this idea the attempt to apply to the self itself the break with contingency which he identified as occurring during the constitution of values. Just as a permanent value is produced in a particular situation under contingent conditions, so the coincidence of our birth is no barrier to belief in the immortality of the soul. Precisely because we are able to recognize that our actual life does not exhaust our potential, we are able to think of ourselves as existing beyond our reality, as the quintessence of our infinite potential. For Simmel, Christianity radicalizes the idea of the individual's responsibility to himself during his earthly life, which is simultaneously balanced out by a new conviction of his immortality, thus creating a bearable tension. He concludes his chapter with speculations about the meaning of Christian and other basic conceptions about the afterlife (and pre-existence) of the soul, whose substantiality he wishes to be understood in a new way as a 'shorthand symbol for the feeling that personal identity is in the last instance stable and durable'.[42]

However, Simmel's main concern lies not with these speculations, which are apparently sympathetic to mystical experiences, but rather with a new form of ethics. This he brought under the formula of the 'individual law' and elaborated mainly in opposition to Kant. For Kant and the neo-Kantians, the concept of 'individual law' would have sounded like a contradiction in terms, because law is for them defined by its very universality. But it is precisely this identification of the universal with the objective, which forces the individual to be lumped together with the (merely) subjective, that Simmel wants to undermine. He finds it inconsistent and peculiarly narrow of Kant 'that he proclaimed that in cognition the world-stuff is to a large extent shaped through the forms immanent in the mind, but for practical reasons accepted a priori certainties only as demands, as ideal values'.[43] Simmel's counter-strategy arises directly from his version of *Lebensphilosophie*. Like all ideal contents, the 'Ought' does not stand abruptly opposed to life; it is, rather, one of its forms. 'The Ought is not above life in general, nor is it opposed to life; it is, rather, a way in which life becomes conscious of itself, just as being real is another such way.'[44] The self obtains its Ought not from a rational law that exists wholly outside of life, but instead experiences this Ought in the ideal contents that are inscribed in it itself. It is not the Ought itself that is alien to reality if we do not imagine the self without contents of the Ought (*Sollensinhalte*); instead, it is only certain moral principles and moral philosophies that construe the self as free of the concrete contents of the Ought. Simmel is well aware of the difference between him and Nietzsche in this respect, and also of the fact that this difference is the result of Nietzsche's continued dependence on Kant, even though this is contrary to his intentions. The Ought remained for Nietzsche a demand that was alien to life, which he merely rejected in favour of life – unlike Kant. Simmel, however, wants to show that the Ought can be itself a part of life and intrinsically alive.

This vitality of the Ought can only be achieved if the reference point for moral judgement is no longer, as in the Kantian tradition, the moral quality of individual actions and the pure self confronting its own individual actions, but rather the person as a whole in the stream of all his or her actions. Simmel readjusts the reference point by pointing to the abstract character of the individual action. The individual action is the result either of the observer isolating a single part of a continuous process or of a 'scene' formed by the coagulation of action itself. That the meaning of the moral law can lie only in addressing the whole person and demanding of him precisely those acts which are inherent in him as impulsions of the Ought (*Sollensimpulse*) in a particular situation – this Simmel describes as the crux of his whole train of thought.[45] His ethics[46] aims at an ideal way of being for the entire personal life. Out of my self's commitment to value, I experience moral demands directed at me, the fulfilment of which requires my whole person and myself as an unsubstitutable element. It is in this kind of ethical unsubstitutability and not in numerical uniqueness that Simmel sees the essence of individuality.[47] This does not absolve the individual from obeying universal laws; nevertheless, he must relate these to the unrelenting demands of his own individual law.[48] And the individual law does not require the egocentric cultivation of one's own personality, since for Simmel the ideal inherent in the self calls for its expression in life, which, through 'axial rotation', leads away from the individual and pours itself 'into social, altruistic, spiritual, artistic forms'.[49]

Thus, Simmel's answer to the question of the genesis of values gives rise to a new ethics, one which eludes the alternative 'Kant or Nietzsche' and which sets the tone for existentialist ethics.[50] I cannot discuss this novel ethical impulse in greater detail here, since it is not the substance of an ethics which is under the microscope, but the explanatory force of the answers given to the question of the genesis of values.

As far as these answers are concerned, we must return an open verdict. Despite extremely promising points of departure in his theory of religion, Simmel has not really clarified the questions of the relationship between interpretation and experience, of individual and collective, as well as ordinary and extra-ordinary experience. Rooted in *Lebensphilosophie*, his language allows him to overcome both the rigidity of neo-Kantianism and Nietzsche's reductionism, but it is nevertheless too metaphorical to unravel adequately the structure of intersubjective and intrasubjective relationships.[51] The category of social interaction, so central to Simmel's sociology, is actually obscured by the idiom of *Lebensphilosophie*; the relationship between 'individual law' and social order remains just as unclear. Though the radical attempt to tailor Kant's ethics to a world of differentiated individuality anchors the 'Ought' in 'life', the concept of life, as well as that of Ought, are too broadly defined. Simmel not only wishes to understand the latter in the sense of moral demands, but also more comprehensively as a 'quite general state of aggregation of our consciousness of life, in which hopes and drives, eudaimoniacal and aesthetic demands, religious ideals, even whims and anti-ethical movements gather, often together with the ethical and all simul-taneously'.[52] But he thus conceals the internal tensions in the Ought, which we had discovered in the discourse about religion and morality in James and Durkheim, and of which the early Simmel had also been aware. Simmel does not really emerge from Kant's shadow with the formula of 'individual law', because the individualized ethics which he has in mind seems to suggest to him the idea of a law-oriented Ought – and not that of a higher will.

On the other hand, however, Simmel introduces as a necessary component of an answer to the question of the genesis of values an understanding of self-formation and the self's orientation to value, as well as the finitude of the person, and makes clear their role with the greatest intensity. In doing so, he reveals at least one further indis-pensable element to such an answer. That he can only formulate self-formation in terms of *Lebensphilosophie*, and cannot bring it and the interaction of individuals into a fruitful relationship, also holds true in this respect, of course. For this reason, we must devote more attention to the unravelling of our 'Ought' according to the variety of our value-sensations, as well as to the way in which 'life' is differen-tiated in the structure of inter- and intrasubjective interaction.

6

The Value-Feeling and its Object
(Max Scheler)

It was Max Scheler who undertook the most ambitious attempt to advance a phenomenology of emotions in general, and of human value-sensations in particular. In contrast to James's phenomenology of religious experience, we are entitled in Scheler's case to speak of a phenomenology of value-feeling in the more narrow sense as well, since he takes up directly from Husserl's philosophical programme, and was determined to extend it, even if in somewhat unorthodox fashion, to cover the realms of feeling and ethics – realms which Husserl had addressed only hesitantly and cautiously.[1] Such a plan is already far-reaching, yet Scheler envisaged this project as only one step on the path to an even more significant goal: the recovery or refounding of a 'non-formal ethics of value' in opposition to the dominance of a (Protestant or Kantian) tradition of 'formalism in ethics'. By adopting the phenomenological approach, and undertaking a radical critique of Kant, Scheler believed that it was possible to revive the notion of an objective existence of values and to reveal that those values were ordered in an indubitable hierarchy.

At first sight this objective must seem like an anachronistic attempt to ignore or wish to undo the 'subjectivization' of the good, a trend beginning with the emergence of the philosophy of value, if not already with Kant. If this were so, then we could not expect Scheler's work to furnish a helpful answer to our question of the 'genesis of values'. This is indeed the prevailing impression of his philosophy. Outside of Catholic circles, and despite his influence in Germany on the theory of law and administration of justice, his work is nowadays rarely taken very seriously, and is often attacked indiscriminately or even derided.[2] But we should be wary of underestimating Scheler's achievements. For this reason, my aim in what follows is to weigh up the possible contributions which his critique of formalism in ethics and his phenomenology of value-feeling can make to our question. Since Scheler himself gave up his wide-ranging goals in the course of his intellectual development, without thereby wholly repudiating the conclusions he had reached – indeed, he expressly insisted that they continued to be valid[3] – it obviously makes sense not to embrace or to condemn as a whole his argumentation in terms of its furthest-reaching objective, but to assess its individual components separately.

In doing so, we must proceed in a highly selective manner, as we did with our discussion of Georg Simmel – although different reasons are involved here. While it is often difficult to pin Simmel down to an unequivocal commitment to a particular point of view because of his ability to adopt the most varied perspectives, Scheler overwhelms the reader with a torrent of observations and arguments, interpretations and side-swipes, a 'peculiar mixture of astuteness, profoundness and recklessness'.[4] His prose is guided by the most vivid, almost visionary intuitions; its style is characterized more by prophetic proclamation than calm deliberation. Barely a single idea is developed in all its aspects; Scheler stumbles hurriedly on from one assertion to the next, and his references to forthcoming elaborations of these themes are innumerable. Yet few readers can overlook the striking originality of many of his insights and the impression of courage with which he forges his own, new path. Like Simmel, Scheler tries to steer a course between Kant and Nietzsche. For this reason, it does not aid our understanding of Scheler if we mention him in the same breath as the neo-Kantians or brand him the 'Catholic Nietzsche'.[5] It is astonishing that one no longer hears much about this original thinker, whom shortly after his death Heidegger called the 'most potent philosophical force in modern Germany, no, in modern Europe'.[6]

The first step in clarifying Scheler's basic intuition is to address his attempt to call radically into question Kant's dominant role in modern moral philosophy. To my mind, the most vivid instance of this is his critical discussion of the (Christian) notions of 'duties of faith' and (above all) of 'duties of love',[7] and Kant's reflections on these. As is well known, Kant thought this manner of speaking suspicious,[8] because faith and love are thereby made to resemble obligations of the will. Following Kant, Scheler argues, however, that 'indeterminability by imperatives or norms belongs to the essence of the act of faith and the act of love. Strictly speaking, there can be no "obligation" for faith or love.'[9] As soon as faith and love are taken to be the object of obligation, there is the danger that either their emotional intensity will be watered down to mere goodwill and good-doing, or that external works or the symbolic acts of a cult will be considered to be their appropriate manifestations. These dangers are well known from the long history of Protestant polemics against the (purported) Catholic 'sanctification through works'. However, it is precisely not the Catholic Scheler's intention to continue this polemic but, conversely, to attack Kant's misconstrual of the Christian idea of love as a duty of love. For Kant, the idea of 'love your neighbour' becomes a commandment – and thus absurd, because love cannot be commanded. For Scheler, in contrast, what distinguishes the idea of 'love your neighbour' is the very fact that it is the expression of a fundamental relation between an individual, God and his fellow human beings, 'whose meaning lies beyond "command" and "obey" '.[10] Though this fundamental relation expresses the idea that it is good to behave charitably, the actual point is missed if it is reformulated as a norm. The question is, rather, which form the idea of love must assume when it is directed at the will of subjects. An 'invitation to follow'[11] is Scheler's first attempt at describing this form. Kant cannot think along these lines, because his dualism of duty and inclination prevents him from doing so. Because Kant must construe love as a 'sensuous pleasure derived from an object', he asks whether love of God is also to be thought of in this way. Since God is no 'object of the senses', he rules out this possibility. In contrast, Scheler recognizes that the notion of 'inclination' can embrace completely different states of affairs, and that we are by no means constrained to interpret it only in terms of sensuous drives. Inclination can also mean, quite generally, every 'immediate movement toward a value (without a prior norm or commandment)'.[12] If this is so, then a concept of love of God and human beings which does not originate in respect for a commandment and yet has moral value is meaningful. Kant, of course, shrank from the logical conclusion of his thought and did not really reject the supposed commandment of love. He reinterpreted it, rather, in such a way that the full meaning of love is reduced to 'practical love' (Kant): 'To love God means, in this sense, to do what He commands *gladly*; to love one's neighbor means to practice all duties toward him *gladly*.'[13] Scheler, however, does not think this reinterpretation convincing, even given Kant's premises. For if 'practical love' is supposed to be a subspecies of the category of love, why should it then be possible to command it, even though love *per se* cannot be commanded? But if, conversely, the practical ways of comportment are at issue, and these can certainly be commanded, then this shows that Kant has something other than 'love' in mind, and he only obscures this with the conceptual ambiguity of 'practical love'. Goodwill and good-doing can also spring from motives other than those of love, and love can also lead to ways of comportment other than goodwill and good-doing. As Kant had clearly recognized, goodwill and good-doing do not always possess moral value: as when they are inspired by selfishness, for example. Where Kant locates moral value in the performance of duty, Scheler opposes this idea with his interpretation of the message of the gospel: that, namely, 'goodwill and good-doing have only as much moral *value* as there is *love* in them.'[14] Conversely, whether we like doing our duty must in turn be of no consequence for a consistent morality of obligation. This thought prompts the question, well-known ever since Schiller first posed it: whether actions we perform out of love, and whose obligatoriness we accordingly do not experience at all, are, in moral terms, less valuable than those acts carried out in conflict with our inclinations. Scheler expressly defends Kant against the simple reproach that this was indeed his position and that he regarded as morally good only those actions which are performed against our inclinations. According to Scheler's reading of Kant, it is not Kant's arguments, but rather the pathos of his exposition that gives the impression of moral rigorism. Kant certainly conceded that a 'beautiful soul' who performs what duty dictates of his own accord is of equal value to the man of duty. But Scheler criticizes this concession as unsatisfactory, since for him the 'beautiful soul', in whose inclinations the good is inextricably intertwined, is not only of equal, but of higher, value. Kant could never have conceded this higher value.

Kant was nevertheless consistent enough to hold that the absurdity of a commandment of love must also apply to the notion of the enjoyment of duty. If enjoyment, too, cannot be commanded, then once again the commandment cannot be directed at the attitude itself, but only at a striving towards it. Thus, after several steps, Kant creates out of the Christian idea of love a commandment to strive for 'practical love'. 'This almost unbelievable change in meaning to which Kant has subjected these powerful words should become apparent at *first* glance. "Love God above all and your neighbor as yourself" has now become "Strive to like obeying God's commandments and fulfilling your duties to your neighbor."'[15] For Scheler, this reinterpretation is a crass expression of the intellectual constraints and fundamental errors inherent in every 'ethics of imperatives'. He sets about the source of the error more thoroughly than the thinkers we have hitherto discussed, in so far as he does not, like James, largely ignore Kant or, like Nietzsche, pervert Kant's premises. In Scheler's work, even more so than in that of Simmel or even Durkheim, there begins to emerge a fundamentally alternative model to Kantian moral philosophy.

We have already encountered the key concept underlying this alternative model in our passing reference to Scheler's emphatic understanding of the Christian idea of love. It was on this basis – as I have already discussed in detail[16] – that Scheler had refuted Nietzsche's thesis that Christianity originated in *ressentiment*. 'Love' in this sense is more an overflowing and channelling of strength than an ideology of the disadvantaged. In illuminating fashion, Scheler himself links his argument about the questionable nature of a commandment of love with his analysis of *ressentiment*. He makes this connection when discussing the issue of how much the moral value of persons and acts increases when the costs incurred and the sacrifices made become greater. The important aspect of this for us is his claim that there is a fundamental difference between a renunciation made for the sake of a higher value, yet which acknowledges the worth of the competing value, and a renunciation that simultaneously devalues the sacrificed good and asserts its valuelessness. The latter is characteristic of the 'illusory asceticism of *ressentiment*',[17] while genuine asceticism does not deny the value of a good, but is able to renounce these goods, despite their value, out of love for higher values. 'For a Christian, for instance, a *free* renunciation of possessions, marriage, and self-will for the sake of higher goods represents a morally valuable act only when such goods are positive.'[18] In opposition to Kant *and* Nietzsche, Scheler draws attention to the exuberance of the Christian idea of love, from which he intends to develop his alternative to an 'ethics of imperatives'.

Scheler defines 'love' as that 'original act through which an existent – without ceasing to be this limited existent – leaves itself in order to share and participate in another existent as an *ens intentionale* in such a way that both do not actually become real parts of one another'.[19] In his essay *Ressentiment*, Scheler argues that the Christian idea of love, in contrast to the ancient Greek conception, represents a fundamental 'reversal in movement',[20] in so far as love is no longer restricted to the striving of the inferior towards the higher being, but now becomes the defining characteristic of God, of the highest being. 'But a *new way of grounding* love and cognition or value and being also forms the basis of this very reversal in the movement of love.'[21] Scheler vigorously resists ascribing only secondary importance to the role of love in cognition, as if we first produced a purely cognitive relation to objects of knowledge, in order then to direct feelings towards the objects thus constituted. For him, rather, 'value-ceiving' (*Wertnehmen*) always precedes 'perceiving' (*Wahrnehmen*). The assumption that 'love makes one "blind" rather than "seeing", that therefore all genuine knowledge of the world can be based only on the most extreme *restraint* of emotional acts and on the simultaneous ignoring of the value differences of the objects, whose values are profoundly connected in the unity of experience with these experiences of acts' – this he scathingly describes as a 'specifically modern, bourgeois judgement'.[22] The rise of the bourgeoisie means that the object of the original Christian elevation of love to the constitutive principle of cognition has once again been defeated. Although the Greek, as well as the Indian, philosophical traditions have maintained that love is a means by which knowledge advances, only Christianity has incorporated into this idea the claim that love first makes knowledge itself *possible*. According to the Christian idea of love 'all new contents of knowledge about God are sustained by the *loving act* of His *self-manifestation in Christ* as its creative ground'[23] and love remains a relationship between loving beings – between God and the believer. The latter does not, however, despite his total devotion, surrender or strive to overcome his personal form, but instead strengthens it: 'The person finds himself by losing himself in God.'[24]

Nevertheless, Scheler finds the history of Christian philosophy wholly inadequate. The fundamental experience of love in this sense has mostly been distorted, rather than articulated, by the categories of Greek philosophy – although Scheler regards Augustine, Pascal and, above all, mysticism as exceptions. With enormous pretension, he views his own thought as the fulfilment of the mission to find an appropriate philosophical idiom through which to articulate the Christian idea of love and thereby to introduce this idea into modern debates. This intention has nothing in common with a backwards-looking orientation to Scholasticism, so characteristic of Catholic thought. This is also not the voice of a Catholic Nietzsche, but rather of a thinker who, as a modern-day Augustine, longs to make effective the unsurpassed radicality of the Christian idea of love in the cultural crisis which Nietzsche symbolized.

In the business of philosophy these grandiose aims must of course be cashed in for the small change of detailed argumentation. My exposition of Scheler's thought is not intended to convey the impression that he made no effort whatsoever in this direction. He develops, with respect to both 'pure' and 'practical' reason, a thorough critique of Kant, whose ethics represents for him – despite his many objections – 'the most *perfect* we have in the area of philosophical ethics – although not in the form of a *Weltanschauung* or a consciousness of faith, but rather in the form of strict scientific insight'.[25] The question as to whether his individual arguments are compelling and do full justice to Kant need not interest us here[26] – or at least need interest us only in so far as it contributes towards answering the question of the genesis of values. For our purposes, we can therefore ignore his detailed account of Kant's equation of the distinction between formal/ non-formal and that between a priori/a posteriori. However, it is worth mentioning how Scheler attempts – in a very similar fashion to the pragmatists[27] – to undermine Kant's epistemological and ethical constructions through a critique of their psychological foundations. It is by precisely these means that he hopes to be able to bring an 'emotive apriorism' to bear against the 'false unity of apriorism and rationalism that has hitherto existed'.[28]

For Scheler, Kant's formalism and rationalism are only comprehensible when they are understood as counterbalancing a psychology that conceives the outer and inner world of human beings as 'chaos' – as a chaos of sense impressions and instinctive impulses – faced with which the ordering intellect must first create coherence and structure. Kant uncritically borrowed this way of thinking from the British philosophical tradition (above all from Hume); only on the basis of these premises are his constructions completely sound.

> In short, *Hume's notion of nature required a Kantian understanding*, and *Hobbes's notion of man required a Kantian practical reason*, insofar as these theories were to be brought back to the facts of natural experience. But *without* this erroneous presupposition of a Humean nature and a Hobbesian man there is *no* need for such a hypothesis and *hence* no need for an interpretation of the a priori as a 'law of functions' of such organizing activities.[29]

Neither the faculty of perception nor the drive-structure of human beings corresponds, therefore, to this erroneous, 'sensualist' conception. What attracted Scheler to Husserl's phenomenology was the fact that it had uncovered a completely different structure of human perception, and developed its methodology on the basis of this. Nevertheless, Scheler is interested in ethics even more than he is in perception and cognition, and consequently he wants to prove, by following the phenomenological method, that Kant's concept of inclination is quite misleading. The 'inclinations' are for Kant morally indifferent; they belong, as it were, to the human being's animal nature and wrestle with the rationally constituted will, which first opens up the sphere of possible moral evaluation. If we do not construe the human being in this dualistic fashion, that is, as composed of base inclinations and a higher will, then there is no obstacle to our recognizing that an orientation to values can be established even at the level of our 'conations' (*Strebungen*) – to use the term which Scheler prefers. Our conations are already directed towards or away from something before they are transformed into desires by the goal-contents being represented to consciousness, or further into purposes of willing by a decision to realize the goal-contents. The conations have goals, and our purpose-oriented action arises on the basis of this pre-reflective directedness of our conations. 'Nothing can become a purpose that was not first a goal! The purpose is grounded in the goal! Goals can be given *without* purposes, but no purposes can be given without previous goals. We are not able to create a purpose out of nothing, or to "posit" a purpose without a prior "conation toward something".'[30] Because Scheler thereby breaks through the deep-rooted and momentous equation of intentionality and the positing of purposes,[31] he opens up the possibility that it is not the will which first establishes a relationship between the person and values. His ideal is not strength of will, but rather the person's complete moral development. A person is of high moral standing when 'the involuntary and automatic appearances of his inner conations, and the non-formal values at which the conations "aim", follow an *order of preference*'.[32] Completely different objects can be operative for different people – and, according to Scheler, what these objects are is not unimportant for judging a person morally. He consequently devotes large parts of his work to proving that, contrary to Kant's assumption, a non-formal ethics need not become an ethics of success or pleasure. The 'conations' belong to the substance of action – unlike the consequences of action, they are immanently oriented towards values, however, and are not a relic of pre-human nature in the person.

Scheler therefore seeks to construct his ethics on a radically different understanding of human action, and of the role of perception and the instinctive impulses, from that of Kant. Yet this alternative understanding was not actually worked out in *Formalism*; his arguments are scattered throughout that work, which itself was intended as a mere prolegomenon to a future ethics. In later works that were fundamental to the development of 'philosophical anthropology' in Germany,[33] Scheler took further steps to substantiate his theory, which goes beyond the opposition between utilitarian and normativist models of action.[34] But it is not this action-theoretical strand that I propose to follow up here. My aim, rather, is to demonstrate that, on the basis of this alternative understanding of action, Scheler opens up two related prospects: the possibility of a 'non-formal ethics of value' and a 'phenomenology of emotions'; the potential of both is certainly not exhausted by his own work, with its often idiosyncratic features. With Scheler, the Christian idea of love does not remain a mere postulate, powerless and lacking efficacy in the world; instead, it motivates him to elaborate, in an anthropological theory of action and in ethics, a far-reaching, albeit unsystematic, alternative to utilitarianism and Kantianism. We must take an even closer look at Scheler's two projects combined in his work on ethics and examine whether they actually deliver, or could at least point us in the direction of, an answer to the question of the 'genesis of values'.

What, then, does Scheler's notion of a 'non-formal ethics of value' mean? It does *not* mean that Scheler wished to return to a religious or metaphysical grounding of ethics. Or to an ethics of goods or an objective ethics of purposes, which claim, respectively, a knowledge of the highest goods or the real, ultimate purpose of all the will's efforts. Scheler sets the greatest store on not being construed as an Aristotelian or a Scholastic; he even scorns Nicolai Hartmann, who praised his philosophy as having effected a 'synthesis of ancient and contemporary ethics'.[35] At least in terms of its intentions, the 'non-formal ethics of value' does not represent an attempt to return to pre-Kantian ethics, but to go beyond Kant's moral philosophy. 'It is only *after* the collapse of ethics of goods and purposes, with their self-reliant "absolute" worlds of goods, that "non-formal value-ethics" *could* come into being. It *presupposes* Kant's *destruction* of these forms of ethics.'[36] Scheler can pursue this aim, which to many sounds paradoxical, because he sees a way of avoiding ending up in the cul-de-sac of Kantian formalism, despite subscribing to Kant's critique of the inadmissibility of ethics of goods or purposes. He sees this possibility because he maintains that there is already an orientation to value in the human being's pre-reflective conations. He is able to locate this value orientation there because he construes values as 'objects of intentional emotional acts'.

Just as Husserl proved that cognition provides us with access to 'ideal' objects (like colours or geometric shapes), Scheler wants to prove that our emotional life provides us with access to another class of ideal objects, namely, to values. In order to understand this idea, we must first consider his distinction between the *'feeling of something'* and mere *'feeling-states'*.[37] As examples of feeling-states Scheler cites states of pain or pleasure, even those of the vaguest kind like 'indeterminate' moods of sadness and joyfulness. They have no inherent relation to an object. Although I can relate to them intellectually – I can learn, for instance, to regard certain feeling-states as symptoms of incipient illness – this connection need not exist of itself: I can be mistaken in the interpretation of my symptoms! Feeling is a completely different matter: 'For here we do not feel "about something"; we immediately feel *something*, i.e., a specific value-quality.'[38] When I love, I cannot deceive myself; even if my intellect can give reasons why I should not love, this does not change anything about the directedness of my feeling. Intentional feeling does not arise through an act of imagination or judgement. According to Scheler, the originality of intentional feeling is best demonstrated when it is itself directed towards a feeling-state. I can emotionally relate to a state of pain, for example, in various ways, with the spectrum extending from suffering through to endurance and tolerance, and finally to enjoyment.

It is not the feeling-states, but rather the 'intentional functions of feeling' that are crucial for Scheler's project. In detailed arguments, which admittedly often owe more to the history of ideas than to the phenomenological method, he attempts to demonstrate that we only do justice to this feeling if we understand it in terms of its objects. These objects of intentional feeling – that is to say, 'values' – are for him not products of abstraction; he deems false every interpretation that disputes their independent existence and traces them back to the actually existent feeling person or to the goods which embody values. Likewise, he rejects the interpretation of value judgements as the expression of emotion or as the expression of a desire or command. All such reductionist reinterpretations of our value-feeling make it seem ultimately incomprehensible why there are value judgements at all. 'It is necessary to ask why men mummify their interests and desires in value-judgments instead of giving expression to them.'[39] Only if we assume that values actually exist as autonomous objects does it make sense for us to refer to these deceitfully, in accordance with the old adage that hypocrisy pays homage to virtue.

To be sure, Scheler should have elucidated the precise character of the intentionality of our value-feeling more thoroughly, instead of only repudiating rival philosophical positions. His impatience, however, drives him on, and in several directions at once. On the one hand, he is not satisfied with deriving arguments for the objective existence of values from the analysis of feeling; he also wants to use our feelings to map the inner structures of the world of values. According to Scheler, in 'preferring' and 'rejecting' we comprehend not only values as such, as we do in general forms of feeling, but also their order of rank. He elaborates a comprehensive typology of values which is made accessible to us in our feeling.[40] Values stand in identifiable hierarchical structures, and these structures are ascertainable by phenomenological means. On the other hand, Scheler insists on doing justice to the diverse forms of our value-feeling and devotes individual investigations to them. Not so much in *Formalism*, but in a spate of separate, penetrating studies, he sets out to analyse morally relevant emotions: remorse and shame, respect and humility, the various forms of sympathy and, of course, *ressentiment*.[41] In a separate investigation, Scheler even addresses the 'religious acts' which, though always lurking conspicuously in the background of his ethics, never attracted his full attention there.[42] We must leave all details of these works to one side here. But it seems beyond dispute that, with these studies, Scheler has done important spadework for every future ethics that is to reserve an important place for moral feelings. Although he sets his sights on a hierarchicalized, though richly structured, world of value, his phenomenology of value-feeling is guided by a profound sense of the irreducible plurality of our feelings; the feelings which he examines are not variations of a unitary sub-stance, but arise, rather, from the complexity of interpersonal action embedded in a world of values. Whilst many thinkers concentrate exclusively on a few intentional feelings – what does Durkheim know other than moral outrage (in *Division of Labour*) and collective ecstasy (in his theory of religion)? what does the Heidegger of *Being and Time* know other than anxiety (*Angst*) and care (*Sorge*)? – Scheler attempts, with truly anthropological detail, to set forth a typology of all morally relevant emotions.

According to Scheler's own understanding of his project, there is no contradiction between his sensitivity to the broad palette of our morally relevant feelings on the one hand, and his assertion of a 'rigid ethical absolutism and objectivism' on the other.[43] He can characterize his ethics as both 'emotional intuitionism' and 'non-formal aprior-ism'.[44] Nor does he see any problem in combining the rich cultural and historical variety of value systems with his theory of the self-evidence of uniform value orientation. His belief in 'eternal values' is accompanied by an extraordinarily profound historical erudition and an acute sense of the historical and cultural variability of value systems. In opposition to the formalist universalism of Kant's ethics, Scheler maintains that his non-formal ethics of value is imbued with a stronger spirit of historical relativism, in so far as it is possible, within its framework, to view the 'rational humanism of Kant's ethics as only one moment in the history of the human spirit'.[45] Scheler's anthropological and psychological interests also lead him to dynamize Kant's apriorism from the point of view of natural history; after all, Scheler is, furthermore, one of the founding fathers of the sociology of knowledge. Evidently, he was less interested in actually elaborating a positive, systematic ethics than in a '*philosophy of the development of moral consciousness* in history and society'.[46] This further development was already mapped out in *Formalism*; in that book, Scheler had already adopted a by no means defensive attitude towards the historical relativity of ethical value-estimations. He is not afraid that this insight leads inexorably to sceptical conclusions *vis-à-vis* the existence of a world of value; he even goes on the offensive, proposing to develop a systematic theory concerning the dimensions of the possible relativity of value-estimations. Such a theory will, he hopes, shed light on what is at first sight the apparently muddled cultural history of valuations and gradually reveal it to be the appropriation of an objectively existing world, in much the same way that the history of knowledge is. The 'realm of value-estimations and their contents, which at first appears like a palette daubed with paint', can then

> gradually assume the interconnection of sense of a grandiose painting, or at least the fragments of one. And in this painting, one will be able to see mankind, mixed as it is, beginning to take possession, through love, feeling, and action, of a realm of objective values and their objective order, a realm that is independent of mankind as well as of its own manifestations; and one will be able to see mankind draw this realm into existence.[47]

But is this hope well-founded? The fact that Scheler so vociferously denies that tension exists between his ethical objectivism and his historical-sociological awareness of the diversity of valuations is not by itself convincing. Does this tension not in fact exist – or was Scheler a master of denial, constantly concealing it from himself? Only if we turn our attention to Scheler's account of the *genesis* of values will we find an answer to this question, without which we cannot pass judgement on his project. After all, we can only discover and comprehend an independent world of values; its genesis – provided that this should be at all conceivable – would have nothing to do with the actions of human beings. Can Scheler maintain on this issue his linkage of a phenomenology of moral feelings and the claim to ground a non-formal ethics of values?

To begin with, the fact that Scheler is definitely looking for an answer to this question is itself noteworthy. We would not expect this of a value objectivist seeking to return to a pre-Kantian understanding of value. But, as the subtitle of *Formalism* has it, Scheler understands his ethics as a 'new attempt toward the foundation of an ethical personalism', and the whole second half of that work is indeed dedicated to this task. No impression of the richness of Scheler's doctrine of the person can be conveyed here. What is significant for us is that here too he wants to go beyond Kant, and not to retreat behind him. He readily concedes that ethics of goods and purposes, as Kant had argued, diminishes the value of the person in so far as it ranks it below the value of the highest goods, or measures it in terms of the person's achievement in realizing an end. But he goes further and asks whether Kantian ethics and every 'formalistic and rational ethics of laws does not also *de*grade the person . . . by virtue of its subordination of the person to an impersonal *nomos* under whose domination he can become a person only through obedience.'[48] This question seems to push Scheler in the same direction as Simmel's reflections on the 'individual law'.[49] However, his radical critique of imperative ethics prevents him from having to establish the relation to the individual by individualizing the Ought. Scheler expressly criticizes Simmel for having become entangled in irreconcilable contradictions because of his dependence on Kant. Simmel's 'attempt to adhere to Kant's theory that "good" is what ought to be and, at the same time, to oppose Kant's theory concerning the necessary universality of duty'[50] is doomed to failure, since it will never permit us to distinguish between true oughtness and mere capricious impulses without reintroducing the principle of universality he had just rejected. The only way to escape this dilemma is by breaking with imperativist ethics, i.e. by adopting the non-formal ethics of value, which in this respect also promises to do more justice to Simmel's radical, individual-related motifs than his own theory. Though there is no 'individual law', there is an 'individual value-essence' whence there can also arise the experience of an individual Ought, 'an experiencing of the ought-to-be of a content, an action, a deed, or a project through *me*, and, in certain cases, *only* through me as this individual'.[51] The individual value-essence – like every value – can be apprehended objectively. The values of the person, and, among these, the value of my person, have priority amongst the objectively apprehended values. Scheler coins the seemingly paradoxical formula that there is 'evidential knowledge of a "good-in-itself" but precisely in the sense of a "good-in-itself-for-*me*" '.[52] This formula would be truly paradoxical if in it Scheler had wanted to force together into a contradictory whole the 'in-itself', which is supposed to express a value's existence independent of its being experienced, and the value's relation to the person. But it is not this that he is seeking to express; rather, it is the experience of a 'calling', 'mission' and 'election': that the insight into objective values can be experienced as a personal invitation to act in the name of these values. For Scheler, the belief in a 'good-in-itself' does not conflict with the individualization of the value-experience; on the contrary, this belief is the logical precondition for being able to construe the idea of a good-for-me as an individual person, and for not obscuring it with the maxim of universal validity. Again and again in this context and in his critique of Simmel, Scheler swaps over into religious language, because he finds it easier to articulate his thoughts in this tradition that is saturated with experience and wisdom. The individual value-essence is then personal 'salvation'; God's love is, so to speak, directed at me as an individual, and sets me free to strive after the ideal image that He has of me: 'under the influence of the *goal* of this value-ideal of the individual person, through which the unique place of the person in the realm of the extant good is *fixed*'.[53]

Thus for Scheler, the individualization of the experience of value is compatible with his value-theoretical objectivism; but what about the transmission and genesis of values? The great essay *Ressentiment*, in which he launched his critique of Nietzsche, already implied that he was seeking an answer to the question of origin. For if he had wanted to declare this question itself nonsensical, then he would have had to reject completely Nietzsche's claim that a value system can originate in *ressentiment*. Instead, Scheler only disputed its validity as an explanation of the genesis of Christianity, and himself maintained that the bourgeois work ethic emanated from a revaluation of truly Christian values under the pressure of *ressentiment*.[54] On a general level, however, we have so far as the basis of an answer only the formula 'invitation to follow', which Scheler had opposed to the misinterpretation of the idea of love as a duty of love. In *Formalism*, he develops this idea further in his discussion of the role of the 'model person'.[55] In this respect, too, Scheler distances himself from Kant, for whom the role model can only illustrate, but of course cannot replace, the moral law; this is thoroughly consistent in a prescriptive ethics. In an ethics of value, in contrast, the model person has far greater significance. One's relationship to the model represents a relationship to the individualized 'value-essence' of another person. This relationship differs from a moral ought in three respects. Firstly, it is not directed at an action, but at a 'To-Be'. Scheler distinguishes sharply between 'imitation' and 'following'. A model's concrete actions are not supposed to be blindly imitated; rather, the model motivates us to orient ourselves through our own insight to those values embodied in him. Secondly, the relationship to the model is grounded in love, and all oughtness arises from this reverential relationship. Scheler describes this relationship in terms of a 'tug' and an 'enticement', and distinguishes it not only from the experience of obligation, but also from the conscious positing of ends and mere suggestion.

> Models draw persons toward them. One does *not* actively move toward them. Models *become* goal-*determining*; the model is not a goal after which

one strives or an end that one posits. But this tug does not appear in the form of a blind compulsion, say, the 'suggestive powers' of a certain person. Rather, it possesses a consciousness of the ought-to-be and the being-right as its foundation.[56]

The possibility of a '*free* devotion to the content of personal value which is accessible to autonomous insight'[57] is given and appropriate *vis-à-vis* a model understood in this sense. Thirdly, Scheler emphasizes the genetic priority of personal models over norms, and asserts that every respect for a norm is ultimately founded not only genetically, but also structurally upon a respect for persons, and the latter in turn in a love of these persons. The model is actually the '*primary* vehicle for all changes in the moral world'.[58] At the same time, Scheler recognizes that a 'countermodel' can also take the place of a model; that is to say, it can be the very rejection of a person embodying value that informs an individual's ethical orientations. The doctrine of the model person, which Scheler himself regarded as only the starting-point for wide-ranging reflections on a typology of value-persons and a sociologically conceived taxonomy of the developments character-istic of a particular social unit, remains, like the doctrine of the individualization of value-experience, wholly within the framework of value objectivism. For Scheler there is no doubt that an act of feeling value-cognition (of love, say) – and by no means a value judgement – precedes the act of taking a model. Even love, expressly described as 'creative',[59] can only be designated as such within the framework of value objectivism because it plays the role of discovery, and not an actually creative role as such. 'Values cannot be created or destroyed. They exist independently of the organization of all beings endowed with spirit.'[60] This creative role is thus attributed to love as far as 'the range and nature of feelable and preferable values of a being, but not the existing values themselves are concerned'.[61] In opposition to Kant *and* Nietzsche, in opposition to a transcendental, as well as an empirical, subjectivism, Scheler puts forward the thesis that 'the person alone is the ultimate *bearer* of values, but in no respect whatsoever is the person a *positor* of values.'[62] Although his ethics focuses on the person, for him the objective existence of the world of values cannot be called into question.

Nevertheless, the tension between the two poles in Scheler's ethical thought increases when he asks whether the highest 'value-persons', i.e. the models issuing the most powerful invitation to follow, are likewise to be regarded only as bearers of value, or whether they can be seen as positors of value as well.[63] This question becomes unavoid-able with respect to the founders of religions in particular, in so far as the sacred embodied in them is precisely not to be thought of as a 'blanket-conception covering "the good, the true and the beautiful"',[64] but instead as a *sui generis* phenomenon. If, in order to remain faithful to his value objectivism, Scheler had needed to view Jesus Christ as a mere embodiment of pre-existent values, then he would have moved far closer to Kant than he wants to, and would have been led astray from key aspects of his emphatic conception of love. At this point of his argument, Scheler introduces the concept of the 'original holy man' – a holy man who not only follows another holy man, but who himself first creates the ideals which he and his disciples follow.[65] For Scheler, the paradigmatic expression of this is contained in Jesus' words: 'I am the way, the truth and the life'. What is intended here is not the communication of a true proposition, but the personal embodiment of a path to be followed. 'There is no universally valid standard *above* the person of the original holy man, no norm against which his desires, actions, effects and his own value can be measured.'[66] It is precisely in this that the 'charismatic' quality of an original holy man consists,[67] as examples of whom he names, in addition to Jesus Christ, Buddha, Muhammad, Confucius and Lao Tze. His thesis of their value-creative character is certainly plausible for all of them; it cannot, however, be reconciled with his postulation of an eternal world of values. For this reason, Scheler's phenomenological analyses lead him into inconsistency as soon as he wants to do justice to the phenomena of the sacred above and beyond the realm of ethics. If the original holy men can create values, then the world of values does not exist prior to them or independently of them. Scheler could most likely escape this conclusion if, for dogmatic religious reasons, he were to bestow the epithet of the original holy man upon just one of the founders of religion – so that the eternally valid order of value were revealed solely in him. But Scheler does not do this; any broader use of the concept of charisma, such as we find with Max Weber, would anyway make the tension between it and value objectivism unmistakably apparent. The phenomenon of personal following can also be found in situations where Scheler himself would certainly not speak of a value being embodied. It is precisely the charismatic features of the twentieth century's totalitarian movements which make it difficult today to reconstruct Scheler's ideas on model and following in an adequate form at all. Scheler distanced himself in the last years of his life, albeit not clearly and consistently, from the value objectivism for which he had argued so vehemently – not, though, to the extent that he dropped it completely or retracted all his earlier theses, but in so far as he credited human beings in general – and not just the founders of religions – with a 'co-creative' role in reality, as well as in the reality of values. He turns against the notion of a providential order existing prior to the creation of the world. Because no such thing exists, 'our co-performance of these acts is also not merely a finding or discovery of an independent existent or essence, but rather a true *co*-production, a co-creation, out of the centre and *origin* of the things themselves, of the entities, ideas, values and goals belonging to the eternal Logos and eternal love and the eternal will.'[68] That is how he formulated it in his later anthropological work, which formed part of a new metaphysics that was, however, to remain only fragmentary.

Does this winding path through Scheler's tangled thoughts thus end in perplexity? By no means. The first thought we should hold on to is that Scheler undertook perhaps the most reflective and complex attempt to ground and develop an ethics of value under postmetaphysical conditions and based on a phenomenology of emotions. But so radical was his approach that he overshot the mark in two respects, thus burdening himself with problems that any modern attempt to break the spell of an 'ethics of imperatives' must avoid. On the one hand, Scheler overestimated from the very beginning the actual scope of his phenomenological analyses of intentional emotional acts. Though he convincingly demonstrated in these analyses that we can indeed have many and diverse experiences of the affective charge of value which are quite distinct from experiences of the Ought, he mistook this successful proof for an ontological one, as if the certain experience of value attested to the pre-existence of values independent of experience.[69] It is in the area of religious experience in particular that it becomes clear how much Scheler overestimates his argument, so that ultimately it sounds like a mere postulate. He infers the existence of God from the fact of religion and simply declares a world with religion but without God to be 'wholly irrational'.[70] With the same self-confidence, however, Durkheim had announced that he had unveiled by means of sociology the mystery of all religion – just as Feuerbach, Marx, Nietzsche and Freud also claimed to have found the definitive answer. In contrast, William James had proceeded more cautiously, tentatively, dialogically. Sure enough, Scheler misconstrues James's phenomenology of religious experience, in which an intentional object of that experience was asserted, but remained ultimately undefined, as a mere empirical psychology of religion with no religious significance itself.[71] He cannot see that the modest pragmatist attitude had remained James's guiding spirit, even informing his attitude towards salvation and redemption: his investigation does not proclaim certain knowledge of redemption, but is instead characterized by the curious, tolerant and receptive search for it.[72] Scheler's notion of the intentionality of emotional acts can, therefore, also be retained without claiming for value-cognition an allegedly completely evident character. There must be other ways to articulate our experience of values and their hold on us than through Scheler's talk of values as 'true objects'.[73]

On the other hand, Scheler also overshot the mark by completely subsuming the Ought under values. As splendid as his attempt is to make the dimension of values visible once more, flying in the face of those attempts to reduce ethics to the Ought and religious ethics to a form of obedience to God,[74] this argumentation becomes equally one-sided when he ascribes to the Ought a status that is only derived from values. Scheler does not only repudiate the notion that value judgements might have their origin in moral judgements; in fact, he asserts precisely the opposite: 'Whenever we speak of an ought, the comprehension of a *value* must have occurred ... *every ought has its foundation in a value.*'[75] But the tension between 'value' and 'ought', which James construed as a tension existing between religion and morality and Durkheim as present within morality itself, is thereby occluded and misjudged. Where Nietzsche had largely retained the Kantian dualism of duty and inclination, however much he reversed the valuations; where Simmel, despite all his efforts to liberate himself from the influence of Kant and Nietzsche, had remained under the sway of prescriptive ethics, Scheler believes every concession to an independent origin of the Ought to be a return to the very prescriptive ethics he is combating. It is for this reason that, like Nietzsche and Simmel, he failed to recognize the conflict between these two principles within ethics which James and Durkheim both discerned.

Moreover, the two respects in which Scheler's argument over-reaches itself, namely, the ontologization of the experience of value and the total subordination of the experience of Ought under the experience of value, are, I would argue, interlinked. Precisely because Scheler, in his ethics, lets everything ride on values and does not, like Kant and his successors, ascribe to the Ought an independent dimension of objectification and universalization, he can only escape the radical contingency of valuations if he ascribes to them an alternative foothold in an objectively existing world of values. This chimes with the fact that Scheler, mainly in his late work, interprets religion as an 'urge to be saved',[76] that is, as man's attempt to save himself in the face of the irrefutable experience of contingency. But his own philosophy of value represents an attempt, by no means free of rhetoric and forcible closure, quickly to stifle once more the experience of contingency in modernity – instead of courageously and openly exploring, like William James, the possibilities of value commitment under modern conditions. The impression can thus arise that the only alternative to the 'eternal struggle' is the belief in an 'eternal hierarchy of values'.[77] Both alternatives, however, are equally inappropriate. The way first shown by William James led – once again on the other side of the Atlantic – to insights which circumvent this poor alternative.

Shattering Intersubjectivity
(John Dewey)

No thinker overcomes the abrupt opposition of value objectivism and
value relativism in so thoroughgoing and original a fashion as John
Dewey, whose work elaborates motifs first articulated by William
James. We must investigate whether he thereby opens up a perspective which allows us to draw together the strands of the foregoing
argument.

It was not until late in his career that Dewey addressed in detail the
question of values, their role in action and their genesis. Though with
hindsight we can establish that the threads he later consciously took
up already run throughout his entire previous work, the outlines of
his answer to the question of the genesis of values become clearer
only in the works he produced during the 1930s. For Dewey, as with
most of the other thinkers we have discussed so far, the most
important of these is a book devoted to the subject of religion. In 1934,
the same year that his work on aesthetics appeared, Dewey published
a book entitled *A Common Faith*, which sketches a theory of religion
that, while brief, none the less contains a wealth of ideas. This book
has even more bearing on our question than his works on ethics and
the theory of value, from which one would perhaps more likely expect
an answer. I shall cite other writings from Dewey's enormous oeuvre,
which encompasses all the main areas of philosophical inquiry, only
to elucidate the often truncated-seeming argument of *A Common
Faith*.[1]

For a variety of reasons, it might at first seem improbable to expect
Dewey to contribute a productive answer to the question of the
genesis of values at all. This remains the case even when we leave
aside the grossest clichés about pragmatism, whose leading represent-

ative Dewey had become after James's death. Those who presume pragmatism to be a school of thought determined to view all natural and historical phenomena exclusively from an everyday and practical viewpoint, must surely be surprised to discover that there is such a thing as a pragmatist theory of art or religion. That contemporaries reacted in some cases with consternation shows that such gross clichés had by this time become common currency even in the United States, that is, not only in Europe.[2] As unfounded as these accusations against James and Dewey (and the other pragmatists) were,[3] there are none the less more serious indications to support the suspicion that Dewey maintained a reductionist position towards issues in the theory of value. In his work, we do indeed find statements bluntly rejecting any talk of 'ultimates and finalities',[4] of ultimate values, absolute validities or inherent qualities. And this rejection becomes clear not only in passing; it is also announced programmatically and unequivocally. For this reason, it must perhaps seem truly paradoxical to expect the very thinker who was almost unequalled in his efforts to open up the possibility of 'questioning' values to shed light on the genesis of unquestioned value commitments. To resolve this apparent paradox, it will be helpful to turn our attention first of all to Dewey's under- standing of values and their role in action.

Certainly, we would be misconstruing Dewey's position if we supposed his rejection of attempts to reify values and posit them as a special kind of entity located in a separate, pre-existing realm to be motivated by the contrary intention to ascribe to them a purely subjective quality. Instead, he begins his *Theory of Valuation* by repu- diating an interpretation of values as mere expressions of feeling. Even in the concepts 'feeling' and 'expression' he detects dualistic ways of thinking, where feeling is opposed to the intellect, or the inner to the outer. Such dualistic ways of thinking would certainly not do justice to the phenomenal facts. An elementary case of pur- ported emotional expression like the smiling or crying of a baby represents, according to Dewey, nothing more than organic behaviour, which is taken by other persons as a sign or symptom and thereby evokes responses. What is at first a purely causal connection becomes, as the child matures, an intentional one; the scream is thus no longer merely part of an organic process, but exists in a medium of com- munication. However, this enormously important transformation does not mean that the organic states develop into a mysterious inner world of purely individual feelings; they remain, rather, embedded in interpersonal activity. For this reason, if valuation is to be traced back to purely subjective expressive behaviour, more careful reflection upon the meaning of the concepts 'feeling' and 'expression' compels one to conclude that they cannot be removed from the reciprocal social relationships between organisms, and that they can – as signs – assume in principle the character of propositions.[5] With this anthropological argument, which I have outlined only briefly here, Dewey believes he has undermined value-theoretical subjectivism and the relativism to which it gives rise.

For Dewey, the alternative of value-theoretical subjectivism and objectivism does not only not represent an inescapable dilemma; he even sees a hidden complicity between these two seemingly so diametrically opposed ways of thinking. He argues that both the assumption that values exist completely independently of human action and the assumption that they are the expression of arbitrary valuation from case to case ignore the observable role values play in action.

Dewey is evidently less interested in the critique of value-theoretical subjectivism than that of its objectivist counterpart. To the latter he returns again and again, and in his debate with value objectivism we find his religious biography in more or less undisguised form. Early in his life, Dewey had already rebelled against the puritanical religiosity of his roots, which seemed to him to compel an abrupt separation of the ideal from the real. His strong impulse towards political reformism, as well as his early enthusiasm for the philosophy of Hegel, had their origins in his search for ways to overcome this cleavage. In early writings which still bear the heavy imprint of Christianity, he makes known his impatience with a religiosity that reveres ideals sentimentally, but does not let them have a practical effect in everyday life: he presses for a 'practical idealism'. To him it seems that the reliance on God is not a boost to one's confidence, but an unwarranted optimism that paralyses action; the belief in another world a flight from, not an intensification of, ordinary life.

Dewey expects Hegel's philosophy to mediate historically between the reasonable and the real and to overcome all the pernicious dualisms inherent in puritanical culture.[6] Though Dewey was from the outset more inclined to embrace historical openendedness and contingency than Hegel was, in this respect resembling the Young Hegelians more than the master himself, the orientation to Hegel enabled him for a while to sublimate his religious orientation intellectually. With the move away from Hegel (which took place around 1894) and his ever stronger emphasis on human praxis in everyday life, Dewey also jettisoned what was for him the last form of intellectually respectable religiosity. From that point on, he continued to view idealism and religiosity as two forms of a hypostatization of the ideal, and he could find no good reasons for perpetuating this hypostatization. Scornfully, he defined idealism as that group of philosophical orientations attempting 'to prove by one method or another, cosmological, ontological or epistemological, that the Real and the Ideal are one, while at the same time they introduce qualifying additions to explain why after all they are not one'.[7] Dewey's resistance in his theory of value to any talk of 'inherent', 'intrinsic' or 'immediate' values can only be understood against this backdrop. He suspects in all such language a tendency to remove values from the means–end chains of human action, to oppose them in particular to the realm of means, thereby devaluing it. But those who hold ends to be justifiable, without at the same time thinking of the available means, or those who believe a value is something that does not correspond to any human positing of ends – such people offend against our everyday experience of life and the concepts of human maturity and personal wisdom we employ there. Dewey does not see an indifference to means and realizable ends as the expression of an ethics of conviction ignorant of the world, but as the indicator of weak value commitment, regardless of the pathos with which this commitment might be asserted.

Of course, a mere compromise formula, according to which valuations are produced by subjects interacting with the objectively given world, does not help us to escape from the alternative of value subjectivism or objectivism. At least this holds true if subjectivity and objectivity are construed as pre-constructed givens. Dewey – and here is his decisive crucial idea – does not think this necessary. What he has in mind, rather, is a process of interaction through which subjectivity and objectivity first constitute themselves and where, as part of this process, valuations simultaneously arise. The above allusions to his concepts of expression and purpose-oriented action in the respective critiques of subjectivism and objectivism give the first indications of the direction in which Dewey would like to lead us. We can, he claims, resolve the aporias of the value-theoretical debates if we base the understanding of values on an appropriate understanding of action.

We can deduce the following basic framework from Dewey's work on the theory of value. In order to understand what values are, we must start with organic behaviour itself. Even this contains preferences, i.e. pre-reflective correspondences between the organism's needs and the particular environmental situations which it encounters. The state of nature is not one of apathy. Preferences do not emanate from conscious decisions of choice. Rather, such decisions only become necessary when the various preferences conflict either with one another or with the conditions prevailing in a given situation.

When this happens, it becomes necessary to reflect the preferences and their realizability. This reflection then not only touches on the external conditions necessary for realizing the need-dispositions that guide action, but also penetrates into the inner core of these needs. For this reason, organic impulses are for Dewey only necessary, not sufficient, conditions for the desires that enter into action: 'Vital impulses are doubtless conditions *sine qua non* for the existence of desires and interests. But the latter include foreseen consequences along with ideas in the form of the signs of the measures (involving expenditure of energy) required to bring the ends into existence.'[8] For Dewey, deliberations on the realizability of desires under particular conditions and in view of scarce resources do not, therefore, rebound off those desires; the character of these desires can itself be altered under the influence of such reflection. Dewey designates as 'value' only that which sustains such a reflected character – not the vital impulses in the background. When he consequently says that values only exist when problems of action arise, he is not trying to suggest that we are not guided by orientations which extend beyond particular situations, or that we can never take over generalized orientations from another actor. He expressly dismisses this misunderstanding;[9] such generalizations, however, do not represent a complete independence from the situations in which we act, but only an abstraction from a certain number of particular action situations. Only when a problem arises is there any need to evaluate consciously which of the orientations we originally followed without reflection should be given precedence, how it can be pursued in the face of adverse circumstances, and how the desires themselves are to be interpreted and modified.[10] Desires can be changed through insight because what Dewey calls an 'ideational component' is characteristic of them. Desires can even be made the object of joint reflection. He does not believe that he is thereby exaggerating in rationalist fashion the importance of reason-based insight and undervaluing the instinctual substratum of our needs; every person who is able to learn from his experience constantly accomplishes the feat of relating his desires to the means of his action and its foreseeable consequences. To ignore this would mean declaring spoilt children and irresponsible adults to be prototypes of human action.[11] Everyone else, however, is familiar from their experience of everyday life with a distinction that Dewey now introduces into his argument, and which plays a key role in his theory of value. It is the distinction between that which is simply 'desired', and that which an actor holds to be 'desirable' after critical reflection on his situation.[12] Through their ability to learn from their experiences, the actors themselves necessarily come to adopt a reflective attitude towards their desires and needs. Thus, in the realm of human action the 'is' does not stand diametrically opposed to the 'ought'. It is not the scientist or the philosopher who first evaluates desires or actions; the actors themselves cannot avoid revising their desires and actions. Just as actors themselves cannot act over an extended period of time without reflecting on and evaluating their action, so the valuations cannot be thought of as existing independently of these acts of internal revision.

> The 'desirable', or the object which *should* be desired (valued), does not descend out of the a priori blue nor descend as an imperative from a moral Mount Sinai. It presents itself because past experience has shown that hasty action upon uncriticized desire leads to defeat and possibly to catastrophe. The 'desirable' as distinct from the 'desired' does not then designate something at large or a priori. It points to the difference between the operation and consequences of unexamined impulses and those of desires and interests that are the product of investigation of conditions and consequences ... the distinction between the 'is' in the sense of the object of a casually emerging desire and the 'should be' of a desire framed in relation to actual conditions is a distinction which in any case is bound to offer itself as human beings grow in maturity and part with the childish disposition to 'indulge' every impulse that arises.[13]

Dewey does not intend with these deliberations to eliminate the distinction between 'is' and 'ought'; instead, in good pragmatist fashion, he opposes all dualistic tendencies and emphasizes the continuity between the terms which have been differentiated. Just as valuation originates in reflection on the pre-reflective impulses under the compulsion to act, so improved valuations arise in reflection on reflection – and once again this does not imply a differentiation of separate levels, but rather a continuous extension of reflection, expanded to include further consequences of action and other needs which have to be taken into account. One of the most important achievements of Dewey's thought in this connection is that he supersedes a concept of purposes or ends thought to be independent of situations, and develops instead a notion of ends that are appropriate for given situations: the 'ends-in-view'.[14] Every fixing of goals or ends outside all relation to the situation distorts, Dewey argues, not only the theoretical comprehension of action, but even action itself. It leads one to ignore and to brush aside the side-effects and unintended consequences of action, of the means employed and of the abandoned courses of action.[15] According to Dewey's pragmatism, however, all values and goals must be able to become objects of reflection and discussion for both actors and scientists.

Thus far our discussion of Dewey's theory of value has enabled us to correct the prejudice that the framework of pragmatism only allows a reduction of values to facts or subjective sensations. Yet, conversely, these very corrections can give rise to the sceptical suspicion that Dewey's pragmatism is rationalistic in the sense that he ascribes unlimited effect to the rational revision of values in the light of experience. As illuminating as Dewey's account of the role of values in the dynamics of action is, it might be argued that this analysis contributes little to an explanation of the genesis of values, if by that we mean something other than the rational reinterpretation of action orientations in the light of the experience of problematic situations. Dewey's polemic against the origin of the Commandments of Mount Sinai must then lend weight to the suspicion that he is not alive to cases where there is a radical reorientation in values, like the 'conversions' that James had foregrounded. This suspicion is counterbalanced by the fact that Dewey, in his philosophy of nature and even more in his aesthetics, had already sketched a theory of action and experience which extends far beyond a pragmatic understanding of action in the everyday sense of the term.[16] In these works, he develops at length the ideal of both a holistic experience and an action completely pervaded with meaning, and opposes it to all action that satisfies the actor only when the goal has been attained. Here Dewey is thinking of a kind of action which is oriented in all its phases towards the realization of ideals,[17] a perspective that allows us to look beyond a pragmatic relativization of situation-independent purposes. It is in his theory of religion, and not in his theory of value, that Dewey applies this ambitious concept of action and experience to the role of values and to their genesis.

A Common Faith cannot be compared with the great works of Dewey's late philosophy (on nature and art, logic and ethics), for it succeeds all of them in terms either of its sheer brevity, or the richness of its argument or the amount of attention that it receives today. The leading Protestant theologian among Dewey's contemporaries in the United States, Reinhold Niebuhr, called *A Common Faith* quite conceivably a mere footnote to his impressive oeuvre.[18] Nevertheless, the three lectures that Dewey published in this volume are extremely significant, and, in order to do them justice, it is in my view necessary to distinguish the two levels on which the book operates. On the one hand, it represents the attempt to intervene in religious debates taking place in the United States during the 1930s between liberal Christians, fundamentalist currents, those who sought to place fresh emphasis on the concepts of evil and sin, and secular humanist enterprises.[19] In this context, Dewey expresses his personal views on the contemporary state of religion, on its effects and its future. On the other hand, Dewey's work on the theory of religion extends his theory of action and experience to encompass a further area of inquiry in which one can see at least an application, perhaps even a further development or culmination, of his own thought, and thus of the approach inaugurated by William James.[20] Dewey's contribution to a systematic understanding of the genesis of values should be expected on this level. For this reason, we shall first turn our attention to Dewey's theory of religious experience, before then discussing his peculiar attempt at a sacralization of democracy.

Like James, Dewey separates at the very beginning of his discussion – in the lecture entitled 'Religion versus the Religious' – the 'religious' from institutionalized forms of religion, which he defines as 'a special body of beliefs and practices having some kind of institutional organization, loose or tight'.[21] Thus, his approach to the phenomenon of the religious is intended to run parallel to the argument he had employed in his book on aesthetics, where it had proved fruitful not to start out from ossified art hanging in museums, or its professionalized or commercialized forms, but to investigate 'art as experience'. Dewey immediately defends himself against a possible misunderstanding. Under no circumstances does he intend to trace ossified cultural forms back to their origin in human experience merely in order to reproduce conceptually, by distinguishing types of experience, the rigid boundaries between the culturally differentiated value spheres. Hence Dewey does not believe in a specifically 'aesthetic' or 'religious' form of experience, but in aesthetic or religious dimensions of human experience in general. This distinction seems to Dewey to be of fundamental importance as far as religion is concerned, even greater than its significance in the domain of art. He views every assumption of a separate kind of experience that is uniquely religious as disguised theology. Any theory starting from the premise of such 'experience' would perpetuate the dualism of the natural and supernatural which Dewey had resisted throughout his entire career. Theories of religious experience had become almost fashionable during the years separating James's pioneering achievement and Dewey's book – that is, between 1902 and 1934.[22] Dewey sees two reasons for this development. Firstly, the old ontological, cosmological and teleological proofs of the existence of God had been discredited not only by Kant's epochal critique, but also by the realization that such rationalism was unlikely to inspire religious motivation. Secondly, in a scientifically oriented age the prospect of justifying religion in an analogous way to science is an enticing one: that is, as based on a separate type of experience clearly distinguishable from the scientific type. Just as the scientists 'rely upon certain kinds of experience to prove the existence of certain kinds of objects, so the religionists rely upon a certain kind of experience to prove the existence of the object of religion, especially the supreme object, God'.[23]

But this proof from experience, Dewey argues, does not really produce the desired result. Like Durkheim seeking to differentiate his own position from that of James,[24] Dewey objects that experience does not itself determine its correct interpretation. On no account does he wish to doubt that experiences of the kind documented in accounts of religious experience actually occur. However, a person who has such experiences obtains his or her interpretations of them from the culture in which he or she has grown up. Dewey does not put forward his own interpretation with quite the same unshakeable belief in its truth as does Durkheim; but neither does he admit all the interpretations made by those involved, as James did in the spirit of unrestrained curiosity. Rather, in a manner that is clearly directed against organized and traditional religions, he wants to put a limit on the religious interpretation of such experiences in the narrower sense. Thus, at least at first sight, the real origins of these experiences remain obscure. For, as a pragmatist, Dewey approaches the question of origins by illuminating the effects: we first ascertain a phenomenon on the basis of its effects. With respect to religious experience, this means that the existence of such experiences cannot prove their 'supernatural' origin, but only the fact of 'an orientation, that brings with it a sense of security and peace'.[25]

If Dewey rejects the notion of a separate type of religious experience and the proof of the existence of God based upon it, in what, then, does the religious quality of experiences consist for him? What is the essence of the reorientations in life brought about by such experiences? Dewey's first step in answering these questions is to introduce a conceptual distinction. He distinguishes three kinds of such orientation in life and offers three different concepts for them: 'adaptation', 'accommodation' and 'adjustment', all of which are commonly employed as synonyms. Yet to do so is to ignore the fundamental differences Dewey wishes to address, and insufficient attention to this distinction has frequently hindered the understanding of pragmatism.[26] All these terms imply a coming to terms with unalterable circumstances; we always act under given conditions and must always take account of these. Dewey refers to a predominantly passive reorientation of particular modes of conduct to such conditions as

'accommodation'; if this unavoidable form of reorientation is generalized and determines our whole behaviour, we call it fatalistic resignation or submission to circumstances.

A second form, clearly distinguishable from the first, could best be
described as the world adapting to us, or as our transformation of it
to serve the purposes of life. Dewey terms this second type of
reorientation 'adaptation'; what stands out here is the active element
in the organism's relation to its environment. The third form, which
goes beyond either of these two, is what Dewey calls 'adjustment'; it
is the goal of these conceptual distinctions to clarify the specificities of
this third type. The main difference between this third type and the
two others lies in its holistic character. Here our whole person is at
issue, and not only individual desires or needs in their relation to
environmental conditions. Because of their holistic character, Dewey
maintains, such modifications to our person are permanent and stabilized against changes in the environmental conditions. It is no simple
thing to compare 'adjustment' with the other two types of reorientation in terms of activity and passivity. Although fundamental reorientations of our person can be called voluntary, they are not so in the
same way that our volitions are. Not only does something change in
and through our will, our will itself changes in them. 'It is a change *of*
will conceived as the organic plenitude of our being, rather than any
special change *in* will.'[27] There is quite clearly a passive element in the
voluntariness here. This should not be confused with a stoical resolution to remain calm in the face of the vicissitudes of fate: this attitude
is 'more outgoing, more ready and glad' than mere stoicism.[28]

It still remains rather unclear as to what kind of experiences Dewey
wants to lay hold of with these terminological distinctions and tenta-
tive descriptions. We are inevitably reminded of James's vivid descriptions of the liberating effects of religious experiences. Dewey does
indeed have in mind the claim made by religions that it is through
them that such holistic and permanent transformations take place in a
person's attitudes. However, in keeping with his objective of distinguishing between experience and interpretation, he wants at the very
least to question this claim's self-evidence. His method is therefore to
reverse the relationship between cause and effect. He thus does not
attribute fundamental reorientations in values to a person opening
himself or herself up to supernatural influences in religious experiences; instead, he simply designates as religious every such fundamental change in orientation. 'It is not *a* religion that brings it about,
but when it occurs, from whatever cause and by whatever means,
there is a religious outlook and function.'[29]

At first sight this move can seem like a mere pseudo-solution to the problem, circumventing it by redefining the terms. We can quite happily concede to Dewey that it is by no means only religions in the usual sense of the word that can bring about fundamental reorientations in a person's outlook; the same goes for the fact that religion only permeates into superficial regions of many believers' characters, so that the influence of religion on personal development can also be easily overestimated. If this were all that Dewey wished to assert, then we would have no qualms in agreeing with him; perhaps we might only want to object that one doesn't necessarily make things any clearer by terming all such reorientations 'religious', even and precisely those which are not connected with institutionalized forms of religiosity. Dewey could then even have saved himself the bother of distinguishing between 'religious experiences' and the 'religious dimension of experiences', since for him the concept of the religious would have surrendered all relation to institutionalized forms of religion and especially to a supernatural realm. But such an interpretation would entirely underestimate the profundity of Dewey's thought. We can avoid this underestimation only by reading Dewey's account against the background of his understanding of action and experience. His roundabout way of dealing with the concept of the religious is therefore not merely pedantry or a consequence of his difficult relationship with organized religion. It stems, rather, from his attempt actually to identify in the potentially religious dimension of all experience a phenomenon which differs from the fragmentation of everyday experience, and yet which also represents more than the situation-bound overcoming of this fragmentation through aesthetic experience.[30]

Dewey's crucial step consists in connecting religious experience with the *imaginary* orientation to a *whole self*. Before Dewey, both William James and Georg Simmel had already thought along these lines. James had interpreted conversion as a transformation of the self from a state of division and turmoil to a newly unified one; Simmel had recognized the self's awareness of its finitude as the necessary co-ordinating point in the genesis of ideal validities, and had elaborated the value-relatedness of self-formation.[31] But neither succeeded in translating these insights from intuitions into clear concepts. At any rate, Dewey contributes to the clarification of their approaches.

He makes it clear that the idea of a whole self is thoroughly imaginary. The holistic self no more exists somewhere, say in a person's inner being, in static perfection waiting to be realized in practical life, than do values exist in a transcendental ideal realm.[32] There is no possibility of ever perceiving the self as a whole through the senses, visually for example. But neither is an integral relation to ourselves possible in any practical activity, or in an act of reflection. Even our interaction with other people in everyday life always touches on only one aspect of our person.

Yet we still speak of a whole self or of self-realization, which only makes sense if the present real self can be ascribed something not yet realized, something that nevertheless must somehow have already existed before, and is not first produced in, its realization. Dewey does not attack the notion of the given self in order to destroy the idea of wholeness and self-realization,[33] but in order to underscore the imaginary character of this idea. 'The *whole* self is an ideal, an imaginative projection.'[34] This emphasis on the imaginary should not be understood as reducing this ideal to the status of mere illusion; Dewey resists such a misunderstanding by pointing out that it is only through our imagination that we can be aware of all possibilities.[35] The dualism of the real and the possible simply does not exist for Dewey; rather, the real contains possibilities, and the imagination is an organ through which human beings can apprehend the possible. Dewey praises his contemporary and adversary George Santayana for having introduced into the discussion of religion the dimension of the imaginary in this sense. Dewey describes as a 'penetrating insight'[36] Santayana's interest in the difference between an 'intervening' and a merely 'supervening' role of the imagination, instead of seeking an essential difference between the aesthetic and the religious. The question is whether the imagination only enhances our life, or whether it permeates and transforms life; this, however, can happen through art *and* religion, just as art *and* religion could remain merely superficial accessories adorning one's conduct of life. Without a 'creative movement of the imagination' all perception remains limited and all discipline mere repression. With it, however, the ideals arise which pervade our perception of the world and our morality. By insisting on their relation to the imaginary, Dewey can recognize ideals without attributing to them a separate, prior existence. In an earlier work he had already asserted: 'The ideal is not a goal to be attained. It is a significance to be felt, appreciated.'[37] But now he extends this determination by defining values or ideals *as the product of creative processes in which contingent possibilities are idealized.* An ideal arises, Dewey writes,

> when the imagination idealizes existence by laying hold of the possibilities offered to thought and action ... The idealizing imagination seizes upon the most precious things found in the climacteric moments of experience and projects them. We need no external criterion and

guarantees for their goodness. They are had, they exist as good, and out of them we frame our ideal ends.[38]

Dewey has far more in mind here than merely a clever modification of goals in response to the conditions for their realization; he sees the genesis of values as the creative work of our imagination.

At the same time, however, this insight brings him closer to understanding the ideas of the whole self and of self-realization. Amidst all the contradictions between our desires, or between duty and inclination, and amidst all the anguish we feel over missed opportunities and unrealized potential, creative idealization allows us to imagine a wholeness which never existed, never will exist, and yet still seems to us to be more real than all partial realizations. It seems real to us because we have experienced it as real with the greatest intensity. This can happen in religious experiences, or for Dewey in any experiences which involve this kind of religious dimension because they 'completely interpenetrat[e] all the elements of our being'[39] and give our self meaning and coherence. When, in intense emotional experiences, we have this feeling of breaking through to our own wholeness, this 'sense of values' sustains us through 'periods of darkness and despair to such an extent that they lose their usual depressive character'.[40] Lack of success in our practical endeavours, blows of fortune or failures in meeting the moral demands we make on ourselves – none of these can destroy this essence of our self. Ideals make permanent that which briefly flares up in these fleeting experiences: ideals integrate. To believe in them is to unify our self 'through allegiance to inclusive ideal ends, which imagination presents to us and to which the human will responds as worthy of controlling our desires and choices'.[41]

However, the unification of the self should not, Dewey argues, be understood as cutting the self off from the world. It is only possible for a person to experience himself as a unity throughout all his actions and the events which befall him, and even in his unrealized possibilities, if the world is introduced into the process of self-unification. 'The self is always directed toward something beyond itself and so its own unification depends upon the idea of the integration of the shifting scenes of the world into that imaginative totality we call the Universe.'[42] He defines the 'Universe' as the totality of conditions with which the self feels itself to be connected. The wholeness of this Universe has the same imaginary character as the wholeness of the self. Dewey is well aware that all religions are characterized by the feeling of 'absolute dependence'[43] on something greater existing beyond our self, supporting and sustaining our endeavours. For this reason, he designates as areligious only those views which attribute human achievements exclusively to humanity itself and ignore the co-operation of its environment. 'Our successes are dependent upon the co-operation of nature. The sense of the dignity of human nature is as religious as is the sense of awe and reverence when it rests upon a sense of human nature as a co-operative part of a larger whole.'[44] Dewey describes this quasi-religious sentiment towards the environment as 'natural piety', a term whose origins lie in English Romanticism. He does not wish this term to be misconstrued as Romantic enthusiasm for nature as such or as a fatalistic belief in the determinism of the universe, for he claims that a sense of what is specifically human in nature can certainly be combined with this kind of piety towards nature as a whole.[45]

The recognition of the imaginary wholeness of self and universe also leads Dewey to emphasize the active-passive character of such an experience of wholeness, which he had already delineated when introducing the concept of 'adjustment'. Like all acts of the imagination and all creative actions, a firm will does not help to bring about this experience. 'An "adjustment" possesses the will rather than is its express product.'[46] For this reason, we cannot directly strive for and deliberately attain experiences of wholeness. Rather, they require an openness to forces that flow from sources beyond conscious deliberation and purpose.[47] For Dewey, this explains the affinity such experiences have with 'supernatural' interpretations. Traditionally, such interpretations have rested on the idea that religious experiences, and the faith which develops from them, are themselves an expression of divine mercy. Wholly independent of all theological contexts, Dewey – like James – advocates a concept of faith premised not on a cognitive holding-to-be-true of facts, but rather on a conviction of the presence of ideals which attract us and govern our conduct. This conviction is the product of captivation, not of a conscious decision, and although cognition and reflection are involved, they do not constitute its essence. 'Conviction in the moral sense signifies being conquered, vanquished, in our active nature by an ideal end; it signifies acknowledgement of its rightful claim over our desire and purposes.'[48]

Thus, Dewey's answer to the question of the genesis of values rather resembles that given by the other thinkers we have previously discussed. Like James and Durkheim, but also like Simmel and Scheler, he anchors the genesis of value commitments in experiences of self-transcendence and self-formation. With far greater perspicacity than the others, he establishes the connection between the theory of values and the theory of self-formation; yet his description of the phenomenal form of the experiences in which value commitments have their origin is less explicit. Dewey does not give any clear metaphors which would guide us and which would be comparable to James's descriptions of prayer and conversion, Durkheim's account of collective states of ecstasy, Simmel's reflections on death and immortality or Scheler's phenomenology of moral feelings. Scattered over many of his writings from all phases of his work, and drawn from various contexts, we find examples of experiences with a religious dimension. To these belong experiences of communion with nature, aesthetic experiences and mystical intuitions, just as much as do deep shocks in compassion and love, or feelings of togetherness that accompany happy, communal life. But these experiences – with the exception of aesthetic experiences – are rarely analysed in detail; rather, they are merely enlisted for conceptual arguments or used as final chords full of pathos.

It is in the chapter on communication in *Experience and Nature* that the experiential content of Dewey's philosophy of value-constitutive experience probably finds its most concrete expression.[49] Here Dewey loads the anthropological theory of the specifics of human communication, as it had been developed by his friend George Herbert Mead, with a quasi-religious meaning: 'Of all affairs, communication is the most wonderful. That things should be able to pass from the plane of external pushing and pulling to that of revealing themselves to man, and thereby to themselves; and that the fruit of communication should be participation, sharing, is a wonder by the side of which transubstantiation pales.'[50] He regards communication not only as a functional agency for co-ordinating the action of different people, but as an event which can open up individual human beings to others; in doing so, it itself makes possible the experience in which value commitment arises. When communication leads to 'shared experience', Dewey sees it as a way of overcoming self-centredness. In his early work, he had still appealed to the Christian concept of love to support this idea.[51] Yet even if he no longer establishes the connection in this way in his later work, it is still evident that Dewey advocates an emphatic conception of altruism. He understands it not as renouncing one's own interests to increase the benefit of others, nor as self-development through one's commitment to others. Instead, Dewey understands it as the radical readiness to let oneself be shaken by the Other in order thereby to realize oneself with and through other people: as shattering intersubjectivity.

I want to emphasize two aspects of Dewey's argument at this point. Firstly, it becomes clear that, by focusing on communication, intersubjectivity and shared experience, he finds a way out from the inadequate dualism of individual and collective experience that we noted in James and Durkheim. Although James's work contained the seeds of an intersubjective interpretation of solitary religious experience,[52] these had remained scattered and of no consequence for the construction of his theory. Dewey, in contrast, is so heavily influenced by George Herbert Mead's anthropological theory of communication that he links the structure of extra-ordinary experiences to the intersubjectivist understanding of human action in general. Dewey construes the opening of the self, which James and Durkheim also described as essential for extra-ordinary experiences, as the decentring of the actor towards another – even where this other is nature or God. We should immediately add the rider, however, that although Dewey constantly appeals to the genesis of the self in ordinary and extra-ordinary intersubjective experiences, he never really follows up this insight.[53] Although he gestures towards combining an intersubjectivist theory of the self with the questions of the genesis of value commitments, he does not take this idea very far.

The second aspect to stress is that Dewey does not only maintain that extra-ordinary experience has an intersubjective character; he also holds that it is possible to find in everyday communication itself an ideal inspiring reverence. Participation in a conversation can itself yield the experience of wholeness. The attitudes of participants requisite for a successful dialogue resemble the opening of the self which he described in the analysis of religious experiences. In turn, the genesis of these experiences in conversation becomes more likely through that very opening of the self. The opening of the self is both the precondition for and consequence of the experience of shattering intersubjectivity. For Dewey, conversation or dialogue is the place where we are confronted with the values of others, and, when we truly open ourselves up, where we consider our own values anew. At the same time, however, provided that it grants us this experience, conversation produces a value commitment to the consummation of intercommunication itself.

With his description of communication as being simultaneously both means and goal, instrumental and final, Dewey repeatedly expresses the possibility of experiencing a 'religious' dimension in conversation itself.[54]

> Communication is an exchange which procures something wanted; it involves a claim, appeal, order, direction or request, which realizes want at less cost than personal labour exacts, since it procures the co-operative assistance of others. Communication is also an immediate enhancement of life, enjoyed for its own sake. . . . Language is always a form of action

and in its instrumental use is always a means of concerted action for an end, while at the same time it finds in itself all the goods of its possible consequences. For there is no mode of action as fulfilling and as rewarding as is concerted consensus of action. It brings with it the sense of sharing and merging in a whole. . . . Shared experience is the greatest of human goods . . . Because of its characteristic agency and finality, communication and its congenial objects are objects ultimately worthy of awe, admiration, and loyal appreciation. They are worthy as means, because they are the only means that make life rich and varied in meanings. They are worthy as ends, because in such ends man is lifted from his immediate isolation and shares in a communion of meanings. Here, as in so many other things, the great evil lies in separating instrumental and final functions . . . When the instrumental and final functions of communication live together in experience, there exists an intelligence which is the method and reward of the common life, and a society worthy to command affection, admiration, and loyalty.[55]

Dewey's emphasis here is on the experience of communication, on communication as experience. The transition from interpersonal relationship to the value of community and democracy takes place not through the justification of democratic principles in an idealized discourse, but through the genesis of a value commitment to the practice of communicating, which is itself rooted in the experience of communication.[56] For Dewey, the unlimited nature of everyday communication and its institutionalization in the form of the procedures and institutions of democratic society become the highest ideal. Replying to critics of his philosophy in 1939, in an essay which simultaneously served as a retrospective on his intellectual development, Dewey could claim that he had endeavoured all his life to make explicit the religious values implicit in the spirit of science and likewise 'the religious values implicit in our common life, especially in the moral significance of democracy as a way of living together'.[57] Democracy becomes Dewey's secular religion. Should we give our allegiance to him as the prophet of this religion?

With this question we return to that contemporary line of attack in *A Common Faith* which we bracketed off at the beginning of our discussion of this work. To facilitate our understanding of this argument, it is useful briefly to recall at what stage of his life Dewey wrote this book. In his neo-Hegelian, still Christian, early phase he had indeed, as he claimed in his retrospective, already ascribed a quasi-sacred character to pragmatic intelligence and democratic will-formation. At first glance, the sermon he delivered to Christian students in Michigan in 1892[58] reads like an attempt at a Christian justification of democracy. In the course of the lecture, however, it becomes increasingly clear that Dewey is interested in far more than just this; in keeping with the character of American spirituality, by positing a radical relation of the divine to the everyday life of humanity, he opens up the perspective of surpassing Christianity in a sacralized democracy. The spirit of revelation is then 'sublated' in scientific inquiry, as the incarnation of God in man is 'sublated' in the democratic community. Dewey asks himself whether religious institutions, with their origins in a pre-democratic and pre-scientific age, can welcome their replacement by democracy and science, or whether, in defending their independence, they are condemned to ossify because they can only look backwards to the past. For Dewey himself, it was already clear by this time that the future could belong only to the sacralization of science and democracy. After the end of his neo-Hegelian phase, he only rarely comments on religion and its place in democracy,[59] but when he does so, his early optimism about the process of secularization is couched in even more radical terms.[60] Specifically, he does not interpret progressive secularization as a symptom of moral and cultural decay; instead, he understands it as a change in the way religious motifs are expressed, as their liberation from dogmatic doctrine and narrow forms of institutionalization. According to him, the disappearance of individual churches as institutions need not represent a loss; such a development might instead express the universalization of Christian impulses, and thus historical progress. This combination of declining interest in religion and democratic optimism did not, to be sure, withstand the turmoil of the twentieth century. After the First World War, and particularly after the beginning of the Great Depression, Dewey became increasingly convinced that his philosophical conception of democracy would not stand up to the events of the age if it did not also find the means of seizing the hearts and minds of the people and inspiring them to make the necessary radical reforms.[61] Therefore, Dewey's attempts to attribute a sacred character to democracy itself already begin in the 1920s, and find their culmination in *A Common Faith*, his book on religion.

In Dewey's view, the most important thing is to avoid the infelicitous association of the religious with a belief in supernatural forces. Since modern science has gradually reduced the cognitive claims of religion to represent a knowledge of such forces and has devalued such a knowledge altogether, this linkage leads to a poor alternative: either to remain a believer, but then pay the price of defending conceptions of the world which have lost their credibility – or, as a scientifically minded atheist, to become unable to find any meaning at all in religious ideals. Those who refuse to accept this poor alternative, as Dewey is well aware, stand to be denounced by both sides – with the religionists seeing an opponent of their doctrines and the militant atheists a half-hearted supporter of a religion that is beyond rescue. Dewey, however, thinks he has found a way out from this alternative, which is to uncouple the notion of ideals and values from the cognitive belief in supernatural forces. If it is possible (and this is exactly what the theoretical nub of his argument was driving at) to preserve a rational core at the centre of the religious by interpreting experience and action in a new way, and yet simultaneously to cast off all the mythological and dogmatic baggage that has weighed down traditional religions, then the way is clear for the sacralization of the everyday social relationships of human beings and their action in nature. What Dewey finds repellent about mere atheism is that, in rejecting the supernatural, it also tends to devalue the natural. In the belief in a 'supernatural' realm, however, he sees the prototypical case of a rupture between the ideal and the real, which he had sought his whole life long to repair. Dewey would have us believe that the catalogue of the misdeeds perpetrated by religions is long. By hypostatizing all that is ideal into the notion of a prior existing being, 'God', they distract us from everyday action, lull us into a false sense of security and seduce us into idleness; they impoverish our everyday life because they discourage our recognition of its potential; they divert our attention from other people because they fix our gaze on individual salvation; and they delude us into believing in unattainable objectives, thus overtaxing and suffocating our natural powers. All this can be laid squarely at the door of a belief in a 'supernatural' being. Moreover, further problems arise because this belief assumes the form of institutionalized churches, each one of which claims a monopoly on our religious experience. In doing so, they hinder such experience more than they make it possible, competing with one another and thereby erecting artificial boundaries within a community. In order to protect their untenable claims, they obstruct unprejudiced scientific research and the free communication of democratic citizens.

On no account does Dewey express his opposition to all these consequences of religion by proposing a programme for its abolition by coercive or even violent means; his goal is not to destroy religion, but rather to recast it. He defines this recasting as the emancipation of the religious attitude from the institutional forms of religion. For the first time in the history of humanity, 'the religious aspect of experience will be free to develop freely on its own account',[62] and people who feel 'repelled from what exists as a religion by its intellectual and moral implications' will become aware 'of attitudes in themselves that if they came to fruition would be genuinely religious'.[63] In this new form of religiosity, the word 'God' would no longer designate a particular being beyond the human world, but instead the *'active relation between ideal and actual'*.[64] If this were to become the new meaning of the term, then even Dewey, the atheist, would be ready to accept again the notion of a 'God'.[65] There would then arise, he maintains, a 'common faith of mankind', a faith which has always resided *in nuce* in human beings, but whose realization has awaited philosophical explication.[66]

But can anyone believe in such a God? Is it really true that organized religion has always inhibited intellectual and moral progress? Can we today, more than six decades later, still share Dewey's optimism that the de-institutionalization of religion will release and emancipate authentic religious impulses? The answer to all three questions must be 'no'. The idea that a philosopher's decision to use or to admit the concept of 'God' to denote an intellectual abstraction could move someone to achieve something, and would exercise some kind of transformative influence, seems almost laughable. If we take away Dewey's casting of the concept of God, then the sociological hole in his argument looms large. Admittedly, he asks which ideals today 'can direct action and generate the heat of emotion and the light of intelligence'[67] in order to ground democratic institutions in particular. Yet his answer to this question of where the deep affective roots of democracy could lie in individuals and societies remains weak and abstract. Likewise, it is all too easy to read Dewey's objections to the cultural and social impact of institutionalized religion as a fallacious generalization of his experiences of the pietistic Protestantism of his childhood and youth. Indeed, religion has often been not an obstacle, but rather the impetus for intellectual and moral progress. Dewey had never sufficiently devoted himself to studying the history and sociology of religion in order to be able to advance such theses. One need only think of Max Weber's intensive studies of the active or passive features, this-worldly or other-worldly orientations, of the major world religions for it to be clear that, if the consequences of institutionalized religiosity are to be assessed, we require more evidence than that which Dewey adduces.[68] Hence not only does he offer no interpretations of concrete religiosity; nowhere does the particular style of his account betray the passionate curiosity for the variety of religious phenomena which was so characteristic of James's work. Dewey brings the debate to a close before it has even begun.[69] In stark contrast to his constant efforts to circumvent all abrupt dualisms, he sets institutionalized religion against the free-floating religious in the experience of democracy without seeking to mediate between them.

However much he may have been right in individual cases with his critique of the churches' claim to exclusivity, or with his assertion that religious institutions may hinder religious experience, he overshoots the mark with his plea for radical de-institutionalization. Today it could be said that the de-institutionalization of religion does not, in all probability, lead to the consequences Dewey expected, but rather to a subjectivization of religion – to what the group around Robert Bellah has described as 'Sheila-ism'.[70] This term refers to a purely personal form of religion, where the only person who currently holds such a belief proclaims her idiosyncratic mixture of views to be a new variant of religion. This kind of religiosity, however, cuts itself off from the rationalizing effects of the intersubjective assimilation of religious experience, from the wealth of traditions spanning millennia and the wisdom of specialists in religious experience. Whoever wishes to be religious without following a particular religion succumbs to the same paradox as one who would like to speak without using a particular language.[71]

Dewey's sacralization of democracy thus ends in a paradox. The same thinker who related the questions of the genesis of values to the value-forming experience of communication eschews any attempt at clarifying particular binding forces. He skips over the particularism of each individual experience and lands, with his 'common faith of mankind', in an empty universalism of the democratic ideal, the motivating force of which remains unfathomable.[72] This leads to what Charles Taylor has harshly and accurately called 'post-Enlightenment banalities'.[73] For this reason, our task now is to continue and go beyond what Dewey started – the combination of the theory of value-genesis with a theory of self-formation – yet without at the same time ending up in his paradoxes.

8

Identity and the Good
(Charles Taylor)

From Nietzsche to Scheler, from James to Dewey – for a few decades there existed a rich discourse on the question of the genesis of values. The thinkers I have hitherto discussed by no means wrote in isolation from one another; they frequently refer to one another either explicitly or implicitly, and often see their own work as elaborating or replying to that of others. Also, they are not the only voices in this discourse; it is just that their answers can be singled out as especially succinct forms in this fluid discourse, and I do not attempt an encyclopaedic survey here.[1] None the less, after the 1930s this discourse seems largely to dry up. For this reason, it is less arbitrary than it might initially appear for the following discussion to skip over a period of fifty years and only take up the thread again with the writings of the Canadian philosopher Charles Taylor from the 1980s. Motifs from the works of the thinkers we have discussed here were of course followed up in various ways in the intervening years; likewise, new approaches to the question were attempted, drawing on completely different sources. In this connection, Taylor himself cites works by Iris Murdoch, Harry Frankfurt, Bernard Williams and Alasdair MacIntyre.[2] However, it can be argued that none of the attempts to develop existing theories, and none of these new approaches, attained the systematic unity of Taylor's work. This is enough to justify concentrating exclusively on Taylor's answer to the question of the genesis of values. In doing so, it will be especially important to consider how his answer relates to the solution we have seen beginning to emerge in John Dewey's writings – to decide whether Taylor can surpass it or whether he ties us up in new difficulties. I shall therefore pay particular attention to the combination of a theory of values with an intersubjectivist theory of identity formation.

Such a link between the philosophy of value and the theory of
identity formation was not only not followed up during the years that
separate the work of Dewey and Taylor; it was actually consciously
avoided. The philosophy of value in the sense of a systematics of
values increasingly became a sterile discipline, widely regarded as
obsolete and rarely pursued further. The international discussion in
philosophical ethics was dominated by entirely different trends. Ethical naturalism reduced values to subjective emotions or projections
against the backdrop of a value-neutral world. The Kantians, who
concentrated exclusively on the Ought and its justification, also could
not find an appropriate place in their systems for the ideals that attract
us and give our life meaning. In analytic philosophy, substantive
clarifications of ethical questions were temporarily replaced by the
attempt to construct a neutral metaethics, that is to say, a discipline
that sets itself the goal of clarifying ethical statements, but is itself at
the same time governed by the norm of value-freedom. This development made it possible to include philosophical ethics in the universe
of empirical sciences, in which this same norm had become self-
evidently valid. For this reason, any connection between the analysis
of data and the philosophy of value in the empirical sciences themselves could only appear suspect. Although those who subscribed to
this way of thinking readily conceded that values guide the choice of
objects of scientific inquiry, they could scarcely imagine that their
investigations might have a retroactive effect upon the valuative
presuppositions which served as their point of departure. This lack of
awareness of the reciprocity obtaining between values and research
applied throughout all the social-scientific disciplines, even for
research on identity formation. Whereas reflections on socialization
theory and ethics still seemed to evolve organically from one another
in the work of George Herbert Mead, undisputedly the classic exponent of this research tradition,[3] this link was by and large forgotten in
the tradition of symbolic interactionism, a school of thought which
appeals to Mead's authority. Its central programmatic work, written
by Herbert Blumer,[4] thematizes the intersubjective genesis of meanings, but not valuations; whereas for William James and Émile Durkheim meaning and valuation coalesce in the experience of the sacred,
it seems perfectly natural to Blumer to detach the horizon of value
from the semantic fields of human action. Although the subsequent
research on identity formation often takes interpersonal processes into
consideration in exemplary fashion, it neglects to analyse the values
that are necessarily simultaneously posited in those persons who play

a role in our identity formation.[5] For this reason, the establishment or re-establishment of the linkage between the philosophy of value and research on identity formation presupposed a shift in fundamental assumptions, a resistance to the hegemony of scientism in the sciences and the prevailing trends in philosophical ethics.

In view of the way in which his academic career developed, Charles Taylor was particularly favourably predisposed to this situation.[6] He first made his mark with an exhaustive critique of behaviourism and other attempts to analyse human action on the basis of models stemming from the natural sciences. In doing so, his argument was fashioned in the style of analytic philosophy, yet he had essentially advanced motifs influenced by so-called 'Continental' thought, the phenomenology of Maurice Merleau-Ponty in particular. This aspect of his work dealing with the philosophy of science and with methodology also led him in subsequent years to write several pieces which have since become classics of their kind: an extensive critical discussion of the issue of value-freedom and neutrality in political science, for example.[7] In this work he argued that value orientations were unavoidable within the great explanatory frames of reference in the social sciences, and warned that there was a danger that these sciences could become impoverished if research were guided by an orientation to avoid such value-relatedness. Increasingly, however, Taylor pushed beyond this narrow area of inquiry, and asked why scientism and naturalism enjoyed such great prestige in the social sciences – even when such orientations had not shown themselves to be especially fruitful for research and theory construction. This question led him to examine the historical roots of this way of thinking and to search for alternative traditions. Influenced by Isaiah Berlin, he stumbled upon the counter-tradition of expressivism, which sought to analyse human language and action neither according to the schema of cause and effect, nor according to that of means and ends, but understood them rather as the *expression* of the speaker or actor.[8] Taylor's style of thinking and argumentation, however, is characterized more by an impulse towards integration than polarization. The overriding impression one has when reading his work is that he does not by any means dismiss rival positions or those he intends to criticize, but treats them rather as the voices of interlocutors who are to be taken extremely seriously. With polished interpretative skill, Taylor extracts from these viewpoints a confession of the concealed assumptions or thoughtless inconsistencies that underlie them. Thus, he did not simply oppose the prevailing social-scientific and philosophical schools of thought with the anthropology of expression, which goes back to Herder, Hamann and Humboldt and was consti-

tutive of the hermeneutic tradition; instead, he endeavoured to synthesize legitimate motifs from the rival traditions. It is therefore not
surprising that Hegel became the crucial reference point for him, for
it was Hegel who, perhaps more than any other thinker in modern
intellectual history, sought to integrate not only the various disciplines
amongst which knowledge was divided, but also the great currents of
thought dominating his age. Taylor devoted a monograph to him,[9]
which brought him fame as a philosopher, but also gave rise to the
impression that he was merely 'a kind of late Hegelian peripheral
phenomenon on the Anglo-Saxon philosophy scene'.[10] Not until he
had completed the Hegel book – although this development was fully
consistent with the motifs expressed therein – did Taylor gradually
introduce those conceptual innovations which allowed the outlines of
his own philosophical anthropology to emerge in his understanding
of action and evaluation. These same steps also led to an answer to
the question of the genesis of values, which is why Taylor's work is
important for the train of thought we are pursuing here. He developed
his answer most consistently in the systematic part of his major work
published in 1989, *Sources of the Self*.[11] The following discussion is
based on this work, although it also draws on several of the preliminary studies and his subsequent attempts to clarify his position in
reply to his critics.[12]

The first, most important and most momentous step in Charles
Taylor's theory of value consists in his distinguishing between 'strong'
and 'weak' evaluations. In doing so, Taylor adopts and modifies
Harry Frankfurt's suggestive distinction between first- and second-
order desires. Within the framework of a philosophical discussion
about the specifics of the concept of a person, and thus at the same
time about the characteristics of the human personality that set it
apart from other creatures, Frankfurt had drawn attention to a distinctive feature of the human will which unambiguously distinguishes
human beings from other creatures. This distinctive feature consists
in the fact that humans not only have desires like other creatures;
above and beyond these desires they also have desires directed at
their desires. They can desire to have or not to have a desire, and they
can desire that one of their desires could actually be strong enough to
influence the will.

> Besides wanting and choosing and being moved *to do* this or that, men
> may also want to have (or not to have) certain desires and motives. They
> are capable of wanting to be different, in their preferences and purposes,
> from what they are. Many animals appear to have the capacity for what

I shall call 'first-order desires' or 'desires of the first order', which are simply desires to do or not to do one thing or another. No animal other than man, however, appears to have the *capacity for reflective self-evaluation* that is manifested in the formation of second-order desires.[13]

Frankfurt has two goals: to explain the principally reflective structure of both human desire and human willing. In order to admit a reflective relation to our own desires in cases where we none the less do not transform them into willing that is relevant to a particular action, he distinguishes within the category of second-order desires itself those which can be characterized as second-order 'volitions'. It is only the second-order volitions that define for him the human person. He calls wanton and irresponsible a being that only reflects its own desires without itself ever willing that higher desires determine the will; such an imaginary sloven does not yet fulfil the criteria of the concept of a person. By introducing a level on which humans relate reflectively to their desires, Frankfurt does not wish to create an image of a person calmly in harmony with himself, constantly oriented towards a stable self-evaluation; on the contrary: 'There is as much opportunity for ambivalence, conflict, and self-deception with regard to desires of the second order, for example, as there is with regard to first-order desires.'[14] Our second-order desires can conflict with one another so that we become unable to transform one of them into an act of will. Also, we cannot rule out the possibility that such a conflict will drive us to ever higher and more abstract levels of self-reflection. As a rule, however, this is prevented because we 'identify',[15] as Frankfurt puts it, so completely and decisively with one of our first-order desires that there is no room left for any wavering of the will or for higher reflection.

Taylor seamlessly picks up from this train of thought, but adds to it a further distinction within the class of second-order desires: he distinguishes between so-called 'weak' and 'strong' evaluations.[16] At issue in this distinction is the question as to whether we rule out or prefer the satisfaction of certain desires in an action situation on contingent or categorial grounds. In simpler terms: we are all familiar with decisions in which we have to choose between desires that seem to us to be equally legitimate, but which, for practical reasons, we cannot fulfil simultaneously. In such a situation we are forced to choose and that means that we must at least postpone, or even, if necessary, renounce completely, the satisfaction of one of our desires. We can try to develop shrewd strategies of action which permit an optimal satisfaction of as many of our desires as possible. To realize such a strategy we can also cultivate desires directed at our desires in such a way, for example, that the intensity of a desire – of the feeling of hunger, say – does not increase, or increase too quickly, and thus foil our complex strategy. All evaluation of desires in the mode Taylor designates as 'weak evaluation' remains limited to situation-bound or pragmatic considerations about the realization of desires. It is a different matter when we reject perfectly realizable desires because we hold their satisfaction to be unacceptable.

> In this kind of case our desires are classified in such categories as higher and lower, virtuous and vicious, more and less fulfilling, more and less refined, profound and superficial, noble and base. They are judged as belonging to qualitatively different modes of life: fragmented or inte- grated, alienated or free, saintly, or merely human, courageous or pusillanimous and so on.[17]

In this case we evaluate our desires not only from the viewpoint of practical realizability, but according to standards that represent some- thing other than simply another kind of desiring.

Taylor moves on to clarify further what kind of standards these are, and how our orientation to them is constituted, by referring to the dynamics of our moods and moral feelings. In a way that is very reminiscent of Scheler, Taylor stresses the simultaneously affectual and cognitive character of moral feelings. We do not apply standards to our desires in an emotionally neutral state; instead, feelings of outrage, shame or guilt, respect or admiration take hold of us. These feelings are the emotional expression of our recognizing standards which must be applied to our desires, even if we perhaps wish to be free of these standards, or even if we are not aware that we have these standards. In our moral feelings we sense that something lies beyond our mere desires and interests, something which we cannot identify until we reflect on the grounds of our moral feelings. This reference point indicates a way of life that we hold to be of higher value than others, an ideal, a conception of what kind of person we want to be on the basis of our own standards. This sensation of the higher value of a way of life can be transformed into propositions that designate something as desirable, and not only as actually desired. Such prop- ositions express the content of our moral feelings, but are by no means the origin of these feelings. If Taylor's earlier formulations seemed to give the impression that he defined strong evaluations in terms of their reflective and articulated character, then his replies to critics have since made clear that this was not his intention.[18] Rather, his aim was to establish the qualitative distinction between 'desired' and 'desirable'; the question of how that which is experienced as desirable comes to be reflected and articulated leads us deeper into Taylor's philosophical anthropology.

The subject experiences his own strong evaluations not as being posited by himself, but as givens with an independent existence that demand his respect and to defend which he can adduce reasons. 'We sense in the very experience of being moved by some higher good that we are moved by what is good in it rather than that it is valuable because of our reaction. We are moved by it seeing its point as something infinitely valuable.'[19] Taylor has no doubt that a phenomenology of moral feelings reveals that our value-standards are in this sense objective. Moreover, these value-standards are not given individually in our experience; rather, they themselves forge meaningful links with one another. Taylor speaks of 'frameworks' of qualitative distinctions incorporating our perception of self and others, and the situations in which our action and acts take place. The language with which we make ourselves understood both to others and to ourselves is permeated with such qualitative distinctions; the practices into which we grow and which remain intact as the foundation of all our conscious action are inconceivable without the strong evaluations woven into them. This hermeneutic-pragmatist anthropology, which I have sketched only roughly here, furnishes Taylor with the arguments to support his thesis that identity formation is necessarily related to such a framework of qualitative distinctions.

Taylor advances three such arguments.[20] Firstly, every answer that I give to the question 'who am I?' involves declaring my social 'commitments and identifications', from which I may keep a certain distance, but which nevertheless open up a space wherein I can determine what I endorse or oppose. Consequently, the question of identity can be answered with reference either to voluntary commitments and identifications, or to those that are not a matter of choice, yet which none the less provide the backdrop framing one's own valuative attitude. In both cases, the answer contains an orientation to strong evaluations. Secondly, Taylor suggests that identity itself is a 'strongly valued good' – it demands that we remain true to it or justify our action according to its demands. In this sense, too, identity cannot simply be understood as a merely actual given. In his third and main argument, Taylor avers that our identity can only play a role in our self-understanding, in our reflection on our own action orientations, if it incorporates qualitative distinctions. 'Our identity is what allows us to define what is important to us and what is not . . . The notion of an identity defined by some merely de facto, not strongly valued preference is incoherent.'[21]

A neutral self-description – if such a thing is at all possible – would have no consequences for our actions. To which question is it supposed to supply an answer? If we understand it as a ruthlessly realistic attitude towards ourselves, then we do so only because we can derive from it a revision of our self-assessment. But we thereby return to the space opened up by the relationship between our design of a self to which we aspire and the reality of our action.

With these arguments Taylor believes he has demonstrated that our identity formation necessarily takes place within 'frameworks' of qualitative distinctions and that such 'frameworks' are inescapable for us. They are not inescapable in the sense that we are compelled by our culture to internalize certain values and will never again have the chance to jettison these values. But they are inescapable in the sense that it belongs to human agency 'to exist in a space of questions about strongly valued goods'[22] on which we must take a stand. In opposition to the existentialist-decisionist pathos of the choice between ultimate values,[23] Taylor emphasizes that, though we do indeed frequently have to make a decision between alternatives ourselves, we have, on the other hand, not chosen the alternatives with which we are faced. This should not be construed as a restriction of our freedom, but rather as a constitutive condition for being able to make a meaningful choice at all. Without pregiven structures in the sphere of alternative choices, choice degenerates into chance.[24] The world in which we attempt to understand ourselves, Taylor argues, is therefore shaped by our experience of such inescapable 'frameworks' and by those values that can be experienced in our moral feelings and which demand our respect.

Taylor uses spatial metaphors to elucidate the relationship between a person and his values. He speaks of a 'moral space' and its 'topography', and takes up the spatial metaphors of everyday language, where we distinguish between higher and lower values, deeper and more superficial persons or inner and outer orientations. If our values take up a position for us in a moral space, then it is also inevitable that we ask ourselves where we stand at a particular point in time in relation to our values. In doing so, we cannot avoid the question of which direction our life is going in, how it can be interpreted as striving and whether our striving is successful.

So the issue for us has to be not only where we *are*, but where we're *going*; and though the first may be a matter of more or less, the latter is a question of towards or away from, an issue of yes or no. That is why an absolute question always frames our relative ones. Since we cannot do without an orientation to the good, and since we cannot be indifferent to our place relative to this good, and since this place is something that

must always change and become, the issue of the direction of our lives
must arise for us.[25]

A temporal dimension of our self-understanding thereby results
from the quasi-spatial structure of our relationship to values. We
make sure of the location of our striving in moral space by telling our
lives as a story. For Taylor, then, the narrative structure of self-
understanding is also inescapable. 'In order to have a sense of who
we are, we have to have a notion of how we have become, and of
where we are going.'[26]

We should not misconstrue this claim as implying that we have to
cling to the same conception of the good throughout our lives and
necessarily narrate our lives as if they were a continuous story.
Usually, it is not only the place to which our striving has led us that
changes: we also alter our conception of what is worth striving for.
But we also retrospectively integrate such alterations – like the conversions on which William James placed such special emphasis, for
example – into our life-story as a whole; the time before the conversion
then appears as a time of error or as preparation for the as yet
unsuspected transformation. In addition, the inescapable nature of the
narrative form of individual self-understanding is not limited to the
individual person's life. Not only do fellow human beings appear as
actors in every autobiography; we must also search, when we are
joined together with others in the 'We', for a collective self-understanding, for which once again the location of the good and the
narrative form of our striving are inescapable.[27]

These reflections on time and place in our relationship to the good
also bring Taylor's conception of the articulation of moral feelings
into sharper focus. This allows us to formulate his answer to the
question of the genesis of values. Moral feelings are distinguished
from other feelings by their internal relation to values and to our self-
understanding. They would simply not be moral feelings if they were
not related to our conception of the good. However, as Taylor endeavours to show, our conception of the good pervades our entire self-
understanding. For this reason, our moral feelings contain a reference
to ourselves, and not just in the sense of something that makes our
feelings precisely *our* feelings. Many of these feelings would lose their
meaning if they were not related to our self-understanding: shame or
guilt are only comprehensible on the basis of their constitutive relation
to that which we acknowledge to be morally prescribed, or how we at
least wish to appear from the point of view of the validity of such
prescriptions. At the same time, the fact that our strong evaluations

are embodied in moral feelings is in itself momentous. A gap can open up between our moral feelings and our reflective values. Perhaps we realize with astonishment that we fail to feel guilt or outrage even though we ourselves or others have infringed what we took to be our values. Conversely, perhaps we are tormented by feelings of guilt or are seized by outrage even though we are under the impression that none of our consciously endorsed values has been infringed. The relationship between strong evaluations embodied in our moral feelings and our consciously endorsed values is therefore not without tension.

The role of articulation consists precisely in bridging the gap between moral feelings and reflective values. When we articulate our moral feelings, we give them a form in which they can be discussed. Discussion can produce a confirmation, a rejection or a modification of our feelings. Confirmation supplies the feelings themselves with new energy and vigour. Rejection does not simply dispel the feelings, but it can be the starting-point for a reflective process in which we recognize the dubiousness of our articulation and either endeavour to articulate our feelings in a way that can reckon with the confirmation of others, or, conversely, resolve to insist upon our previous articulation in order thereby to attack social conventions. Finding and acknowledging another articulation for our moral feelings alters our own understanding of these feelings. Since our self-understanding and our orientation to values are fused together in our moral feelings, the change in the articulation produces a modification in the feelings themselves. The social constraints on articulation must not be understood as a mere restriction, as an obstacle to the realization of one's own authenticity. Without finding a purchase in the reactions of others and the classifications of feelings offered by the repertoire of a language or symbolic order, we could not identify our own feelings at all. We adopt interpretations of diffuse sensations before we can even defend our feelings against expected interpretations. The dependence of our self-interpretation on intersubjective networks – what Taylor calls 'webs of interlocution'[28] – is not only a peculiarity of the development of children; it conditions our experience throughout our lives.

> Even as the most independent adult, there are moments when I cannot clarify what I feel until I talk about it with certain special partner(s), who know me, or have wisdom, or with whom I have an affinity . . . This is the sense in which one cannot be a self on one's own. I am a self only in relation to certain interlocutors: in one way in relation to those conversation partners who were essential to my achieving self-definition; in

another in relation to those who are now crucial to my continuing grasp of languages of self-understanding – and, of course, these classes may overlap.[29]

Without doubt, then, Taylor's theory of identity formation merits the description 'intersubjectivist'.

The process of articulating our moral feelings does not have a clearly determinable direction. Rather, it describes the hermeneutic circle. We move to and fro between the levels of our feelings, of our own interpretation of these feelings and the publicly established interpretations. Our present self-interpretation, despite its intersubjective constitution, is not necessarily identical with the public interpretation of an instance. Our feelings, despite their need for interpretation, are not completely absorbed into our self-interpretations. What is more these three levels are all directed towards incidents, events and situations that likewise bring their own character antagonistically into play. Taylor illustrates the interplay of these four levels with the example of the members of an ethnic minority suffering discrimination.[30] This brings to life the complex interconnectedness of the cultural ascription of inferiority, of the possible feelings of inferiority of those involved should they adopt this cultural ascription, of the transformation of these feelings into servility, resignation or defiance, and of the possible mobilization of them in resistance to the discriminating culture. Something new is produced in this very interplay between the various levels. If it is difficult or impossible to express one's own feelings in the vocabulary available in a given culture, then innovative forms can perhaps be invented or borrowed from other cultures. For Taylor, furthermore, we experience our values themselves as hierarchalized, and the higher values can challenge or reject other values.[31]

In this kind of case, the degraded values need not simply disappear without a trace; they can, rather, offer resistance and even demand fresh expression. The hermeneutic circle is therefore not a real circuit that leads us back to an unaltered starting-point. After their articulation our moral feelings are no longer quite the same; in the process of articulation we can also modify our values or produce new ones. Those values which have difficulty in being articulated because other values enjoy hegemony in the public sphere, and perhaps even in the individual self-interpretation, generally lose their intensity.[32] Articulation thus does not only add to our moral feelings; Taylor believes, rather, that without articulation these feelings must wither away.

Using this differentiated picture of an interplay between articulation and experience, or rather between the situation experienced, pre-

reflective experience, individual articulation and the cultural repertoire of interpretative patterns, Taylor devises the solution to a
problem that had been neglected or left unsolved by his precursors in
the discourse about the genesis of values. In contrast to Nietzsche, he
does not think that uncovering the psychological and historical roots
of a conception of the good leads to a sobering diminution of its
attractive effect; we cannot articulate goods without advocating a
particular reading of their genesis, and this is especially true of the
highest goods.[33]

In contrast to James and Durkheim, for Taylor the interpretation of
an experience does not simply arise out of this experience; rather, he
sees articulation and interpretation as a complex activity in which we
strive for a harmony between several levels that we rarely, and never
permanently, attain. But in this very process – in the attempt to
achieve this harmony – new values are produced. Taylor expressly
keeps all possibilities for this kind of genesis open. Change can
commence on the level of interpretations as well as on the level of
experiences which result from our ways of life and practices.

> It is clear that change can come about in both directions, as it were:
> through mutations and developments in the ideas, including new visions
> and insights, bringing about alterations, ruptures, reforms, revolutions in
> practices; and also through drift, change, constrictions or flourishings of
> practices, bringing about the alteration, flourishing, or decline of ideas.
> But even this is too abstract. It is better to say that in any concrete
> development in history, change is occurring in both ways. The real skein
> of events is interwoven with threads running in both directions. A new
> revolutionary interpretation may arise partly because a practice is under
> threat, perhaps for reasons quite extraneous to the ideas. Or a given
> interpretation of things will gain force because the practice is flourishing,
> again for idea-extraneous reasons. But the resulting changes in outlook
> will have important consequences of their own. The skein of causes is
> inextricable.[34]

Such a declaration that the causal knot cannot be unravelled certainly cannot be the last word for a sociological theory of the genesis
of values. Taylor is clearly aware, as his 'Digression on Historical
Explanation'[35] demonstrates, of the difference between an interpretative articulation of the motive force of ideas and the explanatory
analysis of their dissemination and influence. As far as his own
undertaking is concerned, he has in view only the more modest goal
of articulation, and expressly renounces the more ambitious goal of
explaining the genesis of new values in the strict sense. The pursuit of
the more modest goal of first articulating the values whose genesis is

in question makes sense in any case, since any explanation that is not based on insight into the motive force of these values will be unsatisfactory. This distinction between articulation and explanation already represents a counter-position to those explanatory models starting from reductionist premises; that is, those wishing to deny the contents of culture their independent causal role. Consequently, Taylor defends himself vehemently against those trends in Marxist historiography which are guilty of this. In exactly the same way, however, he counters evolutionist viewpoints that play down the possibility of culturally determined, unexpected new departures. Those sources of value orientation which we can uncover are not the only logically possible ones; they have, rather, arisen contingently. Taylor finds every interpretation of the Enlightenment that construes it as having merely removed the obstacles hindering the evolutionary progression of humanity just as suspect as either optimistic or pessimistic interpretations of the inevitability or irreversibility of secularization.

At the same time, Taylor realizes that the distinction between articulation and explanation should not be understood as comprising a complete separation. Not only must an explanation be – in Max Weber's words – 'adequate as to meaning',[36] and remain to this extent dependent on the process of interpretative articulation; but, conversely, a perspective on genesis that is itself not indifferent to the sociological attempts at a causal explanation also enters into the articulation, as Taylor's argument against Nietzsche's conception of 'genealogy' implied. If we bear in mind Taylor's earlier discussions of value-freedom in the social sciences, then we can conclude that interpretation and articulation become significant at two points in the construction of explanatory theories of the genesis of values. Firstly, only an intermediate hermeneutic phase in which we grasp the meaning of values can help the explanation to be adequate to its subject; secondly, we must reintegrate the explanation as a whole into a comprehensive interpretation of past and present, a frame of reference which itself contains valuations.

While, from this sociological point of view, Taylor quite consciously limits his methodological ambitions, leading us to the threshold of explanatory theories without actually crossing it, his position on the philosophical question of the ontological status of values is clear and decided. Taylor is an avowed value realist – but in a different way from Scheler and especially from the Platonic tradition. If we are to understand the structure of Taylor's project, we must incorporate this element of his thought into our discussion.

Taylor clearly distinguishes his value realism from a Platonism of the good,[37] according to which the good is an entity independent of all human existence. Taylor unambiguously takes the view that a return to a metaphysical theory of the good is not possible for us moderns. Like Scheler, Taylor instead starts, in his phenomenology of moral feelings and his theory of strong evaluations, from the experience of value. In contrast to Scheler, however, whom he does not discuss, Taylor does not mistake the certainty we feel in our experience of value for proof of the pre-existence of values independent of experience.[38] But while still remaining consistent in his commitment to the dimension of experience, he arrives at his own form of value realism.[39]

Taylor does this with the aid of what he calls the 'BA-principle', that is, the principle of the 'Best Account', the best possible articulation of an experience. He introduces this principle with a rhetorical question: 'What better measure of reality do we have in human affairs than those terms which on critical reflection and after the correction of the errors we can detect make the best sense of our lives?'[40] When I articulate my life-experiences I appeal to values without which I cannot express the orientations that guide me. I do not experience these values as having been grafted onto a value-neutral world by me, but rather as existing independently of me. Of course, new experiences or the objections of others can convince me that I have endorsed values which were not worth endorsing. But this transforms the one articulation into another, one that is better for me – it does not lead me to change the level in principle and to adopt a relationship to my experiences other than that of articulation. Taylor vehemently resists the scientistic conception of the world, which describes human beings in categories that cannot in principle be integrated into a person's self-understanding. Nobody can understand himself as, say, an organism merely reacting to external stimuli and simultaneously cope with his everyday life. The same applies, according to Taylor, to the projectivist theories of value: they too do not do justice – this much at least is certain – to moral self-experience. If this is so, then the question arises as to how a scientistic description of my identity should assume a higher degree of reality than my reflective self-description. Taylor sees neither the possibility nor the necessity of making the leap to a descriptive level which no longer leaves any room for the ways in which we experience ourselves.

> Once we have established our best possible account of the questions we have to take seriously in order actually to live our lives, once we have clarified, in other words, what the ontological assumptions are that we can't help making in practice as we go about the business of living;

where in heaven or earth could the epistemological arguments come from that should convince us that we are wrong?[41]

If, therefore, such a leap is neither possible nor desirable, then we are left only with the method of 'practical reasoning',[42] in which we do not establish incontrovertible standards, but instead actually advance in our moral reflection by a step-by-step consideration of additional facts or by resolving contradictions. Not every articulation is, therefore, equally good; but only a proposal for a better interpretation of our experience takes us beyond the best we have hitherto achieved. We can never completely transcend this experience itself. Taylor defends in some detail the possible validity of transcendental argumentation[43] – but of course only in the Kantian sense that indubitable aspects of our experience provide the platform for further investigation of the conditions of possibility of this experience. Through this reflection, Taylor argues, we also arrive at the essential features of a philosophical anthropology which does not lay claim to foundation, but remains part of the articulation of our experience.[44] When we make this kind of effort to achieve the best articulation, however, the fact that certain values are indispensable to our self-description and orientation becomes evident. It is in this very indispensability that the reality of these values then lies. This reality can only be undermined concretely, through a proposal for revaluation that is itself value-related – not abstractly, by fictionalizing the values as such.

My account has thus far deliberately ignored a further aspect of Taylor's theory of value. In a manner that is analogous to Scheler's thesis that we not only experience values as such, but that they become experienceable in their hierarchical gradations, Taylor also distinguishes not only various goods, but also various types of goods. Beyond the level of individual 'lifegoods' lies the level of 'hypergoods', which allow us to evaluate the lifegoods themselves, and, beyond that, the level of the 'constitutive goods', the ultimate sources of our moral orientation. The distinction between the three levels remains blurred in *Sources of the Self* and is not made any clearer in subsequent writings – in fact, it is partly retracted.[45] In our context, it is not necessary to follow up these individual distinctions in detail; the end result of Taylor's reflections is perhaps less important here than characterizing the intentions behind them. He wants not only to emphasize the hierarchy of values, but also to show that the relationship between articulation and experience appears differently on the various levels of goods. The 'constitutive goods', according to Taylor, differ from the lifegoods and hypergoods in the manner in which they depend on articulation. 'A God or the Platonic Good, the Romantic concept of Nature or rational action in Kant's sense – all can only be communicated and comprehended as *articulated* goods. This does not necessarily require their formal definition in doctrinaire theories: mythical and narrative articulations are also admissible. But without explicit formulation in some form, these goods do not even represent options.'[46] Taylor needs this distinction because it is only in this way that he can make clear his own 'best account' – and this is, even if cautiously, a theistic one. The individual's moral and religious experience can call for an interpretation which lies ready in the cultural repertoire of interpretative patterns; it can also strive to alter the interpretation, but it cannot produce an interpretation *ex nihilo* without any reference whatsoever to the cultural repertoire. Taylor claims for himself the right to find convincing, on the basis of his experience, an interpretation in which a God, in the sense of the traditional faith of a particular culture, is indispensable. This does not rule out granting other cultures their own interpretations of equally authentic religious experiences. But the path we must travel in order to enter into dialogue with them leads through the particularities of our religion, not past them into a realm of abstracted common features:

> it is through the particularities that they animate our lives. Even if we suppose that the ultimate reality is neither God's love as I understand it, nor Nirvana as understood by a Buddhist, I cannot relate to it as a 'je ne sais quoi' which is neither. The route of Nathan the Wise is the road to post-Enlightenment banalities, which lose their transforming power very quickly.[47]

In stark contrast to John Dewey's view of religion, Taylor advocates here a universalism which does not lose its foothold in particularism. Like James, Taylor employs the means of postmetaphysical philosophy to defend the right to believe. And like Scheler, Taylor continues the Augustinian tradition, advocating a modern Catholicism that is free of ecclesiastical authoritarianism and resentful antimodernism.

In Taylor's own work, his theoretical reflections on the link between identity formation and valuation, as well as on the relationship between articulation and experience, do indeed have the task of providing the basis for a modern philosophical anthropology. Yet these reflections are mainly presented as mere preparation for the project of rearticulating the evaluations inherent in the self-understanding of modernity. Taylor's book *Sources of the Self* is an heroic and a grandiose attempt to portray comprehensively the ensemble of cultural traditions which have produced living evaluations ('hypergoods') in Western societies up to this day. As the three fundamental traditions of this kind Taylor counts: an understanding of 'inward-ness' that goes back to St Augustine and Descartes; the post-Reforma-tion high esteem for ordinary life; and an expressivist-Romantic interpretation of nature and the creative imagination. It is not neces-sary for the present discussion to follow up the wealth of ideas contained in these accounts, which aim at a substantive understanding of the values of modernity. It is wholly consistent for Taylor to steer this course through the history of ideas, since he wants to make a contribution to the articulation of modern self-experience, and such an articulation requires an interpretation of the genesis of the higher and highest goods. Taylor expects the articulation to reinvigorate these traditions. Precisely because the self-understanding of modern-ity also comprises those conceptions which see it as characterized by the break with all value orientations, or by the end of all value-certainty and value-consensus, the remembrance and revitalization of traditions contributes to a more adequate self-understanding of modernity. Moreover, Taylor hopes that such an articulation can help to reconcile the divergent tendencies in modern culture.

This is not the place to discuss the historical legitimacy of Taylor's reconstruction of the genesis of those values on which Western modernity is based. His reconstruction takes the form of a profound discussion of Western, predominantly European, intellectual history from Plato to Nietzsche. Thus, it today draws the criticism that it is doomed from the very outset to onesidedness, because its scope is limited to Western culture – and high culture at that. However, this restriction to Western culture is obviously justified if it is precisely its specifics that are at issue. Likewise, his emphasis on high culture within the Western tradition would only be intolerable if Taylor were concerned with a comprehensive history of the European mind. On the other hand, it is actually perfectly conceivable that other works will pick up from where Taylor left off and investigate the social dissemination of those cultural paradigms which he only typifies in terms of the history of ideas. For example, even though the pattern of expressive self-realization originated in the eighteenth century, its dissemination across wider social strata might be said to have occurred only in the last three decades.[48] In this respect, Taylor's work is certainly only a beginning; but he himself repeatedly resists confus-ing philosophical ideas with cultural practices, or reducing practices to the philosophical inaugurators supposedly causally responsible for them.[49] For this reason, his side-glances at the development of the family or of architecture are quite clearly intended to be read as only illustrations and signposts pointing the way to a largely unexplored field of inquiry. To criticize Taylor on these two points, therefore, is in my view trite, since every such criticism misconstrues the goal that the author has set himself.

So a possible immanent weakness of Taylor's conception will not be found here. But such a weakness can be exposed if we search for possible oversights within the domain which obviously and indisputably comprises Taylor's area of investigation. Various critics have already noticed such glaring omissions. Why, it was asked, has he neglected to discuss the entire twentieth-century philosophy of value from Max Scheler to John Dewey – those writings, then, which certainly are not guilty of doing what Taylor deplores, i.e. reducing morality to obligations?[50] Why does a book that pleads for a theistic interpretation of our moral sources and dwells exhaustively on aesthetic epiphanies not devote a single word to religious experiences and the existential theologies of the twentieth century?[51] Why does a work on Western intellectual history only touch very superficially on the developments in America?[52] How can it be that, despite the fact that Max Weber's work on the Protestant (and above all Puritan) ethic strongly influences his interpretation of one of the great developments in morality, namely the 'affirmation of the ordinary life', Taylor's book as a whole completely ignores the rest of this classic sociologist's work, as well as sociological theories in general?

It is quite possible that Taylor will understand many of these suggestions as only offering material that would supplement his work, and not as objections to his argumentation as such. He is not of course expected to master the history of theological and sociological theories in the same way that he surveys the history of philosophy; perhaps he sees in the American history of ideas only variations of themes articulated far more clearly in Europe; and, with the exception of allusions to Wittgenstein, Heidegger and Merleau-Ponty, post-Nietzschean philosophy is anyway almost completely overlooked as a positive reference point. But this is precisely the first point of my argument. I maintain that Taylor does not reconstruct the history of philosophy in a way that allows the conditions of possibility for his own position to be grasped reflexively. The story he narrates does not lead to him. This may seem particularly astonishing for a thinker as steeped in Hegel as Taylor. I do not mean, however, that he should have presented his own position as the culmination of world history or the developing self-awareness of absolute Mind. What I do mean, though, is that Taylor's whole argumentation is crying out for his own philosophy of the good to be situated within modern currents of thought.

Above all, the complete neglect of the specifically American tradition of thought, and pragmatism in particular, is downright spectacular. Taylor even owes his fame in part (and justifiably so) to his role as a mediator between Continental and Anglo-American (that is, analytic) ways of doing philosophy. But precisely this linking of the two traditions means that he ends up ignoring non-analytic American philosophy. In what follows, I shall first of all adduce further evidence of this neglect. Then I shall show that this does not merely represent the neglect of a particular theme, but that it even has consequences for Taylor's systematic argumentation.

The book under discussion (as well as Taylor's other writings) only briefly touches upon American intellectual history. Aside from occasional side-glances cast over Emerson and Transcendentalism, he limits himself to brief remarks on Puritanism and present-day American culture. Pragmatism is mentioned only once in *Sources of the Self*,[53] and, characteristically, in a passage discussing the allegedly Puritanical spiritual roots of the universal instrumentalization of things. At this very point he might have taken the opportunity to recognize that, though pragmatism can be viewed very much as the apotheosis of the ethos of ordinary life, it should not, for this very reason, be seen simply as the apotheosis of instrumental reason. Only this would also have brought to light the subtle mixture of Puritanical and anti-Puritanical motifs in pragmatism. The founder of pragmatism, Charles S. Peirce, is not mentioned at all, even though Taylor would have found arguments in this thinker's work to support his efforts to overcome Cartesianism. Heidegger (and not Dewey) and Merleau-Ponty (and not Mead) are Taylor's authorities.

It is even more difficult to understand why Taylor does not appear to be interested in the origin of those key concepts which underlie his entire work (i.e. self and identity). Although he mentions in passing several eighteenth-century precursors in the use of the concept of self,[54] he does not delve deeper into the history of these concepts. He does not refer at all to the thinker who introduced the concept of self from philosophy into the empirical sciences: William James. Charles Cooley, James's most important successor in this respect, also goes unmentioned. George Herbert Mead, who is today recognized as the influential author of a theory of the social genesis of the self, is dealt with merely in a brief remark.[55] Even the relationship between the two concepts that Taylor employs, 'identity' and 'self', remains somewhat unclear.[56]

What is completely incomprehensible, however, is how Taylor can manage, even in his efforts to rehabilitate a theistic justification of our moral sources, without William James's theory of religious experience, which in our context has turned out to be the crucial modern alternative to Nietzsche's theory of values.[57] What I want to stress with these brief pointers to Taylor's neglect of pragmatism is that this school of thought does not so much diverge from, but in many respects converges with, Taylor's position. The impression of convergence is so strong that Taylor has been called a 'Deweyan without knowing it'.[58] He is not ignoring a tradition that threatens his convictions, but a school of thought which could offer support, indeed inspiration, for his arguments. I shall not speculate here on the biographical reasons for this phenomenon. However, it is certainly to his detriment that Taylor outlines the specifics of his thought only insufficiently *vis-à-vis* pragmatism – as well as *vis-à-vis* other related currents in twentieth-century thought.

Far more important, however, is the question as to whether, despite all the similarities, we can also establish a difference between Taylor's thought and pragmatism; whether his neglect of pragmatism enables us to expose a systematic problematic in his argumentation. There is indeed such a problematic. We find it where Taylor allows himself to be carried beyond his claim that, by undertaking a phenomenology of morality, we can ascertain an experience of captivation, and speaks of the good in essentialist terms that are not covered by his argument and not reconcilable with his declared intention – that is, where Taylor loses sight of the fundamental pragmatist principle of referring all concepts to action. Thus, he criticizes, for example, the currently prevailing moral philosophy in the following way: 'The focus is on the principles, or injunctions, or standards which guide *action*, while visions of the good are altogether neglected. Morality is narrowly conceived with what we ought to *do*, and not also with what is valuable in itself, or what we should admire and love.'[59] What this contrast fails to grasp is that, after we have lost a metaphysical grounding of the good, even what is valuable in itself, admirable or lovable is only accessible to us from the perspective of our actions – the actions in which it is constituted and operative for us. This is precisely what pragmatist ethics and the pragmatist theory of religion and value were driving at: there is a good, but it is necessarily a good-for-us. It seems to me that Taylor sees the matter in like manner in those sections of his work in which he discusses the 'subtler languages' of modernity (Part V) – and yet, in his critique of action-related moral philosophy, he goes too far and then goes astray when he not only finds fault with its reduction of the good to desires or obligations, but also wishes to transcend the good's action-relatedness in general. Rather, the question must be: *in which actions* do persons have the experience that something is 'good-in-itself-for-them'?[60] If Taylor had pursued this question more carefully in his phenomenology of moral and religious experience, then the question of the primacy of the good or the right would also have given rise to the prospect of a surprising mediatory position. It might then be that the good and the right are each grounded in different experiences. Between these grounding experiences, however, there need not exist a relationship of grounding. In the concluding chapter, I shall discuss whether Taylor, like Scheler, has also allowed himself to be carried away, and subordinated the experience of the Ought to the experience of value because he has not sufficiently determined the location of this type of experience in action. However, this does not detract from his contribution to our understanding of the experience and genesis of value.

The Concept of Self and its Postmodern Challenge

In the writings of John Dewey and Charles Taylor, we see a link between the theory of value and an intersubjective theory of identity formation begin to emerge, a link which has in the course of our discussion proved itself increasingly necessary if we are to find a satisfactory answer to the question of the genesis of values. The thesis that values originate in experiences of self-formation and self-transcendence thus acquires a tangible form. But before we can formulate this thesis more succinctly and bring it to bear on the problem we have already touched on several times, i.e. the relationship between the experience of value and the experience of the Ought, between values and norms, between the good and the right – before we do this by looking back over the entire course of our discussion, we must pause once more. For is not the solution which has begun to emerge the expression of a completely obsolete conception of human beings? Did not philosophy long ago abandon concepts such as value and self? Do not those cultural and social processes of change which are lumped together and described as the 'postmodern' give grounds for declaring such a solution to be hopelessly antiquated and illusory under contemporary conditions – provided that it ever had any meaning?

One way of following up these questions in our context is first of all to contrast Taylor's thought with a thinker whose work represents postmodern motifs. Richard Rorty is best suited for this role, not only because he presents these motifs with a lucidity that is the legacy of his training in analytic philosophy, but also because he explicitly takes issue with Taylor on several occasions.[1] Thus, both thinkers share a certain amount of common ground on which we can base such a critical discussion.

Taylor's theory takes as its starting-point an interpretation of our 'strong evaluations' that suggests that in such states we experience values which we did not deliberately posit. In this sense (and only in this sense), we experience something in our strong evaluations that lies beyond contingency. Taylor regards a person who lacks such experience as shallow. A conflict between strong evaluations represents for him a crisis, even a threat to personal identity. Underlying his linkage of identity formation and value orientation is the notion that we cannot simply preserve our identity when our values collapse, just as we cannot simply maintain our value orientations during an identity crisis. Without strong evaluations, Taylor argues, a person cannot develop a feeling that life has meaning. A loss of strong evaluations results for him in the loss of meaning.

One possible objection which can be raised against this whole train of thought is that it does not so much prove a theory as express a theoretical prejudice. Perhaps we suffer when we experience a conflict of strong evaluations only because we have been inoculated with a cultural ideal that stresses consistency and freedom from contradiction. Perhaps the purported shallowness of a person lacking strong evaluations is not an anthropological fact, but only a certain normative conception of personality which is supposed to deny us the possibility of choosing whether we want to have strong evaluations at all. If, however, we can also aspire to make no such distinctions between higher and lower impulses, then the search for a true self would be at an end, its place having been taken by an acquiescence in our being 'centerless' and 'random assemblages of contingent and idiosyncratic needs'.[2] Perhaps the very rationalist character of the social sciences also urges us to see through the voice of our conscience, and even the attractiveness of our values, and to recognize them as sediments of the contingent conditions of our socialization – so that Taylor's intention of finding in the experience of evaluations an unavoidable orientation to the good must seem like a hopeless attempt to retreat from this rationalism, to bestow once more a higher solemnity upon our contingent experiences of value and the Ought, and if possible even to restore their sacred aura.

Rorty does indeed argue along such lines. He calls upon us to relax when dealing with ourselves. If we can surrender the belief in the substantiality of our inner being, and liberate ourselves from the pressure exerted on us by the demand for consistency, then we can develop a relaxed attitude towards the fissures in our identity and towards the contingency of our particular existence. With this relaxation our curiosity about our inner diversity will grow. We can then develop ourselves in all our variedness and contradictoriness, even playfully experiment with these new dimensions, precisely because we are not constantly forced to deny desires and exclude other aspects of our person in favour of strong evaluations. The contingency of our existence is thus no longer a reason to doubt meaning and to despair, but rather an opportunity for creativity, for self-creation in varying contexts. Irony thus becomes the appropriate response to the recognition of contingency.

This way of thinking is an even more radical expression of the insights into the subjectivity of valuation and the contingency of values which formed the point of departure for the philosophy of value.[3] Rorty considers the tendency to cling on to the binding character of values despite these insights, a tendency discernible in the whole discourse about the genesis of values, to be an error. For him, all that we can derive from the recognition of contingency is an imperative of self-creation – and nothing more. The reflection on the genesis of values thereby returns to its starting-point in Nietzsche's work – although there is, admittedly, an obvious change in tone. We can detect nothing any more of his desperation, suffering and hatred, nor even the shrill tones of his euphoria. In the writings of Michel Foucault, Rorty's precursor in this respect, the dramatic character of Nietzsche's thinking still made itself felt, before giving way in his late work to the wise search for a renewal of the ancient art of life.[4] Rorty offers us a civilized, domesticated variant of Nietzschean motifs. Yet there are two respects in which his thought goes beyond mere neo-Nietzscheanism.

Firstly, Rorty is fully aware of the political dangers which can arise from a radical ethos of self-creation. He takes this into account by relegating this ethos entirely to the private life of the citizens of a liberal democracy – but within this private sphere he wishes it to have the greatest possible effect. 'The compromise advocated in this book amounts to saying: *Privatize* the Nietzschean-Sartrean-Foucauldian attempt at authenticity and purity, in order to prevent yourself from slipping into a political attitude which will lead you to think that there is some social goal more important than avoiding cruelty.'[5] Rorty does not attempt to do precisely what political Romanticism or Marxism attempted to do, namely to hold 'self-creation and justice, private perfection and human solidarity, in a single vision'.[6] In contrast to this aim, he argues:

> The closest we will come to joining these two quests is to see the aim of a just and free society as letting its citizens be as privatistic, 'irrationalist', and aestheticist as they please so long as they do it in their own time – causing no harm to others and using no resources needed by those less

advantaged. There are practical measures to be taken to accomplish this practical goal. But there is no way to bring self-creation together with justice at the level of theory. The vocabulary of self-creation is necessarily private, unshared, unsuited to argument. The vocabulary of justice is necessarily public, shared, a medium for argumentative exchange.[7]

The Nietzschean motifs are thus fenced in in a decidedly liberal manner.

Of course, this quickly prompts the question as to how practicable Rorty's compromise solution is. For can the relating of aspects of our life to either the private or public sphere be carried out easily and unambiguously, or rather, is that not itself dependent on decisions about values in the public sphere? If the border between 'irony' and 'solidarity' is drawn in the manner which Rorty proposes, can the public sphere retain its vitality, and can we safeguard an ethos of respect for the self-realization of others, or even an ethos of renouncing those resources which are 'needed by those less advantaged'? These questions might suggest that we should not dwell for too long on Rorty's proposed compromise solution. However, there can be no doubt that he divides his own life in this way, in his work and public activities.[8] Politically, he is thus as far removed from Nietzsche as can be imagined. In his criticism of Taylor, Rorty accordingly claims John Dewey as his own precursor, regarding him as an excellent example of the ability of a social-liberal philosophical tradition to produce thoroughly motivating 'hypergoods'.[9] He even adopts, if somewhat hesitantly, Dewey's perspective at the end of *A Common Faith*: that in a suitably realized democratic culture the metaphysical isolation of man after the 'death of God' can be offset by the sacralization of human communities themselves.[10]

Dewey is also extremely significant for the other respect in which Rorty differs from pure neo-Nietzscheanism. Rorty, namely, is more circumspect in substantiating his critique than other postmodernist thinkers: he does not count mere quotations from Nietzsche as arguments. Rather, he has elaborated extensively the reasons which compel us to dispense with the conception of knowledge as a mirror of nature, and instead to relate knowledge to human action under contingent circumstances.[11] This is an insight which Heidegger, Wittgenstein and Dewey have each developed in their own ways. In particular, Rorty sees Dewey's pragmatism and certain pragmatist developments within analytic philosophy as supporting this position.[12] He endeavours to show that this pragmatic turn must also sweep away the conception of an essential self, as expressed in the traditional paradigm of subject–object: 'the traditional picture of the human situation has been one in which human beings are not simply networks of beliefs and desires but rather beings which *have* those beliefs and desires. The traditional view is that there is a core self which can look at, decide among, use, and express itself by means of, such beliefs and desires.'[13] Moreover, according to this view, convictions and desires are directed towards an external reality, by reference to which they can be criticized. Beliefs can be wrong if they do not correctly represent reality; desires can be wrong because they do not correspond to the essential nature of the desiring self. Rorty is doubtless correct to claim that such traditional assumptions cannot be simply updated after the pragmatic turn. But he maintains that this simultaneously invalidates the entire normative horizon towards which the premise of an essential core self was oriented. This, at least, is an overhasty step. Rorty might have felt himself called upon to proceed with greater caution if he had considered how this situation was dealt with within pragmatism itself.[14] The conception of self current in the social sciences is indeed a spiritual child of American pragmatism. For this reason, it is appropriate to take a brief look at the history and internal problematics of the sociological conception of the self in order to answer the question as to whether the postmodern challenge to this conception as represented by Rorty necessarily leads to the conclusions he draws.[15]

The origins of the sociological conception of the self are to be found in the intellectual life of the United States during the last decade of the nineteenth century.[16] The thinkers who took part in what was to my mind an epoch-making advance in the social sciences have today partly been forgotten, or their works, precisely owing to this accomplishment, are now treated as classics. The starting-point of this sudden flurry of ideas was William James's psychology, which was published in 1890, and in particular his attempt to construe consciousness no longer as some vessel in which impressions of the outside world were stored, but instead as a stream in which thoughts and feelings cropped up and subsided according to laws of their own.[17] James believed that what he termed the 'self as known' was one of the main islands stabilized in this flow, in other words, the self not as the subject, but as the object of knowledge. This 'empirical self', which together with the 'pure Ego' as the subject of knowledge then formed the 'total self', consisted of, according to James, a 'material self', a 'social self', and a 'spiritual self', depending on whether it was constituted in the confrontation with the world of things, with other people, or with one's own feelings and abilities.[18] A younger generation of thinkers immediately objected to what they saw as James's cursory treatment of this new motif. They all felt that James, by construing the concept of consciousness as something fluid, as a 'stream of thought' or consciousness, had created the basis for a radical conception of the constitution of the 'self' in social relations. They were consequently disappointed that for James the 'social self' had merely remained one of several aspects of the 'empirical self', whereas the constitution of the 'pure Ego' still remained an unsolved problem. We can easily see why they wished to contradict him and press further forward. They attacked any belief in a substantive self, in the pre-social or extra-social character of identity over and above mere biological individuality, because they regarded this as a crutch for possessive individualism; in other words, for them it buttressed that way of thinking so dominant in Britain and the United States and which American intellectuals of the day identified as a major obstacle to far-reaching social reform and a hindrance to any liberation from a Puritanical culture. To go beyond James meant to link the concept of consciousness beyond the metaphor of a stream of consciousness with a concept of action. This enabled them to construe the self and all aspects of it as the result of social interaction. In other words, the relation between person and self could be accorded a radically communicative character. In this manner it simultaneously seemed possible to take on board what was worth preserving from the legacy of Hegelianism and American Transcendentalism. Of the different variants of such an approach, to be found, for example, in the thought of James Mark Baldwin, Charles Horton Cooley and George Herbert Mead, it was the thought of the last which became the most influential. Mead devised an anthropological theory of the specifics of human communication and sociality *per se*. On this basis, he developed a genetic analysis of the child's development of a 'self'. According to his theory,[19] the 'self' was not the gradually emerging structure of an individual's personality, but rather the structure of a person's relation to himself or herself, to the extent that he or she succeeded in creating a synthesis of references to different and competing Others and of the different phases of one's life. Mead's notion was closely interwoven with the concepts of role, the generalized Other, self-control and social control he and others had developed and which constituted the theoretical basis for much social research in the United States.[20] If I see things correctly, no European response to this sociological concept of the self was forthcoming in the first half of the twentieth century at all. Instead, the conception initially marched victoriously forward only in the United States.

Things did not change until, after 1945, another field of thought and research concerned itself with the 'self'. Taking his cue from psychoanalysis, but specifically turning away from Freud's theory of personality, Erik Erikson devised his concept of Ego identity and its development. Freud himself did not speak of identity, but of 'identification', and saw the person as a 'system of relations that is not conflict-free, but under pressure to be coherent'.[21] Although manifestly influenced by the concept of 'self' used in the American tradition, Erikson spoke of 'identity' and therefore took up precisely that concept which had gradually asserted itself both in the Meadian tradition and in German translations from the English, too.[22] Erikson intended the notion of 'identity' to describe conscious or unconscious attempts at Ego synthesis, at constructing or reconstructing the continuity of a person over time, or the consistency of a person in the face of the multiplicity of impulses and the differentiated expectations of the social environment. Almost immediately following his first publications, initial attempts were made in the late 1940s to link the two strands in the conception of identity. Without the concepts used becoming wholly unambiguous, this combination of Mead and Erikson became widespread and, from the 1960s, occupied a central position in debates in the social sciences even outside the United States; in Germany Jürgen Habermas was largely responsible for disseminating these ideas.[23] The interest in the concepts of identity and the self was as strong as it was partly because, at the height of discussions on educational reforms in Germany and other European countries, intellectuals hoped it would enable them to reformulate the old ideals of *Bildung* and emancipation in a modern and scientific manner.

There is, quite evidently, a normative side to this sociological concept of identity. Mead and Erikson, not to mention all their followers and those who advanced this tradition, did not merely describe the achievements the person makes in creating a consistent and ongoing identity. They also shared the tacit assumption that it was good to form an identity – good at least in the empirically verifiable sense that the degree of emotional and physical health and subjective happiness was greater with the successful formation of an identity. They believed that identity formation was also good at a deeper and even more clearly normative level, assuming that identity formation constituted a gain in autonomy and, consequently, that failures in attempts to form an identity amounted to a persistence in self-incurred serfdom (to paraphrase Kant). To imagine that a loss of identity or failures in forming an identity could mean anything other than unhappiness for the person concerned appeared to these thinkers as completely absurd.

However, it was precisely this assumption that was challenged by a train of thought which did not succeed in making itself heard more clearly until around 1968, in spite of some antecedents, such as Friedrich Nietzsche and Theodor Adorno. Authors writing within the post-structuralist, postmodern discourse do not bemoan the greater difficulties involved in identity-formation processes today; instead, they emphasize the compulsion (or self-compulsion) innate in the assumption that a person's character must show consistency and continuity. For a time, the representatives of the sociological conception of identity were able to ignore this questioning of the tacit normative assumptions of their thought, especially as these objections were largely advanced within philosophy and cultural criticism, and thus from outside the domain of professionalized social research. Yet, given the resonance this postmodern questioning of the concept of identity encountered among feminists and members of the gay movements, as well as in debates on racism and ethnicity, sociologists could not go on ignoring it for ever. In addition, empirical evidence from various social domains seemed to suggest a drastic increase in experiences of contingency and difference. The causes of these changes, however, have been interpreted quite differently. The changing organization of work, the rapidly increasing significance of communication technologies, the psychologization of our self-understanding, or simply the multiplication of social relations in which most contemporaries live, are identified as causes for these developments.[24] These developments are then taken as evidence for declaring the communicative (over)saturation of a person and the disintegration of the previously coherent self into a fragmented identity, a 'patchwork' of identities, a person who is not only schizophrenic, but 'multiphrenic'.[25] Other authors with a better sense of proportion[26] do not equate changes in some aspects of social life with total change with quite the same alacrity, although their claims aim in the same direction. How, then, can the traditional sociological conception of the self or identity survive in the face of the postmodern challenge to it?

A simple, if perhaps overly simple, reaction would be to reject the postmodern critique as the result of a misunderstanding. This reaction would suggest itself to the extent that, above all in texts by the epigones, the positions that are attacked or declared to be outdated are indeed frequently presented in a quite misleading manner.[27] For example, the sociological tradition can certainly not be accused of having been unaware of the permanent threat to identity. There can be no talk of it subscribing to the naïve belief that identity formation was a simple and normally successful process. From his *Psychology* to his theory of religion, William James always emphasized the person's inner conflicts and the threats to the coherence of the self.[28] Erikson in particular was fully aware of the enormous strains soldiers, migrants and Native Americans faced in their identity formation. Polemics against, and scorn at, the belief in a substantive self clearly miss the mark if they are used to land a blow against the Mead–Erikson tradition. For nowhere else have thinkers elaborated the constructed character of the self or of Ego identity so carefully. The rupture with the essentialist concept of the person had already occurred in American thinking with pragmatism and was not affected by the reception of 'postmodernism'.[29] Moreover, postmodern critiques often conflate personality structure and the self, a confusion which is occasionally also to be found among the sociological authors themselves. Where a rigid definition of a heterosexual identity or of a clearly differentiated male or female identity is called into question, the description of identity as a compulsive social ascription may sound meaningful. But this has little to do with the understanding of this concept by Mead and Erikson. For at issue here are social expectations *vis-à-vis* specific qualities exhibited by the individual personality, and no longer the communicative structure of the relation of the person to the self as in Mead's and Erikson's work. Nevertheless, even when we have smoothed out all these misunderstandings, the critique still has a certain edge. It also cannot be blunted within a merely normative debate. Of course there may be good reasons for defending the value of individual or collective autonomy and for rejecting the frequently irresponsible coquetry with which postmodernists refer to apocalypse or catastrophe, or speak in terms of the totalitarian character of the coherent person and liberation from it in favour of a 'patchwork identity'. But any reaction that merely repudiates this critique with normative arguments side-steps the issues, for, by questioning the underlying normative assumptions of the sociological conception of identity, we arrive at a new view of the processes of identity formation in at least three respects. In what follows I shall discuss three possible ways of productively using the postmodern challenge to the Mead–Erikson tradition.

The first of these three points involves perhaps a clarification rather than a revision of the tradition, or a revision of individual variants but not of all variants of the conception of identity. The question here is whether the conception of identity is wedded to an understanding of the autonomy of the individual which, as it were, neglects Freud's insight that the Ego is not master of its own house. If the theory of the social constitution of the self relies on such an understanding of autonomy, then the result is unavoidably an 'over-socialized' notion of the individual. This was the slogan on the banner under which Dennis Wrong attacked Talcott Parsons's theory of personality,[30] but it can also be taken up when attacking other variants of the theory of socialization. However, to my mind the objection hardly holds water if it is levelled against Mead and Erikson. In the shape of the category of the 'I', Mead's theory of personality possesses an agency precisely intended to designate the biological root of impulsiveness and spontaneity. Initially, Mead probably had assumptions in mind based on a psychology of the instincts. Yet he later tended to opt more for Freud's distinction between basic impulses that promote solidarity, on the one hand, and those that foster aggression, on the other. Irrespective of how exactly this agency is construed, Mead emphasizes that the individual can, for better or worse, be taken by surprise at any time by his or her own instinctual impulses. These impulses are never completely incorporated into the conscious coherence of the person. How they are unleashed in a controlled manner plays a key role in the pragmatic analysis of creativity. And Erikson, unlike Parsons, certainly remained an orthodox Freudian to the extent that he did not forego the natural traits in the agency of the Id when he expanded the Freudian model of personality to include the concept of Ego identity. This is not to deny that we cannot rely on this line of defence for all sociological representatives of the concept of identity. It is true that even Habermas, like Parsons, runs the danger of simplifying the conception of identity in this regard, as is shown, for example, by his critique of Cornelius Castoriadis in his lectures on the *Philosophical Discourse of Modernity*.[31] Here he objects to Castoriadis's talk of the infant's 'monadic primordial state', claiming it involves an inadequate mediation of individual and society. However, with this formulation Castoriadis does not wish to capture an original isolation of the child, which would indeed be absurd, but the original experience of unity, in other words a symbiotic primordial state, as the basis for the development of impulses.

In stark contrast to Jacques Lacan, Castoriadis develops ideas for a concept of moral autonomy that does not rely on self-repression.[32] The decisive step he takes in this regard is to position the conflict between impulses and reality in the imaginary processing of the two. Imagination allows the person autonomy from both external reality and internal impulses. 'An autonomous subject is one that knows itself to be justified in concluding: this is true indeed and: this is indeed my desire.'[33] There are manifest links here to the sociological conception of identity. Here, identity formation does not mean definitive self-control, but rather the establishment of open communicative relations between the person and his or her world. In this scheme, the achievements of the creative imagination are constitutive the person's ability to communicate with reality, other people, and himself or herself.

The second of the three aspects in which I believe the postmodernist debate fruitfully compels a clarification of the sociological conception of identity perhaps only involves a clearer emphasis of what was always meant by the concept. What I have in mind is that merely proposing that Ego identity and personality structure are both socially constituted should not lead one to underestimate *the radical difference between socialized individuals*. If we construe the individual as a pre-social entity or an extra-social entity, then it is natural to consider the social only as a subset taken from the sum total of individuals, whereby the subset can never encompass the persons in their entirety. If, however, as is the case in sociological research into socialization, the stress is on the social constitution of personality and its self-referentiality, then this can prompt a minimization of the differences between individuated persons by underscoring their common cultural background. Such an approach assumes, then, that because all individuals are formed by a shared language and culture a complete consensus can be achieved between them.[34] A literary example, William Faulkner's *The Sound and the Fury*, may help to clarify this train of thought. This novel describes one and the same series of events involving attraction and rejection among siblings from four different perspectives. However, it does not do so in such a manner that each of these individual perspectives provides a subjective partial view of an objectively given object which allows us to imagine that, at least in the long run, a fully integrated joint viewpoint would emerge through communication under ideal conditions. Instead, interaction among people involves something that is not only viewed from different perspectives, but which is also first constituted by these participants, so that multiperspectivity is an integral aspect of it. Needless to say, in the case of interpersonal processes, the different perspectives can also be brought together in a joint construction of reality. Indeed, sociological research into identity contains a wealth of examples of how a marriage, for example, can lead to the generation of a shared reality.[35] However, this shared reality is a new reality, one that is constructed and not discovered. This new reality is never completely shared and is itself differentiated in terms of individual views of the joint reality, though the constitution of these individual traits still has to be construed as being fully social in nature. The intensity of religious and sexual experiences of fusion with the Other and of self-transcendence stems precisely from the fact that even the socially constituted individuals in a commonly shared culture experience unity with their fellow individuals only in the form of the brief transgression of the boundaries of the self.[36]

In my view, the third aspect is the area in which a revision of the sociological conception of identity is very necessary, but also possible. What I have in mind here is the dimension of *power and exclusion in processes of identity formation*. It is, as already mentioned, certainly wrong to claim that Mead and Erikson advanced a latently totalitarian conception of the person as an entity that completely controls itself, eliding all intrinsic contradictions and compulsively excluding other persons. Yet I believe another objection can be raised that cannot be dismissed so lightly. For Mead and Erikson, one might argue, know only the dialogical, discursive structures of identity formation and ignore the degree to which exclusion and ostracism function to stabilize identity. A 'deconstructionist' reading of Mead could prove this. Mead's explicit theory only construes identity formation via interaction and role-taking. Gradually, according to his theory, the child learns to interact with an ever greater number of persons and acquires the ability to become part of ever more abstract structures of communication and co-operation. This, he believes, constitutes an ongoing universalization of judgement with regard to the child's moral consciousness. However, there are texts by Mead which show clearly that he was also familiar with other, non-dialogical forms of identity formation. Although he rejects these forms on normative grounds, he is aware of them, and we must therefore be permitted to ask to what extent his official theory does justice to these phenomena. His study on the psychology of punitive justice springs to mind here; in it, he investigates how labelling actions as crimes or ostracizing criminals serves to stabilize individual or collective identity.[37] I also have in mind Mead's analyses of nationalism in the context of the First World War and thereafter. In them, Mead contrasts social integration by means of democratic procedures with social integration through the constitution of internal and external enemies.[38] Mead wishes to show us in each case that it is better to achieve identity formation through dialogue and democracy than by means of the exclusion of criminals and enemies. But did his theory ever take the latter possibility into serious empirical consideration? Another question has a similar thrust. May we indeed envisage the steps towards universalizing moral judgements as a form of logical sequence? Is it not rather the case that with each loosening of particular ties, with each act of subsumption under more universal standards of judgement, we run the danger of overtaxing ourselves and thus regressing to lower levels of moral judgement? A developmental psychology of moral judgement, rich in normative content, such as that put forward by Mead, is unable to extricate itself from this dilemma by drawing a sharp line between the logic of moral judgement and the psychology of moral development. How, then, could Mead have answered these questions? He could possibly have reacted by endeavouring to deploy the following distinction. Identity formation can only succeed under dialogical conditions; violence and exclusion may serve to *stabilize* identities and to this extent are functional equivalents of dialogical stabilization, but they are not on their own able to serve as the basis for identity *formation*. They can only stabilize, not constitute, identity. This claim would rest on strong empirical evidence: violence and exclusion cannot enhance the reflexivity of a person's relation to himself or herself, and a structure of primary group relations that is not shaped by violence is absolutely necessary for the elementary stages of identity formation. Yet this counter-claim, although justified, remains somewhat unsatisfying, because it, too, rests on a clear distinction between the two types of identity formation (the one through dialogue, the other through exclusion) as if they were separate domains of reality. But what we are interested in is to pinpoint precisely the interweaving of the two forms in one and the same reality. The idyllic picture of pure dialogical identity formation within the family is not yet disproved, it is true, if we emphasize that such families are not the rule and that violence is frequent within the family. The complexity of the issue becomes more apparent, however, as soon as we realize that the family is itself the result of a drawing of boundaries. The degree of empathy that can be reached among family members is not unspecific: stepchildren and children in care are often excluded from such empathy. Equally, democratic procedures are valid as a rule for a polity clearly delimited in terms of an external and an internal world. And there is no guarantee that those without full citizenship in a democracy, or even countries, are treated in ways imbued with the democratic spirit. The sociological conception of identity in its classical form certainly has not adequately construed this interweaving of dialogue and exclusion.[39]

However, this is no reason to desert to the camp of the postmodern critics of the sociological conception of identity with all banners flying. For the recognition that dialogue and the drawing of boundaries are interwoven actually rescues the notion of discursive identity formation in the face of an approach that claims that all identity formation is based solely on power and arbitrary definition. In Rorty's philosophy, the untenability of such a view, and thus also the impossibility of completely ignoring the self's dialogically constituted consistency, becomes clear at a rather unexpected point. After Rorty abruptly separates the private from the public and strictly limits 'self-creation' to the citizen's private sphere, the question as to whether a mutually binding ethos should be valid in this public domain and in what this might consist of course becomes unavoidable. Encountering this question, Rorty cites the prevention of cruelty as the essence of such an ethos. This sounds at first like a mere minimum condition, like a specification of the classic liberal notion that the pursuit of self-interest is justified so long as it does not interfere with the well-being of others. However, closer examination reveals Rorty's train of thought to be more profound. One might immediately inquire after the more precise determination of the concept of cruelty. Rorty knows that we share the sensitivity to pain not only with all human beings, but also with other life-forms. But what unites us with all humans, and sets us apart from other organisms, is the 'susceptibility to pain and in particular to that special sort of pain which the brutes do not share with humans – humiliation'.[40] Accordingly, the aim of torture is often not to inflict physical pain, but to cause humiliation. Such cruelty does not always require physical violence.

> For the best way to cause people long-lasting pain is to humiliate them by making the things that seemed most important to them look futile, obsolete, and powerless. Consider what happens when a child's precious possessions – the little things around which he weaves fantasies that make him a little different from all other children – are redescribed as 'trash', and thrown away. Or consider what happens when these possessions are made to look ridiculous alongside the possessions of another, richer, child. Something like that presumably happens to a primitive culture when it is conquered by a more advanced one. The same sort of thing sometimes happens to nonintellectuals in the presence of intellectuals.[41]

For Rorty, all these instances are only milder forms of that which achieves its most perfect expression in torture. Using scenes drawn from George Orwell's novel *1984* to illustrate his point, Rorty demonstrates that the particular aspects of a person's orientation to the world are not only devalued in the experience of humiliation; in the vacuum created by this devaluation, the threat of violence can also be employed to compel a person to perform actions which cannot be reintegrated into his or her world:

> the worst thing you can do to somebody is not to make her scream in agony but to use that agony in such a way that even when the agony is over, she cannot reconstitute herself. The idea is to get her to do or say things – and, if possible, believe and desire things, think thoughts – which later she will be unable to cope with having done or thought. You

can thereby ... 'unmake her world' by making it impossible for her to use language to describe what she has been.[42]

Rorty's intentions in this disturbing analysis of cruelty are clear. He sees in the protection from humiliation the common ground shared by all human beings, the ethos for shaping public life, the meaning of 'solidarity'. Here, solidarity is not given by a shared goal or shared values, but, rather, only by the shared hope that we can be protected from humiliation. Rorty wants to teach us not to seek mutually binding values, but to put into practice the minimalist ethos of the prevention of cruelty by becoming more sensitive to the views of others, and thus to the dangers of humiliating them.[43] But in thus grounding his understanding of solidarity, which leads him to make a sympathetic analysis of different forms of humiliation, he encounters a phenomenon that, according to his attack on the traditional concept of self, cannot exist at all: the loss of self-esteem. It may well be true that the loss of an indispensable, personal vocabulary adequately describes the experience of humiliation itself. But the only reason why acts that are performed under the threat of torture, where the 'world is unmade', cannot be reintegrated is that the person cannot live without internal consistency. If, as Rorty proclaimed, we are only an idiosyncratic conglomeration of impulses and conceptions, without a centre and lacking the strong evaluations that create identity, why, then, should it be at all possible for acts ceaselessly and morally to torment us?; why should it not be possible for us simply to divide off the acts carried out under the threat of violence from our present self without any problems whatsoever?

Thus, in grounding his call for a minimum degree of public solidarity, Rorty stumbles, contrary to his intentions, across that very dimension of moral feelings and that same notion of the consistent self which the postmodern critique wished to leave behind. In an empirical respect, his remarks on humiliation show how fruitful the interweaving of dialogue and exclusion can be for our understanding of the formation and loss of identity.[44] In a normative respect, the recognition of this interweaving presents us with the task of reflecting on possible ways of drawing boundaries in which the excluded can nevertheless be tolerated as the Other. This applies as much to the 'internal foreign territory' (Sigmund Freud) of our impulses as to the foreignness of other persons and cultures. Thus, the postmodern discussion teaches us that the decentring of the notion of the subject need not by any means lead us to renounce the normative contents of the concept of identity; rather, it suggests that this normativity can be retained and recovered if we achieve a decentring of the idea of moral autonomy as well.[45]

Even Charles Taylor, the contemporary thinker who has been the most consistent in elaborating the intrinsic relationship between values and identity, has long since abandoned the conception of a unified self as a centring that can be fixed once and for all. He too is 'postmodern', if we take this to mean that he sees the road leading back to the Enlightenment vision of the rational self or to the Romantic vision of the expressive self as closed forever. 'One can't live by either one alone, but neither can they be combined or synthesized. Human life is irreducibly multilevelled. The epiphanic and the ordinary but indispensable real can never be fully aligned, and we are condemned to live on more than one level – or else suffer the impoverishment of repression.'[46] In the differences that are imposed upon us, and in the indissoluble tension between ideals of life in which we find ourselves, there is for Taylor, however, a better and worse, there is criticism and self-criticism – and not only, as for Rorty, a mute, if friendly *laissez-faire*. 'Ironism is not the only alternative to Platonism.'[47] And Taylor claims that, paradoxically, a strong evaluation and thus 'a moment of recognition of something which is not made or decided by human beings, and which shows a certain way of being to be good and admirable',[48] still lurks in Rorty's plea to escape the pressure exerted by strong evaluations on our desires and self-conception itself – as there is in every ethos, no matter how far removed it is from theology and metaphysics.

Expanded and reformulated, the theory of identity formation can thus certainly stand up to the challenge of the postmodern. Nor does the combination of value-genesis and identity formation break down under this challenge; rather, it is able to adduce sound reasons for repudiating an ethos of difference set up in abstract opposition to it. However correct it may be that rigid identity and rigid consensus stifle the creative potential of difference, it is also true that this potential recedes if the difference exists free of tension because none of the parties any longer feels bound to that which is specifically his own, because none experiences the Other as a potentially salutary provocation to serious self-transformation, and because all orientation towards a possible consensus – even if it is only a consensus on agreeing to differ – has disappeared.[49] Identity, not in the sense of stable features, but of a communicative and constructive relationship of the person to himself and to that which does not belong to the self, is the precondition for creative intercourse with the Other and for an ethos of difference.

Values and Norms: The Good and the Right

Hermeneutic efforts elude an easy summary of their results. The very diversity of coexisting conceptual constructs and competing languages that made these efforts necessary in the first place also prevents the one conceptualization which might be independent of the interpreted thought processes from being ultimately available to us. This book made no attempt either to infer general laws inductively from empirical findings, or to derive special claims deductively from clear initial assumptions and definitions. Rather, the aim was to shed light step by step on an idea identified right from the outset as it passed through a diverse world of discourse. After the hermeneutic efforts, this initial idea is no longer the same as it was at the beginning. It has become, rather, more reflective; its internal consistency, as well as its context-specificity, emerge more clearly. This also means that the critical introduction of an idea into new contexts – ours – is now possible.

This book has attempted to answer what is today the theoretically and practically pressing question of the genesis of values in the light of a discourse dedicated to this question from Nietzsche through to Dewey. In the last few decades, this discourse has been neglected to such a large extent that contemporary writers, even if they are more or less explicitly concerned with the question posed here, tend to be so without recalling the answers which have been put forward ever since Nietzsche.[1] Along the way we have encountered highly diverse theoretical assumptions and a multiplicity of phenomena related to the genesis of values. The question concerning us here was clearly posed for the first time in Nietzsche's work. In his answer, the claim that the (Judaeo-Christian) values of justice and love originate in *ressentiment* stands directly opposed to the prospect of the autonomous positing of one's proper value by the sovereign individual. In the work of William James we found a more fruitful answer to the question – posed just as radically – in his attempt to do justice to the variety of religious experience. His investigation of religious experience, particularly of conversion and prayer, yields insights which should be valid for the genesis of all value commitments. Émile Durkheim takes up directly from James's founding of the theory of religion upon the interpretation of experiences, but opposes James's one-sided individualism with an equally one-sided collectivism. This approach, and particularly the investigation of ritual and collective ecstasy, opens up a wide field of inquiry for the sociological study of religion. However, fundamental problems which James left unclear or unresolved remain equally so with Durkheim. These include the unexplained relationship between individuality, intersubjectivity and collectivity; the lack of appreciation of the need for, and openendedness of, the interpretation of all experience; and, finally, the issue of the relationship between ordinary action and extra-ordinary experience. Searching for solutions to these problems, we subsequently turned our attention to Georg Simmel. Despite a few promising ideas, it turned out that his theory of religion cannot, as a whole, really take us very far towards an answer to our question. With its origins in *Lebensphilosophie*, Simmel's terminology does not supply us with the distinctions that are necessary for an answer to these questions. In Simmel's case, it was only by extending our field of reference beyond the paradigmatic area of religion that we could identify his most important contributions. In phenomenological terms, this broader perspective first of all embraced the experience of war and the enthusiastic experience of the suddenly united nation, in which – according to him – could be glimpsed, for one historical moment, the revelation of a modern equivalent of the social integration that had formerly been vouchsafed by religion. After resignedly retracting this claim, Simmel produces more fertile ideas – particularly in his reflections on death and immortality which are prefigured in some of his earlier work. He introduces the subject's constitutive value-relatedness and the personality which becomes aware of its own finitude as necessary components in the answer to the question of the genesis of values.

In order to escape the restrictions of a point of view centred on morality conceived as a sense of duty and the experience of 'Ought', a viewpoint discernible in Simmel as well as in all other writers oriented to Kant (including Nietzsche), our discussion turned to the work of Max Scheler. Here we find a rich phenomenology of moral feelings and the experience of attractive values, part of his audacious project to construct a modern ethics of value and overcome the 'ethics of imperatives' through the spirit of the Christian idea of love, an idea which he advocated passionately. However, Scheler burdens his analyses of the experience of value with a thesis which, as it stands, is untenable, and which he himself more or less retracted over the course of his intellectual development. According to this thesis, the certainty which one feels in the experience of values is an indicator of the pre-existence of values independent of experience. John Dewey's theory of value, in contrast, clears a path between value relativism and value objectivism. Even more so than this path that leads via the situation-specific concretization and specification of values, Dewey's theory of religion, despite its time-bound objectives and implausible historical perspective, offers a fruitful answer to our question. In it, Dewey combines an intersubjective understanding of self-formation with a consideration of the role of imagination and creativity in the genesis of values or ideals, thus aiming at the idealization of contingent possibilities and at the imaginary relation to an holistic self. For Dewey, it is the experience of conversation or communication itself, or the shock provided by the Other, which, although he indicates this only tentatively, leads his thought in this theoretical direction.

Half a century later and without allusion to any of these predecessors, we again find similar thoughts in the work of Charles Taylor. He makes the connection between the philosophy of value and the theory of self-formation more deliberately than Dewey. To support his argumentation, he enlists, like Scheler, a phenomenology of moral feelings which, however, he never properly carries out. Intersubjective thinking links him with Dewey (and Mead). Taylor deals with the relation of experience and interpretation more sophisticatedly than all the other thinkers under discussion. He refers us to a hermeneutic circle between these dimensions which prevents their being reduced to one pole: interpretation and experience are neither independent of one another, nor are they reducible to one another. His theory of the 'constitutive goods' also reserves a place for the relationship between everyday action and extra-ordinary experience, even if some questions still remain unanswered. At this point, as with the relationship between value and the 'Ought', it turns out that Taylor's theory is not the last word in the question which concerns us here. The question of contingency with which we had begun this investigation had to be radicalized in the debate with the postmodern challenge to the concepts of 'self' and 'value', represented, for example, by Richard Rorty. Reflection on this question demonstrated the necessity of interweaving the dialogic and 'exclusive' dimensions of self-formation more thoroughly than is usual in the sociological tradition. In Rorty's grounding of public solidarity in the avoidance of cruelty, and in his sensitivity to humiliation as a specifically human form of cruelty, we stumbled once more, as it were in the back of the postmodern critique, upon the dimension of moral feelings and self-consistency in the face of contingency. Along the way, the thought which served as the point of departure for this investigation gained in succinctness, and also proved itself robust in the face of its radical questioning: values originate in experiences of self-formation and self-transcendence.

At this point we should deal with three possible ways in which the precise character of this idea might be misunderstood. With two of these misunderstandings I shall merely allay the doubts which arise from them; a proper working out of the alternatives which they contain would exceed the scope of the present study. The remaining observations, however, will be devoted to the third possible misunderstanding.

The first possible misunderstanding concerns the status which phenomenological analyses of the genesis of value held in our framework. For each individual theory examined here, the elucidation of individual phenomena occupied an important place in the argument as a whole. *Ressentiment* and the sovereign positing of value; conversion and prayer; collective ecstasy in archaic ritual and in nationalistic enthusiasm for war; the confrontation with death; shame and guilt, remorse and humility; the opening of the self in conversation and in the experience of nature; the experience of strong evaluations; and the fear of humiliation – all this and more was cited, but never really expanded upon. Phenomenological analyses were only developed as far as this was useful for the theoretical argument. Yet this need not have been the case, nor must it remain so, and it would therefore be a grave error to charge the present argument with squeezing, on principle, phenomenological analyses into the corset of theoretical reasoning. Rather, it would have been possible to distinguish between the theoretical and empirical results in the case of every one of the thinkers examined here. Though there is often a certain affinity between a theory and the phenomena which it places in the foreground, an improved theory would have to prove its superiority by taking account also of those phenomena cited by its rivals. What would James have had to say about *ressentiment*, Durkheim about the nationalist enthusiasm for war, or Dewey about the individual's confrontation with death? My own contribution to this discussion in particular is urged to expose itself to a rich phenomenology of the experience of value, which would also have to incorporate, more thoroughly than was the case in the present context, formative experiences of loss and traumatization other than humiliation and death –

for the opening of the sacred boundaries of the self through violence, that is, the radical inversion of the experience of self-transcendence, must also become a touchstone of this theory.

A second misunderstanding arises from the ambiguity of the word 'genesis'. The 'genesis' of values can be understood in four different ways. Firstly, it can involve the original historical promulgation of a value; secondly, the defence of this value by a small, but growing, group of disciples; thirdly, the genesis of a new commitment in individuals (through conversion, for example) to values which are by no means historically new; fourthly and finally, a resuscitation of values which have lost their drive or sunk into oblivion. Such a distinction is, of course, crucial for an historical sociology of the genesis and diffusion of values, or of the shift in values. Such an historical sociology has to make clear which kind of processes of value-genesis are the subject of scientific research.[2] In the present context, however, we were able to ignore this distinction. To be sure, values do not always originate in the eruptive form in which charismatic visionaries experience and proclaim them. They can, rather, derive their impetus from a difficult balance between experience, articulation and the stock of interpretations available within a culture.[3] But experiences of self-formation and self-transcendence are indispensable in every case; even the ritually ossified forms of periodic revitalizations of values represent the attempt to facilitate, or at least to quote, such experiences. In this sense, the thesis put forward here is located on a level prior to the differentiation into the various topics of an historical sociology of values. In each of these topics, assumptions are made, which are explicitly or implicitly, about the genesis of values, and which are situated on the same logical level as the idea defended here.

The third and probably most dangerous misunderstanding of the present argument consists in reading into my emphasis on the contingency of the genesis of values a plea against the claims of a universalistic morality – a thrust that is at the very least relativistic, and possibly even antimoral. This would be quite contrary to my real intentions. There is obviously a need for clarification here. The question of the relationship between the attractive character of values and the obligatory character of norms was a continuous undercurrent in my discussion of each of the individual accounts of the genesis of values, but without ever moving to the forefront. After briefly looking back at how the thinkers we have investigated portrayed the relationship of the good and the right, I shall put forward a thesis which integrates the theory of the genesis of values with a universalistic conception of morality. This thesis will then be further explicated in critical dialogue with one of the most influential projects to construct a universalistic moral theory: Jürgen Habermas's 'discourse ethics'. Finally, this thesis will be proposed as a way of resolving the liberalism–communitarianism controversies of the present, which essentially turn on the appropriate relationship between the good and the right.

The relationship between the good and the right had become an issue long before the rise of the philosophy of value in the nineteenth century. That is not to say that the definition of either concept is unanimously agreed upon, and only their relationship is in question;[4] rather, the conceptions of the good and the right depend upon further assumptions of an anthropological or a metaphysical nature. In the period of time under investigation here, which is demarcated by the discourse about the genesis of values, Nietzsche's attempt, first of all, at an 'overcoming of morality' turned out to be so enmeshed in the Kantian dichotomy of duty and inclination and the very premises of the morality he was attacking that it only achieved an inversion, rather than a resolution, of the dilemma he recognized. In the work of William James, on the other hand, in which Kant is almost completely ignored, we encountered an abrupt separation of 'religion' and 'morality', in which morality appears exclusively as imperative and restrictive, and religion, on the other hand, as attractive, creating possibilities for, and motivating, action. And Durkheim, who took Kant far more seriously than James did, locates the tension, which for James exists between religion and morality, within morality itself. Just as the sacred is simultaneously both adored and feared, so the good and the right are contained in all moral actions in complex and varying proportions. Primacy, however, is not accorded to either of these components of the moral.

In Georg Simmel's radical attempt to rethink Kant's ethics under the conditions of a world of differentiated individuality, the concept of the Ought – as his formula of the 'individual law' already intimates – is so broadly defined that the internal tensions between the good and the right, which James and Durkheim were each able to express in their own way, are actually occluded. Far more fruitful is Max Scheler's broadly executed enterprise to break the spell of imperative morality and formalism in ethics, and to break through to a new 'nonformal ethics of value' on the basis of a phenomenology of value-experience. In doing so, however, Scheler ends up with a reversed one-sidedness. For him, the 'Ought' derives from values; he mistrusts every concession to a self-sufficient origin of the 'Ought', which would be a precondition for the existence of tension between the good and the right, believing it to signal a return to the very prescriptive ethics against which he is arguing. In contrast to the other thinkers, John

Dewey's discussion of the theory of value and religion did not itself provide the space to deal with the relationship between the good and the right in his work. This would have required us to incorporate his ethics[5] into our discussion – which, however, did not promise any further gains for the question of the genesis of values. Dewey also starts from the premise that the good and the right are not reducible to one another in either of the conceivable directions. His real interest concerns our practice of reaching a judgement reflectively when different goods conflict with one another. He interprets obligations as goods too, so that these can compete with other goods on an equal basis. Whoever asks Dewey whether the good or the right should ultimately win the upper hand in our reflection will find his answer half-hearted. Dewey aims for a balance, but inclines towards the priority of the good. The real value of his reflections does not lie here, but rather in his focus on the mediation of different goods. We shall return to this issue shortly.

In the course of Taylor's intellectual development, it is possible to establish an increasing appreciation of the relative rights of an ethics of prescription and obligation *vis-à-vis* an ethics of goods and values. Given his starting-point, he initially inclined towards a one-sided emphasis on the good as opposed to the right – even when he was concerned with classic questions of the right.[6] At first, he saw no difficulties in conceiving the right simply as a dimension of the good in the Western cultural tradition – and not necessarily only here. Seen in this way, the right can of course assert its claims against other goods and against situative exigencies, but loses its inevitable, and certainly its unconditional, character, which the Kantian tradition has always emphasized so strongly. Taylor even tries, in his debate with contemporary attempts to construct a formal 'procedural ethics', to turn the tables and show that even the most discriminating variants of such an ethics argue from an implicit horizon of the good, which is then denied in their implementation.[7] A similar argument can also be found in his major work, *Sources of the Self*.[8] The ambition of procedural ethicists, Taylor argues here, opens up a gaping hole when what is at issue is the question of what can motivate us to morality in the first place, to enter into the procedure and to commit ourselves to its results.[9] For this reason, despite his appreciation of the motives of the procedural ethicists and his high regard for the goods they reluctantly articulate, the priority of the good over the right remains intact for him. Consigned to two mere footnotes,[10] though, we find a remarkably more sophisticated argument. First of all, Taylor distinguishes between the moral and the political sphere in such a way that it seems possible to uncouple from one another the opinions prevailing in both spheres on the primacy of the good and the right. According to Taylor, in the political sphere the safeguarding of formal procedures stressed in the liberal tradition actually has the greatest merit, because only through them can the Rousseauistic-Jacobin dangers of a tyranny of unity be averted. Yet he does not fully endorse the defenders of the priority of the right in the political sphere – not because he fails to recognize these merits, but because he finds, as it were, the principles of liberal democracy only insufficiently articulated in an exclusive emphasis on procedures. In moral philosophical respects, Taylor now distinguishes between three different meanings of the thesis of the primacy of the right. If, firstly, it is supposed to mean, in Kant's sense, that moral obligations can never be derived from the goods (understood from a utilitarian point of view) towards which the desires of the agents are directed, then Taylor can agree to this thesis; he would only object to restricting the understanding of our desires to these first-order desires. If the thesis is supposed to mean, secondly, that only duties could arise in moral considerations because all values or situative points of view are to be excluded from the outset, then this entails for him a thoroughly unjustified understanding of morality. Taylor rejects a priority of the right which does not even in principle grant the good a right to compete in our moral reflection. If, however, the thesis is supposed to mean, thirdly, that such competition can indeed arise, but that we should always and under all circumstances accord priority to the right, in the sense of our obligations towards others or everyone, over the good, in the sense of striving for a value-filled life, then Taylor concedes that this conception expresses an authentic ethical position. At the same time, however, he resists it, because he sees a moment of self-overtaxing and hubris bordering on self-destruction in such a monomaniacal orientation to the viewpoint of justice at the expense of all other values. So Taylor ultimately rejects the claim of a priority of the right over the good for the moral sphere, too. It would be wrong, though, if he were to see in this rejection itself a justification for the opposite primacy: of the good over the right. To reject one primacy does not yet exclude the possibility that entirely different relations – other than superordination or subordination – might obtain between the good and the right. Taylor's lack of interest in a grounding of the 'Ought' in experiences of a separate kind, independent of the experience of value, can invite suspicion. On the other hand, in his reply to Richard Rorty's criticism of his major work, Taylor unexpectedly expresses another idea, one that is new to his work. In addition to our orientation to 'constitutive' goods and our caution before possible self-delusions, he now mentions our prior sense of the right, and thinks that we must balance these three points of view against each other: 'None of these has primacy. It is a matter of achieving reflective equilibrium, to use the Rawlsian term.'[11] But where does this prior sense of the right come from? If this right is only a right which has been earlier derived from a good, then we would still be left with a primacy of the good. If Taylor wishes, however, to take seriously the notion of a 'reflective equilibrium' between the good and the right, then he must concede the right's own grounding in action, independently of values.

For Rorty himself, finally, the last thinker to crop up in our context, the tension between the good and the right is dispersed through the neat division into private self-realization and public solidarity. However, this dispersion is only apparent, as is shown by the unavoidable questions to which Rorty's philosophy has no ready answers. Are questions of justice never posed in private affairs? Is the minimal ethos of protection from humiliation sufficient for our dealing with the moral questions which arise in public affairs?[12] Is the boundary between the private and the public sphere not in fact controversial, and how should reasons for or against a particular boundary be constituted? The orientation to the good that has for so long gone unarticulated and which lies behind the emphasis on the contingent becomes increasingly apparent with other postmodern thinkers, too; but nowhere in their work can I recognize any contribution which might bring us closer to an answer to the question of the relationship between the good and the right.[13]

The starting-point for the solution I shall propose here is Dewey's emphasis on reflective adjudication and deliberation, as well as Taylor's briefly glimpsed notion of a reflective equilibrium between the good and the right.[14] It is derived from the spirit of pragmatism, of which John Dewey was a representative and which also, though without his assent, makes its presence felt in Taylor's work.[15] In order to give this solution its full weight, and to prevent the rejection of a primacy of either the good or the right being seen merely as the middle road between extremes, or as a hollow compromise, it must be recalled that pragmatism contains not only – as with James and Dewey – a theory of the contingent genesis of values, but also and particularly – as with Dewey and Mead – a conception of moral universalism. How are we to envisage the combination of these two divergent theoretical components in the pragmatist spirit?

In order to answer this question, we should recall two distinctive features of pragmatist ethics which distinguish it from several other approaches.[16] First of all, pragmatist ethics is based on an elaborate anthropological theory of human action in general, and human communication in particular. Dewey and especially Mead developed the essential features of such a theory of the biological preconditions for specifically human achievements.[17] Without going into these in detail, it can nevertheless be emphasized that even the attempt at such a theory involves the assumption that there are universal structures of human action which distinguish it from animal behaviour, and that it is possible to make substantive statements about these anthropological-universal structures. Dewey and Mead have no doubt that typical functional disturbances are located in these universal structures, from which there arises a need for regulation. Above all, George Herbert Mead – and subsequently, under his influence, Dewey – interprets the anthropological-universal capacity for 'role-taking', the decisive characteristic of typically human communication, as the prerequisite for overcoming these disturbances. The development of this capacity and the social conditions which make this development possible are thus of the highest empirical significance. At the same time, however, Dewey and Mead see a substantial ideal located in precisely this empirically verifiable capacity: 'Universal discourse is then the formal ideal of communication.'[18] Mead shows how the capacity to employ significant symbols refers every participant in communication beyond his or her immediate community to a virtual world of ideal meanings. Pragmatist ethics thus stands opposed to culturalistic moral relativism and stresses the universal need for the normative regulation of human co-operation[19] and care, as well as the possibility of seeing a substantial ideal in the solution of these problems of co-operation through communication itself.

The second distinctive feature of pragmatist ethics consists in the fact that it is an ethics based on the perspective of the actor.[20] Of central interest for Dewey and Mead is not the issue of the legitimation of norms, nor even that of the justification of actions, but the issue of the solution to problems of action. What was novel in Mead's critique of Kant's ethics was his suggestion that the categorical imperative as such could only serve to subject actions to a universalization test, but not to discover which actions were adequate in the first place.[21] Action itself demands a creative design. When Mead talked of the experimental method in ethics, he did not mean that moral problems could be solved by experimental research into facts, but rather that an appropriate conception of one's own action can only be developed by experimental means, through a creative design under contingent conditions. The concept of the 'application' of norms or values is hardly appropriate for this emphasis on the creative and risky performances in action. Of course, a value, as well as the 'application' of a value, can be subjected to a discourse of justification, but pragmatist ethics separates the perspective of such a discourse from the existential perspective of the agent.

If we now take these two distinctive features together, then we soon see how the universalistic conception of morality and the theory of the contingent genesis of values can be combined to form a whole along pragmatist lines. According to this point of view, there is no higher authority for the justification of norms than the discourse. From the perspective of the actor, however, who devises his actions under contingent conditions, it is not the justification which is uppermost, but the specification of the good or the right in an action situation. Even if we as agents wish to grant an explicit primacy to a particular good or right as we understand it, we do not have at our disposal certain knowledge of what we must then do. We can honestly strive to increase the good, or to act exclusively according to the right, but this does not furnish us with any certainty that we will actually meet with success in doing this with all the actions that we decide upon and all the direct and indirect consequences which we thus bring about. In the light of the consequences of action, every conception of the good and the right will come under the pressure of revision.[22] Nor can any new specification liberate us from this; a clear termination cannot be envisaged, since the situations in which our action takes place are always new, and the quest for certainty remains forever unfulfilled.[23] We can establish for certain *in abstracto*, that is to say, in the discourse taking place outside action situations, that certain aims of action should enjoy priority on the basis of certain presuppositions about points of view that we must take into account. In the concrete reality of action situations, however, though we often achieve, to be sure, a subjective feeling of certainty, intersubjectively we can achieve only plausibility.[24] In retrospect – having become wiser after the event – we can discover more about the actual appropriateness of our action, but even here a definitive and certain judgement eludes us, because the future will yield further consequences of action and points of view, which again jeopardize our appraisal.

Whilst some might concede that our action has the character I have described here, they might nevertheless dispute that an answer to the question of the relationship between the good and the right follows from it. In which respect, then, should this emphasis on the creativity of action suggest such an answer? It might at first seem as if this emphasis were at best banal and at worst dangerous.[25] It would be dangerous if it exclusively emphasized the situation-specific nature of our decisions, thereby opening the door to arbitrariness and a lack of principles. It would be banal if it only stressed what no one, not even the most ardent proponent of an ethics of conviction, has ever contested – namely, that the right acts do not always follow from a good will. But the way in which the pragmatists present the argument for the creativity of action in ethical contexts does not open the door to unlimited arbitrariness; it declares only certain revisions and specifications to be acceptable. And it is not banal to incorporate into the concept of the good will itself the moral duty to recognize empirical conditions of realization. From the pragmatists' understanding of action, and from the structure of their ethics as an ethics based on the perspective of the actor, it follows that, in the action situation itself, the restrictive point of view of the right *must* inevitably arise, but *can* arise only as one point of view alongside the orientations of the good.

This double assertion requires further clarification. The right *must* arise, according to this view, because it represents the anthropological-universal requirements of the co-ordination of social action, and these are unavoidable in the face of the unavoidable embedding of action in social contexts. All action is unavoidably embedded in the social because the capacity for action is itself already socially constituted, and our co-operation by no means aims only at individually attributable, but also at irreducibly social, goods.[26] This point of view of the right is always present in the manifold diversity of our orientations; the situative revision of our objectives does not degenerate into arbitrariness because it must pass through the potentially universal 'sieve of the norm' (Paul Ricoeur).

The right *can* only arise, according to this view, as one point of view among several in the action situation, because this potentially universal 'sieve of the norm' would have nothing to test if the agent were not oriented to various conceptions of the good, about which he cannot be certain if they are acceptable from the point of view of the right. Even the self-overtaxing moralist described by Taylor, who is thoroughly determined always to give precedence to the universalization procedure, may well want to eliminate his inclinations, but will only be able to test his conceptions of possible actions in this procedure. A decisive point in emphasizing the creativity of action is the recognition that actions cannot be derived from the universalizing point of view itself; the moral agent can only assess whether a possible action is acceptable from this point of view. Even the person who wishes to eliminate his or her inclinations does not thereby eliminate the candidates for the examination which the rule of universalization represents.[27] These candidates are our conceptions of our duty on the one hand, and our conations on the other; they, too, contain a potentially universal validity claim. If with Kant and his followers it remained unclear whether the universalization test of the categorical imperative is directed at our inclinations or at the maxims of our action, then this was due to his failure to understand the interplay obtaining between our pre-reflective conations and our conscious intentions.[28] If, however, one assumes a theory of action which anchors intentionality in the situation-specific reflection on our pre-reflective conations, then it becomes clear that the right can only ever be an examining authority – unless it itself becomes the good, the value of justice.

In the action situation, consequently, there is no primacy of the good or the right. There is a relationship of neither superordination nor subordination, but rather one of complementariness. In the action situation, the irreducible orientations to the good, which are already contained in our conations, encounter the examining authority of the right. In these situations, we can only ever achieve a reflective equilibrium between our orientations. Certainly, the extent to which we subject our orientations to this test may vary. For this reason, there is in the point of view of the right a perpetual, unflagging potential to modify the good, in order to enable it to pass the universalization test. But it does not follow from the universality of the right that, in action situations, we should give precedence to the right over all other considerations as a matter of course – nor that we should not do this. The debate over the question as to whether primacy should be attributed either to the good or the right must be sharply distinguished from the debate over the universalizability of the right. From the pragmatist perspective, the debate over the universalizability of the right need not take place – not because this possibility is rejected, but because it is held to be beyond dispute, in accordance with the premises of the anthropological theory of action. The emphasis here on the situatedness and creativity of action does not involve the slightest scepticism *vis-à-vis* the notion of the universality of the right.[29] On the other hand, however, the pragmatists do not maintain that this idea entails that, within the action situation, the testing of an orientation against the universalization principle *must* self-evidently be given precedence over all other considerations. When, in reply to the question of the primacy of the good and the right, John Dewey answers in his ethics that there is no primacy in the process of deliberation, but that, as far as the weighing up of goods is concerned, priority should be accorded to the good, then this response is neither half-hearted nor inconsistent.[30] Rather, it appears as an empirically convincing solution for the analysis of action situations; and for the weighing up of goods it is at least a feasible and defensible answer, even with full consent to a universalistic morality.

Not only individual agents, but also collectives, entire communities and cultures are located in action situations. From the philosophical conceptualization of the 'good' and the 'right', let us return to the sociological terminology of 'values' and 'norms' when we come to speak of collective actors and aggregations of action. Like individual actors, these, too, exist in a field of tension located between their particular value systems, which have arisen contingently, and the potential of a morality which is pressing towards universality. Universally distributed structures of morality can certainly be ascertained by empirical means. Fundamental norms of fairness, for example, can be discovered by children by merely focusing on the internal need for the regulation of co-operation; such norms, all the way up to the reflective formulation of the 'golden rule', seem to be known in all cultures.[31] A relativist perspective emphasizing the contingency of values has difficulties with this phenomenon; by contrast, the universalistic-deontological tradition of moral theory has always been able to find greater confidence in these facts. We should qualify this allusion to the universal distribution of fundamental norms by immediately adding the rider that every culture fences in the potentially universal morality by defining its areas and conditions of application. Which people (or organisms) and which situations are 'set free' for this morality is a matter of interpretation, and consequently varies across cultures and history. In each case, a justification is produced for excluding people of different nationalities, ethnic groups, races or religions, of another sex or age, of other mentalities and moralities. Without such a justification, the right would become cultural dynamite. But in the exuberance of the plea for a universalistic morality it would again – as in the case of the individual agent – be an error to overlook the fact that no culture can manage without a definite, particular value system and a definite, particular interpretation of the world. 'Particular' here does not, of course, mean 'particularistic'; cultural distinctiveness does not lead to an inability to take universalistic points of view into account. On the contrary, the questions are: which particular cultural traditions from the point of view of the universality of the right be most readily adhered to, and how can other cultural traditions be creatively continued and reshaped from this point of view?

For sociological theory construction, this means that we have to distinguish clearly between cultural and social integration, and, at the same time, at the level of social integration, take the potential universality of norms into consideration. The normative regulation of social integration originates partly in cultural values. It is not, however, simply derived from them, but is rather the upshot of a reflective equilibrium between the co-operating agents reflecting on their collaboration and the cultural interpretations. If with Parsons it seemed as if norms were merely specifications of values in situations, then he fell prey to the fallacy of reducing the social to the cultural.[32] The assertion of the social cannot, however, be permitted to occur at the expense of its potential universality, so that it is reduced to mere conflicts of interest and distribution struggles without considering the potential of norms built into even the antagonistic forms of co-operation. This would only replace the culturalistic-idealistic fallacy with a utilitarian-materialistic one. The analysis of the interplay between cultural and social integration, between values and norms, must take account of the observation that different value systems have a different proximity to those norms which result from the universal structures of co-operation. In the particular value systems of democratic societies, we find rules which can be viewed as transla-tions of universal moral rules into particular political institutions. These none the less inevitably remain particular, and, each time they are imported into another culture, must always be examined in order to assess whether their particularity is a particularism. The notion, however, that in order to overcome particularism, particularity itself must disappear, overlooks the necessarily contingent character of values. Such a notion is condemned to remain a mere morality, and, cut off from the attractiveness of values, to assert the possibility of motivation by morality alone.

The answer to the question of the relationship between the good and the right which I have given here implies, therefore, that in the action situation there can only be a reflective equilibrium between the good and the right; that the point of view of the right, however, inevitably enters into conflict with that of the good and influences its modifica-tion. At the same time, I maintained that this represents the appropri-ate ethical theory from the perspective of pragmatism, which addresses issues from the point of view of the actor. It is now important to point out that what is perhaps the most impressive present-day project to construct a universalistic moral theory, the 'discourse ethics' of Karl-Otto Apel and Jürgen Habermas, also appeals with good reason to pragmatism – although it reaches differ-ent conclusions from those I have drawn. Jürgen Habermas[33] vehe-mently defends the primacy of the right over the good, and emphasizes this idea in his contributions to the discourse theory of law and the democratic constitutional state. Indeed, the idea of discourse goes back to Charles Sanders Peirce's philosophy of science and George Herbert Mead's ethics and theory of communication, and thus to two central components of the pragmatist tradition. The progress of discourse ethics beyond Kant resides essentially in the pragmatist insight that, in moral judgement, no individual *can*

> project himself sufficiently in the situation of everyone else *through his own imagination*. But when the participants can no longer rely on a transcendental preunderstanding grounded in more or less homogeneous conditions of life and interests, the moral point of view can only be realized under conditions of communication that ensure that *everyone* tests the acceptability of a norm, implemented in a general practice, also from the perspective of his own understanding of himself and the world. In this way, the categorical imperative receives a discourse-theoretical interpretation in which its place is taken by the discursive principle (D), according to which only those norms can claim validity that could meet with the agreement of all those concerned in their capacity as participants in a practical discourse.[34]

What, then, is the cause of this divergence between Habermas's interpretation and my own? I do not pose this question here with a view to preserving a pragmatist orthodoxy – nothing could be further from pragmatism's intentions – but in order to find out how the idea of discourse relates to the explanation of the genesis of value commitments I have attempted here.

The first step is to establish that the problem of a possible conflict between two conceptions, both of which derive from the same source, does not result from the idea of the discourse itself, but from the logical status attributed to that idea within the larger framework of a philosophical system. If the task of discourse theory were seen exclusively as expounding a procedure for assessing validity claims outside the actual action situation, and if, accordingly, a discourse ethics had no other objective than presenting and defending this procedure for assessing normative and evaluative validity claims, then discourse ethics would simply not deal at all with the subject-matter covered by a theory of the genesis of values. No argument against such an understanding of discourse theory and discourse ethics can actually be inferred from the train of thought which I have presented in this book. There would then be no conflict within pragmatist ethics; instead, there would be a division of labour between the discursive justification of validity claims and an ethics based on the perspective of situated action. Jürgen Habermas, however,[35] does not see the task of discourse theory in this way. The way in which he delimits the tasks and possible achievements of discourse ethics is problematic, and the significance of these problems points beyond the questions of the internal structures of theories to competing points of view in the public 'values-discourse'.

Habermas's understanding of the status of discourse theory and discourse ethics has undergone considerable modifications over the years. There can be no doubt that compelling and substantial motives have driven him from the very beginning to emphasize the potential of public communication and symbolically mediated interaction.[36] Such motives lurk behind the theory of communicative action as a whole and discourse ethics in particular. In the early phases, the idea of the discourse was consequently understood as the 'foreshadowing of a way of life',[37] as a variant of a way of life that can today be experienced in communication, but which has yet to be comprehensively realized by social criticism and politics. Because Habermas soon recognized that ways of life cannot as a whole be subordinated to a normative point of view, and that hubris lay in the desire to derive the correct form of societal structures from the structures of rational argumentation, he retreated to a formal-procedural understanding of the status of discourses. Habermas's systematic major work of 1981, *The Theory of Communicative Action*,[38] clearly expresses this shift in his understanding. Yet in the same work, namely, in the thesis of the 'linguistification of the sacred',[39] an idea which picks up from where Durkheim left off, the enormous claim with which he burdens rational argumentation in the discourse becomes apparent once again. Habermas defines the 'linguistification of the sacred' here as 'the transfer of cultural reproduction, social integration, and socialization from sacred foundations over to linguistic communication and action oriented to mutual understanding'.[40] His hypothesis is that

> the socially integrative and expressive functions that were at first fulfilled by ritual practice pass over to communicative action; the authority of the holy is gradually replaced by the authority of an achieved consensus . . . The aura of rapture and terror that emanates from the sacred, the spellbinding power of the holy, is sublimated into the binding/bonding force of criticizable validity claims and at the same time turned into an everyday occurrence.[41]

Though this thesis is developed with reference to Durkheim, it corresponds far less to his notion of the persistence of the sacred in modern society than to Dewey's position, which, in an earlier chapter of this book, I characterized and criticized as a 'sacralization of democracy'.[42]

After *The Theory of Communicative Action*, Habermas extends and modifies discourse ethics and his grounding of it in various ways. A chronological presentation of the development of Habermas's thought is, though, of no relevance to the present context. It is therefore better to describe systematically which problems arise when we reflect on the status of discourse ethics and how Habermas reacts to them. In our context, this can, in most cases, only be hinted at; I shall argue in more detail only that point which gives rise to the momentous difference in the train of thought I have set out here.

I propose distinguishing six problems which emerge from reflection on the status of discourse ethics. The first problem (1) consists in the question, which has already arisen whilst looking back at Habermas's development, as to whether discourses as formal procedures are really completely detachable or not from value-related presuppositions. The other five problems are most clearly arranged according to their place in an imaginary chronology that results from the task of the discourses, no matter how mediated and removed they are from the actual action situation, to assess and to justify proposals for solving problems of action. Thus, the following questions are entailed: where do the candidates for the assessment procedure come from in the first place – how, that is, do validity claims themselves originate? (2); where does the motive to enter into a discourse and to keep to its rules come from? (3); what internal differentiation of the discourse must we assume? (4); how should the results be applied in action? (5); and by what means can discourses themselves develop a binding effect for the participants? (6)

As far as the first problem (1) is concerned, Habermas does not himself put forward new ideas – he has made and stuck by his decision regarding a formal-procedural interpretation of the discourse. New ideas have come, rather, from critics sympathetic to him, who either do not want to travel the whole way with him, or who wish to exploit still further the potential of the perspective he has abandoned. Thus, Richard Bernstein, one of the leading authorities on the work of John Dewey, has held it against Habermas that, in the explanation of the discourse as procedure, he himself constantly refers to virtues, which he then denies.[43] Bernstein, following Dewey, and in opposition to Habermas, stresses the indispensability of a 'democratic ethos' for the success of discourses; he refuses to equate the democratic ethos with the antipluralistic characteristics of classic republicanism. Axel Honneth thinks with the earlier Habermas against the later Habermas, and defends implications of discourse ethics that are rich in material content. These he sees in the aspect of an absence of restrictions on the one hand, and, on the other, in the 'egalitarian freedom to take a moral stance'[44] which refers to conditions of social recognition.[45] Habermas himself is unimpressed by these objections; he remonstrates with Bernstein that he has never called into question cultural pre-requisites for democracy in an empirical sense, but certainly does not 'ultimately place the burden of democratically legitimating law *entirely* on the political virtues of united citizens'.[46] It is exactly this with-drawal of a substantial-ethical interpretation of discourse that leaves him free to consider the significance of the law in modern societies and the realizability of democracy under such conditions.

The question of the origin of validity claims (2) is only of peripheral interest to Habermas. If the separation of genesis and validity is carried out abruptly, then a theory of assessing validity claims must not, indeed, occupy itself with the origin of these validity claims. They remain banished to an irrational realm, from which they are unable to escape until they appear in the examination procedure of the dis-course. Now, I certainly do not want to contest this distinction itself; only its abruptness is dubious. Even in the case of empirical validity claims, the origin of a hypothesis cannot always be clearly separated from the examination of its truth content.[47] Normative validity claims in particular are not made arbitrarily. To open certain norms to discussion is morally impossible, and we can value more highly that person to whom moral actions come naturally than the one who must first be convinced of them.[48] Habermas himself concedes that the separation of genesis and validity becomes more difficult with ques-tions of value;[49] this does not, however, lead him to pursue the question of the genesis of values. If, as he asserts, no substantial conclusions can be drawn from the formal procedure of discourses, however, and if it is only in individual discourses that an argumenta-tion can be developed and a particular consensus reached on the basis of the arising validity claims[50] – then it is precisely in the case of a discourse about values that the connection between genesis and validity, between a self-reflexive explanation of the origin of certain validity claims and an assessment of their legitimacy, becomes unavoidable.

In contrast, Habermas is fully aware of the problem of discursive and moral motivation (3). After *The Theory of Communicative Action* he retracts, in his all too rare reflections on religion, his earlier unconsid-ered assumptions about the development of religion in modernity and the complete replacement of religious conceptions of the world by a universalistic ethics of responsibility.[51] Habermas thereby erases at least the traces of an Enlightenment or Nietzschean dogmatism of 'God is dead' which were also discernible in his work. But he does not go beyond an agnostic declaration of openness, and does not pose the question of the possibilities of a 'postmetaphysical religiosity', or, to put it better, a religiosity under postmetaphysical conditions, as was discussed in this book in connection with William James.[52] His attitude towards the question of moral motivation is thoroughly defensive. In his meditations on Horkheimer's religious thought,[53] as well as in his critical dialogue with Taylor's *Sources of the Self*,[54] he declares that postmetaphysical philosophy is unable to take over the task of moral motivation.

> Even today philosophy can explicate the moral point of view from which we can judge something impartially as just or unjust; to this extent, communicative reason is by no means equally indifferent to morality and immorality. However, it is altogether a different matter to provide a motivating response to the question of why we should follow our moral insights or why we should be moral at all.[55]

The almost utopian and optimistic undertone which once clung to Habermas's thesis of the 'linguistification of the sacred' has now completely vanished. Justification and consensus achieved through argumentation are now credited only with the 'weak force of rational motivation'.[56] As with the question of the citizens' virtue, this stance once again pulls Habermas in the direction of the law, which intervenes when the force of these rational motivations is just too weak. 'This is why, in important sectors of social life, the weak motivating force of morality must be supplemented by coercive positive law.'[57]

Habermas also devotes a great deal of attention to the question of a differentiation of the idea of the discourse according to the various tasks it might have to fulfil (4). While *The Theory of Communicative Action* had distinguished between the validity claims of truth, correctness and truthfulness, and developed on the basis of this a typology of possible argumentation,[58] Habermas later introduces another tripartite division, whose relationship to the second and third type of the older division remains somewhat unclear. Since 1988 he has distinguished between the 'pragmatic', 'ethical' and 'moral' employment of practical reason.[59] This means that a different type of discourse is said to be required according to the type of question.

> *Pragmatic questions* pose themselves from the perspective of an actor seeking suitable means for realizing goals and preferences that are already given ... *Ethical-political questions* pose themselves from the perspective of members who, in the face of important life issues, want to gain clarity about their shared form of life and about the ideals they feel should shape their common life ... In *moral questions*, the teleological point of view from which we handle problems through goal-directed co-operation gives way entirely to the normative point of view from which we examine how we can regulate our common life in the equal interest of all.[60]

This distinction is certainly a perceptive response to an important material problem. From a terminological point of view, however, it is unfortunate, since the separation of the ethical from the moral in this way corresponds neither to the prior use of these concepts in philosophy as a whole, nor even to Habermas's own use of them in his work. Habermas himself recognizes that, with this shift in terminology, he is pulling the rug from underneath his concept of 'discourse ethics'; it would instead, he says, have to be called 'a discourse theory of morality'.[61] Even more important than this terminological question is the issue of content: that is, whether Habermas's differentiation is appropriate to the matter in hand. We shall return to this issue when determining the difference between pragmatist ethics and his understanding of discourse ethics.

Under the influence of Albrecht Wellmer and Klaus Günther, Habermas has taken account of the problem of norm-application (5), that is, of the distinction between the establishment of a norm and the justification of the application of a norm, by extending the types of discourse to include the discourse of application.[62] This is certainly a productive amendment to the original conception. However, the gulf separating a discourse theory oriented to justification and an ethics centred on the solution of action problems only appears to have been narrowed. Certainly, the point of view of a context-sensitive application of universalistic norms and of a consideration of the irreducible distinctiveness of each individual person[63] thereby finds a more appropriate place within the framework of discourse ethics. But, as Habermas clearly recognizes, discourses of application remain, like justificatory discourses, 'a purely cognitive undertaking and as such cannot compensate for the uncoupling of moral judgment from the concrete motives that inform action'.[64] Discourses of application are not the place where 'applications' – new actions – are creatively devised, but where we argue about the justifiability of an application in isolation from the action situation.

Finally, the question as to the binding effect of the results of a discourse (6) develops in parallel to the question of motivation for the discourse. The clearer his recognition of the 'weak force of rational motivation', the more feeble becomes Habermas's faith in the binding force of consensus produced by argumentation. The difference between Dewey and Habermas is instructive at this point. While Dewey attributes to conversation – not rational argumentation as such – the potential of an experience of self-transcendence,[65] from which an affective bond with the interlocutor and the possibility of intercommunication may result as a value, Habermas ruins this possibility for himself through the increasingly ascetic tailoring of conversation to an argumentative discourse. One cannot, at least, have it both ways: if the discourse is only a formal procedure, then it cannot develop an affective binding power. Should it develop one, it is necessary to ascribe to it more than the rational exchange of arguments.

Both completed and uncompleted tasks begin to emerge after this cursory look at the problems involved in Habermas's discourse ethics. There are certainly unanswered questions regarding the origin of validity claims, discursive motivation and the binding effect of consensus. All these questions point to the theme of values. The discourse tests that to which people feel themselves evaluatively drawn. Without value commitment, they cannot feel motivated to participate in the discourse and keep to its rules; and they feel themselves bound to the result of the discourse only when this arises from their value commitment, or when the experience of participation itself produces value commitment. Thus, in all three questions, discourse ethics and the theory of the genesis of values touch upon one another. With Habermas himself, however, there is no fruitful contact, because he distinguishes the discourse types in such a way that this contact is prevented.

The way in which Habermas distinguishes between the ethical and the moral, the good and the right, values and norms, is, in particular, deeply problematic. His explanations in this regard are not always consistent; for such a conceptually astute and self-critical thinker, this is already in itself a sign of festering problems. There are basically three characteristics which Habermas invokes to define his distinction. First of all, norms and values are distinguished from one another by their relationship to the obligatory or teleological aspect of action; secondly, they are distinguished in terms of their prescriptive validity in such a way that norms are said to aim at universality, and values, on the other hand, at particularity. Thirdly, Habermas declares that norms are necessarily concerned with the regulation of interpersonal relationships, as opposed to values, which refer to the *telos* of each individual life and therefore 'by no means call for a complete break with the egocentric perspective'.[66]

If one examines these three definitions, one recognizes that the first does indeed correspond to the usual distinction between the good and the right, or the distinction between norms and values which has been current since Durkheim and which also forms the basis of this book.[67] The other two dimensions, however, are a different story entirely. The assertion that ethics contains only maxims that formulate what is good 'for me' or 'for us', whilst it is morality which aims at what is good for all, is wrong. Habermas falls victim to the linguistic ambiguity of the expression 'for me' or 'for us'. Ethics does not describe what is good 'for me' in the sense of my own happiness, but what is good 'for me' in the sense of my honest understanding of the good, of my being captivated by values. The only thing these two meanings have in common is their sound. In the one case, I myself am, or my happiness and well-being are, the standard of my judgement; in the other, I am only aware of the fact that in making a judgement I am the one who judges – the standard, however, lies outside myself. To claim that all ethics are only ever concerned with the happiness of the members of a particular culture or religious denomination is – as Richard Bernstein has written with uncharacteristic causticity[68] – 'a violently distortive fiction'. It does an injustice to all universalistic ethical traditions (like the Christian one), and even to that fund of ideals of justice and value conceptions regarding conduct towards strangers that is present in every cultural ethos. The same goes for the third dimension of the distinction. It is simply inaccurate to say that ethics is not essentially directed at the formation of interpersonal and social relations, and that universalistic ethics does not motivate us to break with egocentric perspectives.

I argue, therefore, that Habermas, in the development of his discourse ethics, and particularly where he is concerned with the question of the primacy of the right or the good, confuses the distinction between obligations and teleology with that between universalism and particularism, as well as that between egocentricity and altruism. These distinctions are definitely not different dimensions of one and the same distinction; they are different distinctions which are to a large extent variable in their relationship with one another. A universalistic value system is logically possible and empirically real. Moreover, none of these three distinctions coincides with that between an ethics centred on argumentation and justification, and an ethics based on the perspective of action. This fourth distinction, which is essential for understanding pragmatist ethics, must also be taken into consideration. Both values *and* norms must arise in an ethics based on the perspective of the actor; as was described, the universalization potential of the normative interacts with the contingent values and produces different ways for the motivating value systems to approach the potential universality of the norms.

If this thought is correct, then a whole sequence of theoretical and empirical conclusions which Habermas draws from his understanding of the status of discourse ethics proves to be invalid. His fear that justice would no longer be available 'as a context-independent standard of impartial judgment,'[69] if it should appear only as one value amongst others, is then unfounded. According to the argument I am putting forward here, the standard of justice can only ever present itself as one point of view amongst others from the perspective of the

actors; this point of view is, however, precisely because of its reference to the anthropological-universal problem of the co-ordination of
action, unavoidable for all social action. While Habermas assumes
that the distinction between norms and values would be invalidated
if universal validity is claimed for the highest values or goods, which
has become untenable under postmetaphysical conditions,[70] the argument I have advanced here asserts that the distinction between the
restrictive-obligatory and the attractive-motivating is not invalidated
under any conceivable conditions. At the same time, however, the
universal validity claim of values is held to be formulable even under
postmetaphysical conditions.[71] – Habermas also relates his distinction
between the three different ways of employing practical reason
to three great moral-philosophical traditions.[72] Seen in this way,
the utilitarian tradition corresponds to the pragmatic; the Kantian-
deontological tradition to the moral; and the Aristotelian tradition
to the ethical employment of practical reason. But this also has a
strategic purpose for Habermas. It serves, namely, to burden all
modern attempts to defend the primacy of the good over the right, or
merely to contest the primacy of the right over the good, with
Aristotle's metaphysical assumptions and thereby to declare them
obsolete from the very outset under the conditions of postmetaphysical thought. Now, it is certainly true that there exists a contemporary
neo-Aristotelianism, for which the reconstruction of the critical potential of a morality aiming at universality is anathema. But Habermas
also speaks of neo-Aristotelianism where the association with Aristotle's metaphysical presuppositions is explicitly contested, and new
syntheses with the deontological tradition are being attempted.[73] What
is even more astonishing, however, is that Habermas omits pragmatist
ethics from his entire account. If he had included it, then it would
have become clear that a synthesis with the Aristotelian and Kantian
tradition is just as possible from the starting-point of the pragmatic
employment of practical reason as it is from that of the discourse, i.e.
of an intersubjective continuation of Kantianism. Because pragmatist
ethics is based on the creativity of action, it relativizes the role of the
discourse, seeing its function as the justification of validity claims. But
it is for this very reason that it is able to do greater justice to the
dynamics of human action than a theory which, with its exclusive
concentration on discursive justification, mistakes the reality of
action.[74]

What follows in an empirical regard from Habermas's theory is a
profound scepticism *vis-à-vis* every contribution made by concrete
value traditions and particular commitments to the social integration
of modern societies. A universalistic morality, and, where this is too

weak, modern law, are for him the royal road to the integration of modern societies. Modern law is supposed to be particularly suitable for the social integration of economic societies because these 'rely on the decentralised decisions of self-interested individuals in morally neutralised spheres of action'.[75] But, Habermas continues, the law must also 'satisfy the precarious conditions of a social integration that ultimately takes place through the achievements of mutual under-standing on the part of communicatively acting subjects'.[76] This pro-cess is made possible by a legal framework which safeguards freedom of action and which derives its own legitimacy from a legislative procedure that for its part stands under the principle of the sover-eignty of the people, so that – according to this ingenious train of thought – legitimacy itself originates in the citizen's rights to freedom. To construe the arguments put forward here as contradicting this conception would be to misunderstand them once again. Our objec-tions arise only when Habermas overruns his evidence and asserts not only the possibility that legitimacy originates in this way, but declares this possibility to be the only acceptable one. This point is reached when he claims that a moral community constitutes itself '*solely* by way of the negative idea of abolishing discrimination and harm and of extending relations of mutual recognition to include marginalized men and women'.[77] There is no doubt that a community can constitute itself in this way; but we must dispute the claim that only a community constituted in this way deserves the predicate 'moral'!

But Habermas is quite ambiguous in this respect. It is possible to deduce from his work another, metaphorical, way of speaking, which seems to me to be more appropriate; Habermas says that morality and the law are *safety nets* 'for the integrative performances of all other institutional orders'.[78] However, we fall back on 'safety nets' only in the case of an emergency; we try to prevent recourse to them. What is therefore attractive about this metaphor is that it reveals how little morality and the law should stand at the forefront of social action. Admittedly, any reliance on integration through community and value commitments would be unacceptable today; nor can such commitment persist without constant correction against the universal-ization potential of the normative. But just as we require the pro-cedural rationality of the law, so must those values themselves be reproduced which can protect us from the wrong use of 'safety nets'. The reproduction of these values cannot rely solely on the weak motivation of the rational consensus and the legitimating effects of civic freedoms. The powers of social solidarity can also regenerate themselves today – but, *contra* Habermas, not only – 'in the forms of communicative practices of self-determination'.[79] It would be an anti-traditionalist affect if one denied this capacity to any traditional commitment to particular values and communities.

The goal of these observations comparing pragmatist ethics and the discourse theory of morality, the law and the democratic constitutional state, would be realized if an unnecessary polarization between the justification of actions and institutions from universalistic points of view on the one hand, and, on the other, the attempts to clarify the conditions for the genesis and transmission of democratic values, could thereby be prevented.[80] This kind of false polarization resides in the controversies about liberalism and communitarianism.[81] Truly, the aim cannot be to oppose undialectically the universalism of the liberal tradition with a mere particularism, the centring on the value of justice with the emphasis of particular commitments, and the orientation to morality and law with the invocation of values and community. The communitarian critique of liberalism only has a chance if it can demonstrate that it represents the more reasonable version of universalism, that it exhibits the more appropriate appreciation of the place of justice in action, and offers a more balanced criticism of 'rights talk'[82] *and* 'values talk'. What we are seeking here is not the polarization of the controversy and not merely its wearying, but the integration of both viewpoints. In reality, liberals and communitarians share the same problem: what degree of respect must the individual accord the social order from which he expects a guarantee of his individual rights?[83]

In political terms, this question removes the 'commandment of silence' (Martin Seel) which individual currents of liberalism impose upon the question of values. Accordingly, a space for the conversation about values in society opens up once again here, and this space must not be allowed either to be reduced to moral or legal argumentation, or to deteriorate into conflict and the distribution struggle among fixed identities.[84] In ethical terms, only the inclusion of the dimension of values suggested by this question averts the ever present threat of the reduction of justice to mere utilitarian reciprocity.[85] And, in sociological-empirical terms, this question refers us to the particular conditions under which the values, which are presupposed for the continuity of the democratic polity, originate and can be maintained.[86] Ultimately, the thoughts presented here on the genesis of values must prove themselves in all three areas.

Notes

Chapter 1 Formulating the Question

1 Cf. Ronald Inglehart, *The Silent Revolution. Changing Values and Political Styles among Western Publics* (Princeton, 1977); idem, *Cultural Change* (Princeton, 1989).
2 Paul Leinberger and Bruce Tucker, *The New Individualists. The Generation after the Organization Man* (New York, 1991); William H. Whyte Jr., *The Organization Man* (Harmondsworth, 1963).
3 See e.g. Helmut Thome, *Wertewandel in der Politik? Eine Auseinandersetzung mit Ingleharts Thesen zum Postmaterialismus* (Berlin, 1985); see also Hans Joas, *The Creativity of Action* (Cambridge, 1996), pp. 252ff.
4 For a more detailed discussion, see Hans Joas, 'Handlungstheorie und Gewaltdynamik', in Wolfgang Vogt (ed.), *Gewalt und Konfliktbearbeitung* (Baden-Baden, 1997), pp. 67–74.
5 Ulrich Wickert, *Der Ehrliche ist der Dumme. Über den Verlust der Werte* (Hamburg, 1994); Ben Wattenberg, *Values Matter Most: How Republicans or Democrats or a Third Party Can Win and Renew the American Way of Life* (New York, 1995); André Comte-Sponville, *Petit Traité des grandes vertus* (Paris, 1995).
6 Amitai Etzioni (ed.), *The Essential Communitarian Reader* (Lanham, Md., 1998).
7 Wickert, *Der Ehrliche ist der Dumme*, p. 40.
8 For a beautiful discussion of this point, see Harry Frankfurt, 'The Importance of What We Care About', *Synthese*, 53 (1982), pp. 257–72.
9 The most sophisticated discussion can be found in David Lockwood's *Solidarity and Schism. The Problem of Disorder in Durkheimian and Marxist Sociology* (Oxford, 1992).
10 For more detail see Joas, *The Creativity of Action*, pp. 209ff.
11 Cf. Judith Squires (ed.), *Principled Positions. Postmodernism and the Rediscovery of Values* (London, 1993).

12 Jean-François Lyotard, *The Postmodern Condition. A Report on Knowledge* (Manchester, 1984).

13 Zygmunt Bauman, *Postmodern Ethics* (Oxford, 1993).

14 Robert Bellah et al., *Habits of the Heart: Individualism and Commitment in American Life* (Berkeley/London, 1985), p. 7.

15 Thus, against Alasdair MacIntyre's assumptions (cf. idem, *After Virtue: A Study in Moral Theory* (London, 1981)) and for those of Charles Taylor (cf. idem, *Sources of the Self: The Making of the Modern Identity* (Cambridge, 1989)). Cf. also Jerome Schneewind's remarks in his review of Taylor in *Journal of Philosophy*, 88 (1991), pp. 422–6, esp. pp. 424ff.

16 Cf. Jeffrey Alexander, 'Theorizing the Good Society: Ethical, Normative and Empirical Discourses', Ms. (Los Angeles, 1996).

17 James S. Coleman, *Foundations of Social Theory* (Cambridge, Mass., 1990). The following quotations are from pp. 249, 251 and 273.

18 Michael Hechter, 'The Role of Values in Rational-Choice Theory', *Rationality and Society*, 6 (1994), pp. 318–33; idem, 'Values Research in the Social and Behavioural Sciences', in Michael Hechter, Lynn Nadel and Richard E. Michod (eds), *The Origin of Values* (New York, 1993), pp. 1–28. Another version of neo-utilitarian thought, the so-called 'exchange theory', has also acknowledged this problem. See Karen S. Cook et al., 'Exchange Theory: A Blueprint for Structure and Process', in George Ritzer (ed.), *Frontiers of Social Theory. The New Syntheses* (New York, 1990), pp. 158–84, here pp. 169ff.

19 Edna Ullmann-Margalit's *The Emergence of Norms* (Oxford, 1977) is an almost classic example of this. For a discussion of this topic and the critique of corresponding approaches, see the excellent remarks by Jens Beckert in his *Grenzen des Marktes. Die sozialen Grundlagen wirtschaftlicher Effizienz* (Frankfurt am Main, 1997), pp. 45ff.

20 Hechter, Values Research, pp. 3, 13, 15.

21 This is already the case in the early essay 'The Place of Ultimate Values in Sociological Theory', *International Journal of Ethics*, 45 (1935), pp. 282–316. Of central importance is of course his main work *The Structure of Social Action* (New York, 1937). From the late work I refer the reader only to Talcott Parsons, 'On the Concept of Value-Commitments', in idem, *Politics and Social Structure* (New York, 1969), pp. 439–72. Harald Wenzel has written an excellent study tracing the development of Parsons's work: *Die Ordnung des Handelns. Talcott Parsons' Theorie des allgemeinen Handlungssystems* (Frankfurt am Main, 1991).

22 An important work here is: Clyde Kluckhohn et al., 'Values and Value-Orientations in the Theory of Action. An Exploration in Definition and Classification', in Talcott Parsons and Edward Shils (eds), *Toward a General Theory of Action* (New York, 1951), pp. 388–433. The quotation is from p. 396.

23 The expression used by the former Parsons student and critic Harold Garfinkel was 'cultural dopes'. Cf. idem, *Studies in Ethnomethodology* (Englewood Cliffs, NJ, 1967), p. 66. This critique became the starting-point for ethnomethodology, which was for a long time an extremely fruitful

branch of research. This serves as a point of departure for other critics, e.g. Ann Swidler, 'Culture in Action', *American Sociological Review*, 51 (1986), pp. 273–86.

24 From within the Parsons tradition, Jeffrey Alexander in particular has, in a number of writings, worked towards an opening in this direction. See e.g. Jeffrey Alexander and Philip Smith, 'The Discourse of American Civil Society: A New Proposal for Cultural Studies', *Theory and Society*, 22 (1993), pp. 151–208.

25 Robert Bellah thus speaks neither of 'values' nor of 'culture', but rather of 'traditions' and 'practices'. Cf. idem, 'The Idea of Practices in 'Habits'. A Response', in Charles H. Reynolds and Ralph V. Norman (eds), *Community in America. The Challenge of 'Habits of the Heart'* (Berkeley, 1988), pp. 269–88.

26 This objection was first raised by Alain Touraine. In the beginning it was intimately bound up with a version of the first objection, which is directed at the problem of the situation-specific application of values. Touraine's starting-point was the experience which he gained from his sociological research in industry and organizations: that decisions cannot as a rule be interpreted as merely applications of general principles to certain situations, but are rather the result of transactions between actors with heterogeneous interests and divergent power potentials. Cf. Alain Touraine, *Production de la société* (Paris, 1964), esp. pp. 92ff. While Touraine was initially in danger of regarding culture as a mere resource in power struggles, he increasingly moves away from this viewpoint in his later works and understands culture as intrinsically diverse and conflictual. The concept 'value' constantly seems to him to be only moderately helpful for his understanding of culture. Even if we were to replace this concept with others (for example with 'cultural orientations'), the problem of genesis still remains. Of all Parsons's successors, Shmuel Eisenstadt has placed the most emphasis on the problem of the genesis of values as a subject for research. His background in Martin Buber's philosophy of creativity provided him with the vantage point from which he could perceive shortcomings in Parsons's work. Cf. Shmuel Eisenstadt, 'Social Structure, Culture, Agency, and Change', in idem, *Power, Trust, and Meaning. Essays in Sociological Theory and Analysis* (Chicago, 1985), pp. 1–40. Amitai Etzioni's *The Active Society* (New York, 1968) also represents an interesting point of departure. In this work Etzioni not only has a broader concept of culture than Parsons, in that he devotes more attention to the dimension of societal knowledge; he is also more interested in the ways in which social systems embody values and in the problems arising from the implementation of democratic values. But he, too, would rather leave open the question of the genesis of values than answer it. See Hans Joas, 'Economic Action, Social Action, and the Genesis of Values. An Essay on Amitai Etzioni's Contribution to Social Theory', in David Sciulli (ed.), *Macro Socio-Economics. From Theory to Activism* (London/Armonk, NY, 1996), pp. 35–50; Edward Lehman, 'The Cultural Dimension of the "Active Society"', unpub. Ms. (New York University, 1995).

27 For an attempt at such a synthesis, see Joas, *The Creativity of Action*.

Chapter 2   *The Genesis of Values as Genealogy of Morality?*
(Friedrich Nietzsche)

1 I base my claims on the following works in particular: Jürgen Gebhardt, 'Die Werte. Zum Ursprung eines Schlüsselbegriffs der politisch-sozialen Sprache der Gegenwart in der deutschen Philosophie des späten 19. Jahrhunderts', in Rupert Hoffmann, Jörg Jantzen and Henning Ottmann (eds), *Anodos. Festschrift für Helmut Kuhn* (Weinheim, 1989), pp. 35–54; Helmut Kuhn, 'Werte – eine Urgegebenheit', in Hans-Georg Gadamer and Paul Vogler (eds), *Neue Anthropologie*, vol. 7 (Stuttgart, 1975), pp. 343–73. See also the excellent philosophical-historical survey by Herbert Schnädelbach, with whose conclusions and outlook, however, I do not agree: *Philosophy in Germany 1831–1933* (Cambridge, 1984), pp. 161–91. For the history of the concept in the United States, see Abraham Edel, 'The Concept of Value and its Travels in Twentieth-Century America', in Murray G. Murphey and Ivar Berg (eds), *Values and Value Theory in Twentieth-Century America. Essays in Honour of Elizabeth Flower* (Philadelphia, 1988), pp. 12–36.
2 Hans-Georg Gadamer has drawn attention to this use of the concept in 'Das ontologische Problem des Wertes', in *Kleine Schriften IV* (Tübingen, 1977), pp. 205–17, here p. 207.
3 Gebhardt, 'Die Werte', p. 48.
4 See e.g. (from the standpoint of a pronounced Catholic scepticism of modernity) Kuhn, 'Werte – eine Urgegebenheit', p. 354.
5 Friedrich Nietzsche, *On the Genealogy of Morality* (Cambridge, 1994), p. 4.
6 Ibid.
7 Ibid., p. 5.
8 Friedrich Nietzsche, *Ecce Homo* (Harmondsworth, 1979), p. 114. I do *not* regard the utilitarians and evolutionists as precursors of a conception of the genesis of values, and for this reason omit a more detailed discussion of them here.
9 Nietzsche, *Genealogy*, p. 7.
10 Ibid., pp. 7–8.
11 Ibid.
12 Friedrich Nietzsche, *Twilight of the Idols and the Antichrist* (Harmondsworth, 1968), p. 187.
13 *Genealogy*, p. 12.
14 Ibid., p. 14.
15 Ibid., p. 18.
16 Ibid., pp. 18–19.
17 Ibid., p. 35.
18 Ferdinand Tönnies, *Der Nietzsche-Kultus. Eine Kritik* (Leipzig, 1897), p. 102.
19 Max Scheler, *Ressentiment* (New York, 1961), p. 43.
20 Ibid., p. 86.
21 Ibid., p. 87.
22 In an early essay, Maurice Merleau-Ponty picks up from where Scheler

leaves off and turns the *ressentiment*-argument back against Nietzsche himself, tracing his misinterpretation of Christianity back to his own feelings of *ressentiment*. Cf. idem, 'Christianisme et ressentiment', *La vie intellectuelle*, 36 (1935), pp. 278–306, esp. p. 292.

23 Scheler, *Ressentiment*, p. 98.

24 Max Weber, *Gesammelte Aufsätze zur Religionssoziologie*, 3 vols (Tübingen, 1920). For an English translation of this introduction, cf. 'The Social Psychology of the World Religions', in *From Max Weber* (London, 1947), pp. 267–301, here pp. 270ff.

25 Ibid., p. 270.

26 This point is energetically developed by Wolfgang Schluchter in *Rationalism, Religion and Domination* (Berkeley/Oxford, 1989).

27 Max Weber, *Economy and Society*, 3 vols (New York, 1968), vol. 2, pp. 494ff.

28 Weber, 'The Social Psychology of the World Religions', p. 271.

29 Ibid.

30 Ibid., p. 272. Admittedly, Nietzsche also acknowledges a positive evaluation of suffering in those cases where it is ennobling and springs from the individual's readiness to embrace danger.

31 Ibid., p. 273.

32 Ibid.

33 Cf. Max Weber, *Ancient Judaism* (Glencoe, Ill., 1952).

34 I speak here of enmity towards Jews and not of anti-Semitism, since Nietzsche was obviously not a racist anti-Semite, although his hatred of Christianity also drove him to assume a hostile attitude towards Jewish religious history. Even so, Nietzsche's work is by no means altogether free from racist tones.

35 Nietzsche, *Genealogy*, p. 29.

36 Ibid., p. 13.

37 Johann Gottfried Herder, *Abhandlung über den Ursprung der Sprache* (1772), in *Werke*, vol. 2 (Berlin/Weimar, 1982), pp. 89–200. See also my exposition in Joas, *The Creativity of Action*, pp. 75–85.

38 Alexander Nehamas's *Nietzsche. Life as Literature* (Cambridge, Mass., 1985) is wholly positive, as is Walter Kaufmann's *Nietzsche. Philosopher. Psychologist. Antichrist* (Princeton, 1950). A more complex and balanced work is Bernard Yack's *The Longing for Total Revolution. Philosophic Sources of Social Discontent from Rousseau to Marx and Nietzsche* (Princeton, 1986), pp. 310–64. Brief and succinct are: Martin Seel, *Versuch über die Form des Glücks. Studien zur Ethik* (Frankfurt am Main, 1995), pp. 27–33; Mirko Wischke, 'Der "Kampf der Moral mit den Grundinstinkten des Lebens". Über die Ambivalenz im Perspektivismus Friedrich Nietzsches', *Synthesis Philosophica*, 21 (1996), pp. 39–48; Robert J. Antonio, 'Nietzsche's Antisociology: Subjectified Culture and the End of History', *American Journal of Sociology*, 101 (1995), pp. 1–43. The following works by Volker Gerhardt are extremely significant: 'Die Moral des Immoralismus. Nietzsches Beitrag zu einer Grundlegung der Ethik', in Günther Abel and Jörg Salaquarda (eds), *Krisis der Metaphysik* (Berlin/New York, 1989), pp. 411–47; idem, 'Selbstbegründung. Nietzsches Moral der Individualität', *Nietzsche-Studien*,

21 (1992), pp. 28–49; idem, 'Die Tugend des freien Geistes. Nietzsche auf dem Weg zum individuellen Gesetz der Moral', in Simone Dietz et al. (eds), *Sich im Denken orientieren. Für Herbert Schnädelbach* (Frankfurt am Main, 1996), pp. 198–213. Georg Simmel argued along similar lines at an early date in *Schopenhauer and Nietzsche* (1907) (Amherst, Mass., 1986).

39 Gerhardt, 'Die Tugend des freien Geistes', p. 203.

40 Hans Joas, 'Kriegsideologien. Der Erste Weltkrieg im Spiegel der zeitgenössischen Sozialwissenschaften', *Leviathan*, 23 (1995), pp. 336–50.

41 Eerily even today. Cf. Botho Strauß, 'Anschwellender Bocksgesang', in Heimo Schwilk and Ulrich Schacht (eds), *Die selbstbewußte Nation* (Berlin, 1994), pp. 19–40.

42 Cf. the literature cited in n. 38, esp. Yack and Seel.

43 Nietzsche, *Twilight of the Idols*, pp. 47–8.

44 Scheler, *Ressentiment*, p. 107.

45 See Joas, *The Creativity of Action*, pp. 124ff.

46 Thus runs Heidegger's critique in 'The Word of Nietzsche "God is Dead"', in idem, *The Question Concerning Technology and Other Essays* (New York, 1977), pp. 53–112.

Chapter 3   *The Varieties of Religious Experience*
(William James)

1 I have demonstrated this in more detail in the chapter entitled 'American Pragmatism and German Thought: A History of Misunderstandings', in my *Pragmatism and Social Theory* (Chicago/London, 1993), pp. 94–121. In this essay the reader will also find the evidence which I adduce to support my argument and which I shall mostly not repeat here.

2 As Werner Bloch claims in 'Der Pragmatismus von Schiller und James', *Zeitschrift für Philosophie und philosophische Kritik*, 152 (1913), pp. 1–41 and 145–214.

3 Simmel's spoken remark was reported by Rudolf Pannwitz in Kurt Gassen and Michael Landmann (eds), *Buch des Dankes an Georg Simmel* (Berlin, 1958), p. 240. Two other contemporary works which deal with the relationship between pragmatism and Nietzsche are worth mentioning: Richard Müller-Freienfels, 'Nietzsche und der Pragmatismus', *Archiv für Geschichte der Philosophie*, 26 (1913), pp. 339–58 and Werner Eggenschwyler, 'War Nietzsche Pragmatist?', ibid., pp. 37–47.

4 To be fair, William James and his American contemporaries are not free from distorting cultural stereotypes either – about German thought, for instance. James himself often made condescending remarks about key figures in German intellectual history, remarks which are characterized by national prejudices. Moreover, his complete ignorance of key figures in modern European religious thought (from Feuerbach to Kierkegaard) corresponded to the European ignorance of many American contributions. His remarks on Schopenhauer may be tolerated as superficial, but witty ('As for Schopenhauer himself, personally, his loud-mouthed pessimism

was that of a dog who would rather see the world ten times worse than it is, than lose his chance of barking at it, and whom nothing would have unsuited so completely as the removal of his cause of complaint' (Ralph Barton Perry, *The Thought and Character of William James*, vol. 1 (Boston, Mass., 1935), p. 724)). His remarks on Nietzsche, in contrast, are mostly completely incompetent. In the *Varieties*, James makes one direct reference to Nietzsche's *On the Genealogy of Morality*, without, however, properly discussing it. His opinion is ambiguous. On the one hand, he thinks that 'poor Nietzsche's antipathy' towards the weak was itself pathological; on the other hand, though, he seems to trace this antipathy back to Nietzsche's character in the following way: 'The carnivorous-minded "strong man", the adult male and cannibal, can see nothing but mouldiness and morbidness in the saint's gentleness and self-severity, and regards him with pure loathing' (William James, *The Varieties of Religious Experience* (1902) (Cambridge, Mass., 1985), p. 297).

5 In contrast, a succession of the most important German thinkers of the early twentieth century was deeply influenced by this book in a way which merits further investigation. Ernst Troeltsch was particularly important for the reception of James's work in Germany. Cf. his review in *Deutsche Literaturzeitung*, vol. 25, no. 2 (1904), pp. 3021–7; and, from a later date: idem, 'Empirismus und Platonismus in der Religionsphilosophie. Zur Erinnerung an William James', in idem, *Gesammelte Schriften*, vol. 2 (Tübingen, 1913), pp. 364–85. Max Weber studied this work, possibly through Troeltsch's mediation. Cf. Wilhelm Hennis, 'The Spiritualist Foundations of Max Weber's "Interpretive Sociology": Weber, Troeltsch and William James's "Varieties of Religious Experience"', in *History of Human Sciences*, vol. II, no. 2 (1998), pp. 83–101. I shall not discuss here James's significance for Heidegger, Wittgenstein, Scheler and Simmel.

6 From the very extensive biographical literature on James, I shall mention only the brilliant book by George Cotkin, *William James, Public Philosopher* (Urbana, Ill., 1994). Henry Samuel Levinson's *The Religious Investigations of William James* (Chapel Hill, NC, 1981) is still unsurpassed and indispensable for the interpretation and genesis of his theory of religion. Cf. also Bennett Ramsey, *Submitting to Freedom* (New York, 1993); and, finally, Ellen Kappy Suckiel, *Heaven's Champion. William James's Philosophy of Religion* (Notre Dame, Ind., 1996). James's modernity is clearly recognized by Martin Marty, *Modern American Religion*, vol. 1, *The Irony of It All, 1893–1919* (Chicago, 1986), pp. 63ff. A selection of important texts on James's theory of religion and a detailed annotated bibliography can be found in Donald Capps and Janet Jacobs (eds), *The Struggle for Life. A Companion to William James's 'The Varieties of Religious Experience'*, Society for the Scientific Study of Religion, Monograph Series, 9 (n.p., 1995).

7 Charles Bernard Renouvier, *Essais de critique générale* (Paris, 1875). The epigraph of the present book also comes from this work, quoted from the 1912 edition, *Deuxième essai*, vol. 1, p. 366: 'A proprement parler, il n'y a pas de certitude; il y a seulement des hommes certains.' It was quoted

approvingly by James in 'Bain and Renouvier' (1876), in idem, *Essays, Comments and Reviews* (Cambridge, Mass., 1987), pp. 321–6, here p. 325. In recent biographical literature on James, the importance of Renouvier's ideas has been somewhat relativized. See Louis Menand, 'W. James and the Case of the Epileptic Patient', *New York Review of Books*, 17 December 1998, pp. 81–93.

8 William James, diary entry from 1870, quoted in Henry James (ed.), *The Letters of William James*, 2 vols (Boston, Mass., 1920), here vol. 1, p. 147.

9 Ibid., p. 148.

10 The significance of a non-deterministic philosophy of science for James is exhaustively demonstrated in Paul Jerome Croce's book *Science and Religion in the Era of William James. Eclipse of Certainty, 1820–1880* (Chapel Hill, NC, 1995).

11 Cf. William James, *The Principles of Psychology* (1890) (Cambridge, Mass., 1981); idem, *A Pluralistic Universe* (1909) (Cambridge, Mass., 1977). My interpretation owes much to Eduard Baumgarten's *Die geistigen Grundlagen des amerikanischen Gemeinwesens*, 2 vols (Frankfurt am Main, 1936 and 1938), vol. 2, pp. 99–211. On situating James within the context of pragmatism as a whole, see also Joas, *The Creativity of Action*, pp. 135ff.

12 Nietzsche, *Twilight of the Idols*, p. 53.

13 Ibid.

14 Cf. William James, 'The Will', in idem, *Talks to Teachers on Psychology and to Students on Some of Life's Ideals* (Cambridge, Mass., 1983), pp. 101–14.

15 Nietzsche, *Twilight of the Idols*, pp. 69–70.

16 William James, 'The Will to Believe' (1897), in idem, *The Will to Believe and Other Essays in Popular Philosophy* (Cambridge, Mass., 1979), pp. 13–33.

17 This misunderstanding seems to be particularly persistent in Germany. It crops up in Peter Sloterdijk's introduction to the new German edition of James's book on religion ('Chancen im Ungeheuren. Notiz zum Gestalt-wandel des Religiösen in der modernen Welt im Anschluß an einige Motive bei William James', in William James, *Die Vielfalt der religiösen Erfahrung* (Frankfurt am Main, 1997), pp. 11–34). He attributes to pragma-tism 'a somewhat naked metaphysics of success in life' (p. 30) and claims, lapsing into the oldest of clichés: 'This is precisely the Americanism in the religious – the combination of an oilman-mentality and the piety of success' (p. 33).

18 This misunderstanding plays an important role in James's reception by the Fascists and the subsequent debates about whether the appropriation of his ideas was justified or not. The argument has its roots in the interview with Benito Mussolini published in the *Sunday Times* of 11 April 1926, where, when asked about his intellectual influences, he mentions James in the same breath as Nietzsche and Sorel. ('The pragmatism of William James was of great use to me in my political career. James taught me that an action should be judged rather by its results than by its doctrinary basis. I learnt of James that faith in action, that ardent will to live and fight, to which Fascism owes a great part of its success.' Quoted in Perry, *The Thought and Character of William James*, vol. 2, p. 575. From the second-

ary literature on this topic see above all John Patrick Diggins, *Mussolini and Fascism. The View from America* (Princeton, 1972), p. 56 and pp. 221f.)

19 Cf. his letter to F. H. Bradley dated 16/6/1904 (quoted in Perry, *The Thought and Character of William James*, vol. 2, p. 488), where he writes: '... my "Will to Believe" – luckless title, which should have been the "Right to Believe"'.

20 Blaise Pascal, *Pensées* (London, 1962), pp. 200–5 (no. 343).

21 James, 'The Will to Believe', p. 16.

22 Ibid., p. 29.

23 Ibid.

24 Ibid., p. 31.

25 William James, 'The Moral Philosopher and the Moral Life' (1897), in idem, *The Will to Believe and Other Essays in Popular Philosophy*, pp. 141–162.

26 Cf. James M. Edie's evaluation in *William James and Phenomenology* (Bloomington, Ind., 1987), pp. 49ff. Edie stresses that James contributed more to a phenomenology of religious experience than the leading phenomenologists, and that the so-called phenomenology of religion, despite its name, by and large does not follow the method of interpreting experience to the same extent that James does.

27 I think it is warranted to see James as having made this innovation, and not to see it already in the discovery of 'religious experience' towards the end of the eighteenth century, initiated above all by Friedrich Schleiermacher. On the one hand, it can be claimed that James, in the second half of the nineteenth century, had to make the same changes in the science of religion that Schleiermacher realized one hundred years before in Protestant theology (cf. Volkhard Krech and Hartmann Tyrell, 'Religionssoziologie um die Jahrhundertwende', in idem (eds), *Religionssoziologie um 1900* (Würzburg, 1995), pp. 11–78, here pp. 35ff). On the other hand, as grandiose as his attempt was to overcome, with Kant, metaphysical justifications of faith, but at the same time, *contra* Kant, to prevent the equation of religion and morality, Schleiermacher ultimately reverts to a 'timeless schematism' in the classification of religious systems. James, though, as will become clear, argues more hermeneutically in this sense. On the connection between Schleiermacher and James, and for a similar critique, see already Wilhelm Dilthey's fragment written as early as 1911, 'Das Problem der Religion', in idem, *Gesammelte Schriften*, vol. 6, (Leipzig/Berlin, 1924), pp. 288–305, esp. pp. 293 and 300.

28 James, *Varieties*, p. 32.

29 Ibid., p. 34.

30 Ibid., p. 39.

31 Ibid., p. 33.

32 Ibid., p. 19.

33 Ibid., p. 387.

34 Ibid., p. 12.

35 Ibid., p. 31.

36 Ibid., p. 41.

37 Ibid., p. 46.

38 Ibid., p. 96.
39 James adopts this expression from James Leuba, 'Studies in the Psychology of Religious Phenomena', *American Journal of Psychology*, 7 (1896),
   pp. 345–7, here p. 345.
40 James, *Varieties*, p. 201.
41 Ibid.
42 Ibid., p. 51.
43 Ibid., p. 66.
44 Ibid., p. 67.
45 Ibid., p. 302.
46 Ibid., p. 321.
47 Ibid., p. 126.
48 Ibid.
49 Ibid., pp. 365f.
50 Ibid., p. 406n.
51 James, *The Principles of Psychology*, vol. 1, p. 301.
52 Here James draws on Edwin Diller Starbuck's *Psychology of Religion* (New
   York, 1899) – that is, on the author whose own collection of documentation
   relating to religious experiences he regularly cites.
53 James, *Varieties*, p. 174.
54 James recognizes that the significance of such individual experiences is
   especially great when – as in most American Christian denominations – a
   marked conviction of sin is accompanied by a lack of confidence in
   institutional (sacramental) absolution of the individual. Catholicism and
   Anglicanism/Episcopalism do not require individual 'rebirth' and collective 'reawakening' to the same extent as these American varieties of
   Christianity (cf. James, *Varieties*, p. 166).
55 See chapter 8 of this book for a more detailed discussion.
56 *Varieties*, p. 143.
57 Ibid., p. 161.
58 Cf. above all his essay 'A Certain Blindness in Human Beings', in idem,
   Talks to Teachers on Psychology and to Students on Some of Life's Ideals,
   pp. 132–49. It is an emphatic plea for respecting cultural difference and
   against imperialistic politics.
59 Cf. the preface to *Varieties*.

Chapter 4   Collective Ecstasy (Émile Durkheim)

1 Émile Durkheim, *The Elementary Forms of Religious Life* (New York, 1995)
  (original title: *Les formes élémentaires de la vie religieuse* (Paris, 1912)).
2 Ibid., p. 3.
3 The best study of Durkheim's early work on religion is Ernest Wallwork,
  'Durkheim's Early Sociology of Religion', *Sociological Analysis*, 46 (1985),
  pp. 201–18. Whereas almost all of the secondary literature on Durkheim
  sees a break between the early and later work (although the precise point
  at which this break was effected has been variously dated), Kurt Meier has

recently cast doubt on this assumption in 'Gibt es einen "Bruch" in Durkheims früher Religionssoziologie?', in Volkhard Krech and Hartmann Tyrell (eds), *Religionssoziologie um 1900* (Würzburg, 1995), pp. 129–57.

4 Cf. Joas, *The Creativity of Action*, pp. 49–65.
5 Mark Cladis has brilliantly demonstrated the modern relevance of Durkheim's 'communitarian liberalism' in his *A Communitarian Defense of Liberalism. Émile Durkheim and Contemporary Social Theory* (Stanford, 1992).
6 Émile Durkheim, *The Division of Labour in Society* (Basingstoke, 1984).
7 Émile Durkheim, *Suicide: A Study in Sociology* (London, 1952).
8 From the extensive secondary literature I refer the reader only to the following material: the corresponding chapters in Steven Lukes's biography, *Émile Durkheim. His Life and Work* (London, 1975); the comprehensive compendium by W. S. F. Pickering, *Durkheim's Sociology of Religion* (London, 1984) – see my discussion of this book in *American Journal of Sociology*, 92 (1986/7), pp. 740–1; Robert Alun Jones's works, which are indispensable from a philological point of view, e.g. idem, 'On Understanding a Sociological Classic', *American Journal of Sociology*, 83 (1977/8), pp. 279–319; idem, 'Robertson Smith, Durkheim and Sacrifice: An Historic Context for "The Elementary Forms of the Religious Life"', *Journal of the History of the Behavioral Sciences*, 17 (1981), pp. 184–205; idem, 'Durkheim, Frazer, and Smith: The Role of Analogies and Exemplars in the Development of Durkheim's Sociology of Religion', *American Journal of Sociology*, 92 (1986/7), pp. 596–627; the works by François-André Isambert which also take into account Durkheim's students, e.g.: idem, 'L'élaboration de la notion de sacré dans l'école durkheimienne', *Archives des sciences sociales des religions*, vol. 21, no. 42 (1976), pp. 35–56, and 'Relire Durkheim' in vol. 35, no. 69 (1990) of the same journal. In Germany, Horst Firsching has made efforts towards locating Durkheim's theories within the context of contemporary political debates. Cf. idem, *Moral und Gesellschaft. Zur Soziologisierung des ethischen Diskurses in der Moderne* (Frankfurt am Main, 1994); idem, 'Die Sakralisierung der Gesellschaft', in Krech and Tyrell (eds), *Religionssoziologie um 1900*, pp. 159–93.
9 Durkheim, *The Elementary Forms*, p. 44.
10 For a more precise analysis of the meaning and problematics of this thesis, see Hans Joas, 'Durkheim and Pragmatism: The Psychology of Consciousness and the Social Constitution of Categories', in idem, *Pragmatism and Social Theory* (Chicago/London, 1993), pp. 55–78.
11 Durkheim, *The Elementary Forms*, p. 33.
12 Ibid., p. 9.
13 Ibid., p. 191.
14 Ibid., p. 202.
15 Ibid., p. 212.
16 Ibid., p. 220.
17 In my account I have replaced this term, which never became current outside specialist sociological circles, with 'collective ecstasy'.
18 Ibid., p. 208.
19 Ibid.

20 Ibid., p. 212.
21 Ibid., p. 213.
22 For a qualification of Durkheim's basic premise about Australian totem-
    ism, see Claude Lévi-Strauss, *Totemism* (London, 1964), as well as the
    literature cited in n. 8.
23 Durkheim, *The Elementary Forms*, pp. 424–5.
24 Ibid., p. 426.
25 In his first major work, Friedrich Nietzsche also develops a concept of
    collective ecstasy; however, he does not, as far as I can see, exploit this
    idea for his genealogy of morality. This is almost certainly due to the fact
    that he starts out with a concept of morality that, in contrast to that of
    Durkheim, is as far removed as possible from the dynamics of ideals. Cf.
    Nietzsche, *The Birth of Tragedy* (New York, 1967).
26 Durkheim, *The Elementary Forms*, p. 420.
27 Ibid., p. 421.
28 Émile Durkheim, *Pragmatism and Sociology* (Cambridge, 1983).
29 See chapter 7 of this book.
30 Émile Durkheim, 'De la définition des phénomènes religieux' (1899), in
    idem, *Journal sociologique* (Paris, 1969), pp. 140–65.
31 Émile Durkheim and Marcel Mauss, *Primitive Classification* (1903) (Chicago,
    1994).
32 Marcel Mauss, review of William James, *Varieties of Religious Experience*, in
    idem, *Oeuvres* (Paris, 1968), vol. 1, pp. 58–65.
33 James, *Varieties*, p. 28.
34 Cf. above all Émile Durkheim, 'The Determination of Moral Facts' and
    'Value Judgments and Judgments of Reality', in idem, *Sociology and Philo-
    sophy* (London, 1952), pp. 35–79 and 80–97 respectively.
35 Durkheim, *Sociology and Philosophy*, p. 36.
36 Ibid.
37 Ibid., p. 45.
38 Ibid., pp. 68ff.
39 Ibid., p. 70.
40 Durkheim also emphasized the twin character of morality in his works on
    moral education, but there referred to it as the simultaneity of discipline
    and motivation in education. Cf. Émile Durkheim, *Essays on Morals and
    Education* (London, 1979); on this see Cladis, *A Communitarian Defense of
    Liberalism*, pp. 185–225.
41 The influence of Albert Mathiez's history of the French Revolution in
    particular has been stressed by Edward Tiryakian in 'Durkheim, Mathiez,
    and the French Revolution. The Political Context of a Sociological Classic',
    Archives européennes de sociologie, 29 (1988), pp. 373–96. Important thinkers
    in the fields of anthropology and sociology have taken up and creatively
    deployed Durkheim's concept of 'collective effervescence'. Cf. Victor
    Turner, *The Ritual Process: Structure and Anti-Structure* (Harmondsworth,
    1974); Roger Caillois, *L'homme et le sacré* (Paris, 1939).
42 Émile Durkheim, 'Individualism and the Intellectuals' (1898), *Political
    Studies*, 42 (1969), pp. 14–30.

43 Léon Brunschvicg· is said to have described the Nazi Party's Nuremberg rallies as religious events in the Durkheimian sense (cf. Steven Lukes, *Émile Durkheim. His Life and Work* (London, 1975), p. 339 n. 71). In letters from the years 1936 and 1939 Marcel Mauss remarked self-critically upon his inability to foresee modern means of mass organization employed in the service of evil. Cf. Svend Ranulf, 'Scholarly Forerunners of Fascism', *Ethics*, 50 (1939), pp. 16–34. On this see also Marcel Fournier, *Marcel Mauss* (Paris, 1994), pp. 683–91.
44 James, *Varieties*, p. 229.
45 Cf. Durkheim, *The Elementary Forms*, p. 420.

Chapter 5 The Immanence of Transcendence (Georg Simmel)

1 On Nietzsche: Georg Simmel, *Schopenhauer and Nietzsche* (1907) (Amherst, Mass., 1986). On pragmatism: idem, 'The Conflict in Modern Culture' (1918), in *Essays on Religion* (New Haven/London, 1997), pp. 20–5 (see also my remarks in: Hans Joas, *Pragmatism and Social Theory* (Chicago, 1993), pp. 101f). On the mutual influence of Durkheim and Simmel, cf. Werner Gephardt, 'Soziologie im Aufbruch. Zur Wechselwirkung von Durkheim, Schäffle, Tönnies und Simmel', *Kölner Zeitschrift für Soziologie und Sozialpsychologie*, 34 (1982), pp. 1–25. On the thesis of Simmel's decisive influence on Durkheim, cf. Simon Deploige, *Le conflit de la morale et de la sociologie* (Paris, 1911); see also Horst Firsching, 'Émile Durkheims Religionssoziologie – Made in Germany?', in Krech and Tyrell (eds), *Religionssoziologie um 1900*, pp. 351–63.
2 Cf. the discussion by Max Frischeisen-Köhler, 'Georg Simmel', *Kant-Studien*, 24 (1920), pp. 1–51 – still well worth reading in many respects. Another interesting periodization, also consisting of three phases (the sociological period; the period of 'inward concentration'; the turn towards metaphysics), was proposed by Hermann Gerson in his little-known but significant dissertation. Cf. idem, 'Die Entwicklung der ethischen Anschauungen bei Georg Simmel', unpublished doctoral dissertation (University of Berlin, 1932).
3 Georg Simmel, *Einleitung in die Moralwissenschaft. Eine Kritik der ethischen Grundbegriffe*, 2 vols (Berlin, 1892–3).
4 Georg Simmel, *Die Religion* (1906/1912), in idem, *Essays on Religion*, pp. 137–214. This volume also contains his scattered works on the sociology of religion. Simmel addresses these questions in other works that are not directly related to the sociology of religion. I omit in my discussion Simmel's debate with the economic theory of value and the question of its psychological foundation. Cf. Georg Simmel, *The Philosophy of Money* (1900) (London, 1978), esp. the first chapter. On this see Joas, *The Creativity of Action*, pp. 42ff.
5 Georg Simmel, *Lebensanschauung* (Munich/Leipzig, 1918 and 1922).
6 The following writers have concerned themselves in the last few years with the interpretation of Simmel's philosophy and sociology of religion:

Horst Müller, *Lebensphilosophie und Religion bei Georg Simmel* (Berlin, 1960); Peter-Otto Ullrich, *Immanente Transcendenz. Georg Simmels Entwurf einer nach-christlichen Religionsphilosophie* (Frankfurt am Main, 1981); Horst Jürgen Helle, 'Einleitung', in Georg Simmel, *Gesammelte Aufsätze zur Religionssoziologie* (Berlin, 1989, pp. 7–35); Volkhard Krech, 'Religion zwischen Soziologie und Philosophie. Entwicklungslinien und Einheit des Religionsverständnisses Georg Simmels', *Simmel-Newsletter*, 2 (1992), pp. 124–38; idem, 'Zwischen Historisierung und Transformation von Religion: Diagnosen zur religiösen Lage um 1900 bei Max Weber, Georg Simmel und Ernst Troeltsch', in Krech and Tyrell (eds), *Religionssoziologie um 1900*, pp. 313–49, esp. pp. 322–7 and *passim* in this book; Hartmann Tyrell's remarks are short and to the point in '"Das Religiöse" in Max Webers Religionssoziologie', *Saeculum*, 43 (1992), pp. 172–230, here pp. 175–8.

7 Georg Simmel, 'A Contribution to the Sociology of Religion', in idem, *Essays on Religion*, pp. 101–20, here p. 102.

8 Ibid., p. 102.

9 Ibid., p. 104.

10 Ibid.

11 In this respect, Jürgen Habermas is doubtless right when he criticizes Simmel accordingly; cf. idem, 'Georg Simmel on Philosophy and Culture: Postscript to a Collection of Essays', *Critical Inquiry*, 22:3 (1995–6), pp. 403–14, here pp. 412–13.

12 This diagnosis can be found scattered throughout Simmel's work, but is at its most concentrated in his *Philosophy of Money*. In what follows I am indebted to the essays by Krech, with whose reading I am broadly in agreement – though with the important qualification that his exclusive focus on the theory of religion leads to different conclusions from those which I draw in this chapter.

13 Georg Simmel, 'On the Salvation of the Soul', in idem, *Essays on Religion*, pp. 29–35, here p. 29.

14 Ibid., p. 29.

15 Ibid., p. 35.

16 Simmel, *Religion*, p. 170.

17 Ibid., p. 186.

18 On the following see Georg Simmel, *Der Krieg und die geistigen Entscheidungen* (Munich, 1917) (a collection of Simmel's speeches and essays from the First World War). In various works in recent years, I have explored how classic sociological thinkers interpreted the war, and I have also discussed Georg Simmel in this context. Cf. Hans Joas, 'Kriegsideologien. Der Erste Weltkrieg im Spiegel der zeitgenössischen Sozialwissenschaften', *Leviathan*, 23 (1995), pp. 336–50. A detailed interpretation of Simmel in particular, which I found suggestive and stimulating, but with whose basic thesis I do not agree, can be found in Michael Reiter's dissertation, 'Opferordnung. Philosophisches Unbehagen in der modernen Kultur und Faszination der Gewalt im Ersten Weltkrieg', unpublished doctoral dissertation (Freie Universität Berlin, 1995) (on Simmel, pp. 169–274).

19 One might find it unjust that I discuss Simmel's war writings and not those of James and Durkheim. Though Durkheim expressed an opinion on the war in two pamphlets, he did not connect it in any way to issues in his theory of religion. Later, Roger Caillois was the first to make such a connection, albeit under completely different circumstances. James did not survive to see the First World War. He was an active campaigner against imperialist wars and in his theories sought a 'moral equivalent of war'. Cf. Joas, 'Kriegsideologien'.

20 Georg Simmel, 'Deutschlands innere Wandlung' (1914), in idem, *Der Krieg*, pp. 20f.

21 Michael Reiter puts this extremely well: 'The willingness to make sacrifices is the subjective sign that an absolute value is recognized; the consummated sacrifice is the objective sign of the absolute validity of a value. Thus is the sacrifice transformed into the practical form of the justification of values' (Reiter, 'Opferordnung', p. 180).

22 Cf. Georg Simmel's letter to Hermann Graf Keyserling, dated 18 May 1918 and published in Georg Simmel, *Das individuelle Gesetz*, ed. by Michael Landmann (Frankfurt am Main, 1968), pp. 244–7, here p. 246.

23 Though, as I must stress once again, every such attempt to trace Simmel's development is highly dangerous. With hindsight, we can appreciate that Simmel recognized the war's tragic character even at the beginning. Much must remain speculative for as long as we lack a philologically thorough study on Simmel's mature work like the one that exists on the early Simmel (cf. Klaus Christian Köhnke, *Der junge Simmel in Theoriebeziehungen und sozialen Bewegungen* (Frankfurt am Main, 1996)).

24 Simmel, *Lebensanschauung*, p. 13.

25 Ibid., p. 19.

26 Ibid., p. 14.

27 Ibid., p. 24.

28 Ibid., p. 37.

29 Ibid., p. 38.

30 In my book *The Creativity of Action*, I have attempted, amongst other things, to break the dominance of the means–end schema over our understanding of human action. I appealed to the late Simmel to support my argument. Cf. *The Creativity of Action*, pp. 148–66.

31 Simmel, *Lebensanschauung*, p. 41.

32 Ibid., p. 49.

33 Ibid., p. 84.

34 Ibid., p. 95.

35 Cf. Georg Simmel, 'The Conflict of Modern Culture', in idem, *Essays on Religion*, pp. 20–5, here p. 21. On this problematic see also Müller, *Lebensphilosophie und Religion bei Georg Simmel*, pp. 137ff.

36 Simmel, *Lebensanschauung*, p. 112.

37 Ibid., pp. 96f.

38 Ibid., p. 109.

39 Ibid., p. 112.

40 Ibid., p. 110.

41 This corrresponds to James's notion of 'self-surrender', so important for his theory of religion.
42 Ibid., p. 141.
43 Ibid., p. 123.
44 Ibid., p. 152.
45 Ibid., p. 191.
46 Simmel's long-standing study of Goethe as an alternative to Kant is crucial for the development of this train of thought. Cf. Simmel, *Kant und Goethe* (Leipzig, 1918).
47 Simmel, *Lebensanschauung*, p. 217.
48 Ibid., p. 230.
49 Ibid., p. 234.
50 Martin Heidegger in his work developed and took up a number of themes from Simmel's late philosophy. Cf. Michael Großheim, *Von Georg Simmel zu Martin Heidegger: Philosophie zwischen Leben und Existenz* (Berlin, 1994); from the older literature see Chr. Ertel, 'Von der Phänomenologie und jüngeren Lebensphilosophie zur Existentialphilosophie M. Heideggers', *Philosophisches Jahrbuch der Görres-Gesellschaft*, 51 (1938), pp. 1–28, esp. pp. 21ff.
51 Heidegger was one of the first to criticize the lack of differentiation in the concept of life, which brings biological and existential problematics too closely together – for him too closely. Cf. idem, *Being and Time* (London, 1962), pp. 494–5 n. vi. Heidegger himself, of course, drew the conclusion that the language of *Lebensphilosophie* had to be replaced by a self-created private language which, though often gripping, is no less metaphorical than the language of *Lebensphilosophie*, often also prevents it from being linked to other intellectual traditions, and seems to express a philosophical will to dominate.
52 Simmel, *Lebensanschauung*, p. 151.

Chapter 6   *The Value-Feeling and its Object* (Max Scheler)

1 The most important work by Scheler in this area, and on which the arguments in this chapter are largely based, is *Formalism in Ethics and Non-Formal Ethics of Value* (Evanston, 1973) (originally: *Der Formalismus in der Ethik und die materiale Wertethik. Neuer Versuch der Grundlegung eines ethischen Personalismus*). It was first published in *Jahrbuch für Philosophie und phänomenologische Forschung* (vol. 1 (1913), Part II, pp. 405–565, and vol. 2 (1916), pp. 21–478), the organ of the phenomenologists and edited by Husserl himself.
2 One of the most prominent exceptions is Alfred Schütz. Cf. the following two essays: 'Max Scheler's Philosophy' and above all the (excellent) 'Max Scheler's Epistemology and Ethics', in idem, *Collected Papers* (The Hague, 1996), vol. 3, pp. 133–44 and pp. 145–78 respectively. In sociology, Scheler has again and again been recognized as a classic figure. Cf. Walter Bühl, 'Max Scheler', in Dirk Käsler (ed.), *Klassiker des soziologischen Denkens*, vol. 2 (Munich, 1978), pp. 178–225; Harold Bershady, 'Introduction', in

Max Scheler, *On Feeling and Knowing and Valuing* (Chicago, 1992), pp. 1–46. The anthology entitled *Max Scheler im Gegenwartsgeschehen der Philosophie* (Berne/Munich, 1975) and edited by Paul Good stands out from the rest of the secondary literature.

3 Cf. the preface to the third edition of *Formalism* (written December 1926), in *Formalism*, pp. xxv–xxvi.

4 Ernst Troeltsch, *Der Historismus und seine Probleme*, in *Gesammelte Schriften*, vol. 3 (Tübingen, 1922), p. 613.

5 Ibid., p. 609. In his book entitled *Kulturkrise und Soziologie um die Jahrhundertwende. Zur Genese der Kultursoziologie in Deutschland* (Frankfurt am Main, 1996), Klaus Lichtblau happily places Scheler within the context which these days is mostly associated with Max Weber, though in my opinion he brings him too close to Nietzsche.

6 Martin Heidegger, 'Andenken an Max Scheler', in Good (ed.), *Max Scheler im Gegenwartsgeschehen der Philosophie*, p. 9. On the relationship between Heidegger and Scheler, see above all Michael Theunissen, 'Wettersturm und Stille. Über die Weltdeutung Schelers und ihr Verhältnis zum Seinsdenken', in Good (ed.), *Max Scheler im Gegenwartsgeschehen der Philosophie*, pp. 91–110; Patrick Gorevan, 'Heidegger and Scheler. A Dialogue', *Journal of the British Society for Phenomenology*, 24 (1993), pp. 276–82 (further literature cited in that article).

7 In the chapter in *Formalism* entitled 'Value Ethics and Ethics of Imperatives', esp. pp. 220ff.

8 Immanuel Kant, *Critique of Practical Reason*, in idem, *Practical Philosophy* (Cambridge, 1997), pp. 137–271, here p. 207.

9 Scheler, *Formalism*, p. 220.

10 Ibid., p. 221.

11 Ibid., p. 222.

12 Ibid., p. 223.

13 Kant, *Critique of Practical Reason*, p. 207.

14 Scheler, *Formalism*, p. 225.

15 Ibid., p. 226.

16 Cf. chapter 2 of this book, pp. 25–37.

17 Scheler, *Formalism*, p. 231.

18 Ibid.

19 Max Scheler, *Schriften aus dem Nachlaß*, vol. 1, in *Gesammelte Werke*, vol. 10 (Berne, 1957), p. 356.

20 Max Scheler, *Ressentiment* (New York, 1961).

21 Max Scheler, 'Liebe und Erkenntnis', in idem, *Schriften zur Soziologie und Weltanschauungslehre*, in *Gesammelte Werke*, vol. 6 (Berne, 1963), pp. 77–98, here p. 88.

22 Ibid., p. 77.

23 Ibid., p. 89.

24 Ibid., p. 90.

25 Scheler, *Formalism*, Preface to the first edition, p. xviii.

26 Of all the secondary literature, I find Imtiaz Moosa's work the most illuminating on the issue of Scheler's relationship to Kant. Cf. idem,

'Formalism of Kant's A Priori versus Scheler's Material A Priori', *International Studies in Philosophy*, 27 (1995), pp. 33–47; idem, 'A Critical Examination of Scheler's Justification of the Existence of Values', *Journal of Value Inquiry*, 25 (1991), pp. 23–41; idem, 'Are Values Independent Entities? Scheler's Discussion of the Relation between Values and Persons', *Journal of the British Society for Phenomenology*, 24 (1993), pp. 265–75.

27 As is well known, Scheler prepared a thorough, if certainly not adequate, critique of pragmatism, devoting a comprehensive study to it. Cf. Max Scheler, *Erkenntnis und Arbeit. Eine Studie über Wert und Grenzen des pragmatischen Motivs in der Erkenntnis der Welt* (Frankfurt am Main, 1997) (also in Max Scheler, *Gesammelte Werke*, vol. 8 (Berne, 1960), pp. 191–382). On this topic see Hans Joas, *Pragmatism and Social Theory* (Chicago/London, 1993), pp. 103ff; Kenneth Stikkers, 'Introduction', in Max Scheler, *Problems of a Sociology of Knowledge* (London, 1980), pp. 1–30, here pp. 24ff.

28 Scheler, *Formalism*, p. 65.

29 Ibid., p. 66.

30 Ibid., p. 40.

31 I have attempted a detailed 'non-teleological' interpretation of the intentionality of action in Joas, *The Creativity of Action*, pp. 148–66.

32 Ibid., p. 43.

33 Cf. for example Max Scheler, 'Die Stellung des Menschen im Kosmos', in idem, *Späte Schriften, Gesammelte Werke*, vol. 9 (Berne, 1976), pp. 7–71. On this German tradition, cf. Axel Honneth and Hans Joas, *Social Action and Human Nature* (Cambridge, 1988).

34 Cf. the introduction of this book, p. 18.

35 Nicolai Hartmann, *Ethik* (Berlin, 1926), p. vii, quoted in Scheler, *Formalism*, p. xxviii.

36 Scheler, *Formalism*, p. xxviii.

37 Ibid., p. 255.

38 Ibid., p. 259.

39 Ibid., p. 176.

40 Ibid., pp. 100ff.

41 For example, on humility and respect: Max Scheler, 'Zur Rehabilitierung der Tugend', in idem, *Vom Umsturz der Werte*, pp. 13–31; on shame: Max Scheler, 'Über Scham und Schamgefühl', in idem, *Schriften aus dem Nachlaß*, vol. 1, in *Gesammelte Werke*, vol. 10 (Berne, 1957), pp. 65–154; on remorse: Max Scheler, 'Repentance and Rebirth', in idem, *On the Eternal in Man* (London, 1960), pp. 35–65; on sympathy: Max Scheler, *The Nature of Sympathy* (London, 1964); on *ressentiment*: Scheler, *Ressentiment*. Perhaps Bühl's prediction (Bühl, 'Max Scheler', p. 219) that Scheler could well become a classic figure in the sociology of emotions may yet be fulfilled.

42 Max Scheler, 'Problems of Religion', in idem, *On the Eternal in Man*, pp. 107–356, esp. pp. 246ff. Admittedly, Scheler's account cannot match the richness of James's phenomenology of religious experience; his scattered critical remarks on James are mostly misleading. It is interesting to see how Scheler defends a concept of religion restricted to a personal God against the late Simmel. Nevertheless, during the war Scheler was initially

just as immoderate as Simmel in his efforts to justify it, and, like the majority of theologians from both denominations, the Catholic Scheler also joined in the consecration of the war. As doubts begin to register as to whether the experience of war can really bring about the longed-for Christianization of modern society, Scheler declares himself to be 'shocked without precedent that the all-too-greedy Moloch that is the Nation' could also destroy 'this deepest and most root-bound supranational solidarity [i.e. the Catholic Church]'. Having just acclaimed the conflict, in 1916 he drops the word 'war' as a description of the crisis and attributes the increasingly apparent 'devastation of Europe' to capitalism! He reinterprets the meaning of the conflict, seeing it as a 'call for change' with its goal the unity of European culture and Christian socialism. Later he even employs pacifist motifs. Cf. Max Scheler, *Der Genius des Krieges und der deutsche Krieg* (Leipzig, 1915); further works in idem, *Gesammelte Werke*, vol. 4 (Berne, 1982); Iring Fetscher, 'Max Schelers Auffassung von Krieg und Frieden', in Good (ed.), *Max Scheler im Gegenwartsgeschehen der Philosophie*, pp. 241–58; Richard van Dülmen, 'Der deutsche Katholizismus und der Erste Weltkrieg', *Francia*, 2 (1974), pp. 347–76. The first quotation is from a letter from Scheler to Carl Muth, dated 6 September 1915, published in Good (ed.), *Max Scheler im Gegenwartsgeschehen der Philosophie*, p. 46; the second is from Scheler's preface to 'Der Krieg als Gesamterlebnis', in idem, *Gesammelte Werke*, vol. 4, pp. 269f. The following work is very useful for the interpretation of Scheler's theory of religion: Georg Pfleiderer, *Theologie als Wirklichkeitswissenschaft. Studien zum Religionsbegriff bei Georg Wobbermin, Rudolf Otto, Heinrich Scholz und Max Scheler* (Tübingen, 1992), esp. pp. 193–224.

43 Scheler, *Formalism*, p. xxiii.
44 Ibid.
45 Ibid., p. xxix.
46 Ibid., p. xxxi.
47 Ibid., pp. 296f. Scheler distinguishes five main dimensions of the 'relativity of morals': variations in feeling values, in value judgements, in types of unity of institutions, in practical morality, and in mores and customs (cf. pp. 299f). I shall not discuss the application of this typology here.
48 Ibid., p. 370.
49 Cf. chapter 5, pp. 81ff.
50 Scheler, *Formalism*, p. 490. For criticism of Simmel, see pp. 489–94. Scheler knew Simmel's essay 'Das individuelle Gesetz' in the form in which it was published in *Logos*, 4 (1913), pp. 117–60.
51 Scheler, *Formalism*, p. 489.
52 Ibid., p. 490.
53 Ibid., p. 491 n. 122.
54 This is not the place to comment on and discuss in detail what today sounds, in view of the dominance in sociology enjoyed by Weber's theory of Protestantism, a very unfamiliar thesis. On this cf. Lichtblau, *Kulturkrise und Soziologie um die Jahrhundertwende*, pp. 158ff. Scheler also falls back on the *ressentiment*-thesis in works with quite different objectives. Cf. idem,

'Die Ursachen des Deutschenhasses', in *Politisch-pädagogische Schriften*, in *Gesammelte Werke*, vol. 4 (Berne, 1982), pp. 283–372.

55 Scheler, *Formalism*, pp. 572ff. There are further discussions of this concept in the unpublished manuscript 'Vorbilder und Führer' in his *Schriften aus dem Nachlaß*, vol. 1, in *Gesammelte Werke*, vol. 10, pp. 255–344.

56 Scheler, *Formalism*, pp. 578–9.

57 Ibid., p. 580.

58 Ibid., p. 575.

59 Ibid., p. 261.

60 Ibid.

61 Ibid.

62 Ibid., p. 516.

63 In this paragraph, I partly follow Moosa's argument in 'Are Values Independent Entities?' Moosa bases his argument mainly on Scheler, 'Vorbilder und Führer'.

64 Scheler, 'Problems of Religion', p. 315.

65 Scheler, 'Vorbilder und Führer', pp. 278ff.

66 Ibid., p. 280.

67 Scheler himself uses the term 'charismatic'; that is, he employs the concept which has become famous above all through Max Weber's sociology of religion and domination. For a discussion of the achievement and limits of Weber's conception of charisma, cf. Joas, *The Creativity of Action*, pp. 44ff and the literature cited there.

68 Scheler, 'Die Stellung des Menschen im Kosmos', p. 40.

69 Cf. Moosa, 'A Critical Examination'.

70 Scheler, *Problems of Religion*, p. 264; cf. also Pfleiderer, *Theologie als Wirklichkeitswissenschaft*, pp. 220ff. Elsewhere Scheler even believes he is able to undertake a 'sociological proof of God' on the basis of the experience of community. Cf. Max Scheler, 'Christian Love and the Twentieth Century', in *On the Eternal in Man*, pp. 357–402, here p. 376.

71 Scheler, *Problems of Religion*, pp. 291f and pp. 309f.

72 Cf. also Stikkers, 'Introduction', in Scheler, *Problems of a Sociology of Knowledge*.

73 Scheler, *Formalism*, p. 19.

74 Scheler sees Schopenhauer as the originator of this tendency; cf. ibid., p. 212.

75 Ibid., p. 184.

76 Scheler, 'Die Stellung des Menschen im Kosmos', p. 69.

77 This is how Lichtblau concludes his instructive comparison of Max Weber and Max Scheler (*Kulturkrise und Soziologie um die Jahrhundertwende*, p. 492). He nevertheless remains under the spell of Nietzsche's thought – which he reconstructs so excellently – and does not inquire after alternatives. It is also worth mentioning that in his polemic against Scheler, Carl Schmitt completely misses the actual point of his argument. Schmitt's invective was triggered by the relations of the 'non-formal ethics of value' to a jurisprudence striving to distance itself from legal positivism, yet not arguing in terms of natural law. He sympathizes with and refers to Max

Weber's conception that the human individual '*posits* the values in his complete freedom to make decisions' – while Scheler's analyses (like those of James) actually confirm a captivation by values which cannot be posited in a voluntarist manner. For this reason, Schmitt can only understand Scheler's non-formal ethics of value in a Nietzschean sense, as covert desires for self-assertion. 'Whoever says value, wants to assert and enforce. Whoever maintains their validity must assert them. Whoever says that they are valid, without someone asserting them, is lying.' It is astonishing how little the Catholic Schmitt seems to understand of the dimension of religious experience in general and its function in the work of the Catholic Scheler in particular. Cf. Carl Schmitt, 'Die Tyrannei der Werte', in *Säkularisation und Utopie. Ebracher Studien. Ernst Forsthoff zum 65. Geburtstag* (Stuttgart, 1967), pp. 37–62 (quotations from pp. 54 and 55).

Chapter 7   Shattering Intersubjectivity (John Dewey)

1 John Dewey, *A Common Faith* (New Haven, Conn., 1934). On the theory of value: John Dewey, 'Theory of Valuation', in *International Encyclopedia of Unified Science*, vol. II, no. 4 (Chicago, 1939). On ethics: John Dewey and James Tufts, *Ethics* (New York, 1908 and, in revised form, 1932). The quantity and quality of the literature on Dewey have both experienced an enormous upturn in the last few years. Robert Westbrook's *John Dewey and American Democracy* (Ithaca, NY, 1991) will, as a portrait of life and work, remain indispensable for a long time to come; cf. also Alan Ryan, *John Dewey and the High Tide of American Liberalism* (New York, 1995). I should also mention the following works dealing with themes that are particularly relevant to this chapter: (on the theory of religion) Steven Rockefeller, *John Dewey. Religious Faith and Democratic Humanism* (New York, 1991); (on the theory of value) James Gouinlock, *John Dewey's Philosophy of Value* (New York, 1972); (on ethics) Jennifer Welchman, *Dewey's Ethical Thought* (Ithaca, NY, 1995); Axel Honneth, 'Between Proceduralism and Teleology. An Unresolved Conflict in John Dewey's Moral Theory', *Transactions of the Charles Sanders Peirce Society*, 34 (1998), pp. 689–711; (on aesthetics) Thomas Alexander, *John Dewey's Theory of Art, Experience and Nature. The Horizon of Feeling* (Albany, NY, 1987).
2 Cf. Richard Bernstein, *John Dewey* (New York, 1967), pp. 147f.
3 Cf. the corresponding discussions in chapter 3 of this book and also in Hans Joas, *Pragmatism and Social Theory*.
4 As he put it in his reply to his critics: John Dewey, 'Experience, Knowledge, and Value: A Rejoinder', in Paul Arthur Schilpp (ed.), *The Philosophy of John Dewey* (Chicago, 1939), pp. 517–608, here p. 594 (also in *Later Works*, vol. 14 (Carbondale, Ill., 1988, pp. 8–91, here p. 77).
5 Dewey, 'Valuation', pp. 6ff, esp. p. 11.
6 Two impressive documents of the development I have described here are John Dewey, 'Christianity and Democracy' (1893), in *Early Works*, vol. 4 (Carbondale, Ill., 1971), pp. 3–10, and the autobiographical retrospective

written in 1930: 'From Absolutism to Experimentalism', in *Later Works*, vol. 5 (Carbondale, Ill., 1984), pp. 147–60.

7 John Dewey, *The Quest for Certainty* (New York, 1980), p. 24 (also in *Later Works*, vol. 4, pp. 19f).

8 Dewey, 'Valuation', p. 18.

9 Ibid., p. 44:

> Generalized ideas of ends and values undoubtedly exist. They exist not only as expressions of habit and as uncritical and probably invalid ideas but also in the same way as valid general ideas arise in any subject. Similar situations recur; desires and interests are carried over from one situation to another and progressively consolidated. A schedule of general ends results, the involved values being 'abstract' in the sense of not being directly connected with any particular existing case but not in the sense of independence of all empirically existent cases.

10 Dewey distinguishes in his terminology between 'wishes' and 'desires' (ibid., p. 15) on the basis of whether 'effort' is either present or absent. 'Vital impulses' are neither the one nor the other, but the organic foundation of both.

11 Ibid., p. 31.

12 Ibid., pp. 31f. Dewey had already introduced this distinction at an earlier date, for the first time in *The Quest for Certainty*, p. 260 (*Later Works*, vol. 4 (Carbondale, Ill., 1984), p. 207). But the idea behind it can be traced back to even earlier works.

13 Ibid., p. 32.

14 Cf. my discussion in Joas, *The Creativity of Action*, pp. 153ff, as well as more generally my critique in that work of the teleological interpretation of the intentionality of action.

15 Dewey, 'Valuation', p. 42. This is the crucial source of Luhmann's critique of the concept of purpose in Niklas Luhmann, *Zweckbegriff und Systemrationalität* (Tübingen, 1968); cf. Joas, *Creativity of Action*, pp. 149ff.

16 John Dewey, *Experience and Nature* (1929) (London, 1958); idem, *Art as Experience* (1934) (New York, 1980).

17 For more detail, see Joas, *The Creativity of Action*, pp. 138ff.

18 Reinhold Niebuhr, 'A Footnote on Religion', *The Nation*, 139 (1934), pp. 358–9 (26 September 1934).

19 The best reconstruction of this debate in relation to Dewey can be found in Rockefeller, *John Dewey*, p. 466.

20 The thesis that Dewey's theory of religion is the pinnacle of his thought, even more than his theory of art, was first advanced by Robert Roth, S.J., *John Dewey and Self-Realization* (Englewood Cliffs, NJ), 1962, esp. pp. 100ff, and idem, *American Religious Philosophy* (New York, 1967), pp. 85ff.

21 Dewey, *A Common Faith*, p. 9.

22 Even more important than James's book for this development, especially in theological circles, was Rudolf Otto's *Das Heilige*, (Breslau, 1918).

23 Dewey, *A Common Faith*, p. 11.
24 See above, chapter 4, pp. 61ff. It is worth mentioning that, as early as c. 1915, Dewey engaged in a study of Durkheim's theory of religion (in the original French). His literary remains contain a handwritten excerpt from this work (as communicated to me in a letter dated 20 April 1993 from the archive of Southern Illinois University, Carbondale, Ill.).
25 Dewey, *A Common Faith*, p. 13.
26 Because of this, pragmatism was frequently understood as a philosophy of adaptation, and not as a philosophy of situated creativity. Admittedly, we might ask whether in his early writings Dewey himself always clearly adhered to this distinction. Our assessment of the differences between Dewey and Scheler depends on the answer to this question. Cf. Kenneth Stikkers, 'Technologies of the World, Technologies of the Self: A Schelerian Critique of Dewey and Hickman', *Journal of Speculative Philosophy*, 10 (1996), pp. 62–73.
27 Dewey, *A Common Faith*, p. 17.
28 Ibid., p. 16.
29 Ibid., p. 17.
30 The details of the relationship between the aesthetic and religious dimensions of experience are controversial. Robert Roth (*John Dewey and Self-Realization*) has been particularly consistent in his emphasis not only on the continuity, but also the differences between both. In addition to his books and the monographs by Richard Bernstein and Steven Rockefeller cited above, I recommend the following works which deal with the question treated below: William Shea, 'John Dewey: Aesthetic and Religious Experience', in idem, *The Naturalists and the Supernatural. Studies in Horizon and an American Philosophy of Religion* (Macon, Ga., 1984), pp. 117–41; John Herman Randall, Jr., 'The Religion of Shared Experience', in Horace M. Kallen (ed.), *The Philosopher of the Common Man. Essays in Honour of John Dewey to Celebrate his Eightieth Birthday* (New York, 1940), pp. 106–45; John Blewett, S.J., 'Democracy as Religion: Unity in Human Relations', in idem (ed.), *John Dewey: His Thought and Influence* (New York, 1966), pp. 33–58; Horace L. Friess, 'Dewey's Philosophy of Religion', in Jo Ann Boydston (ed.), *Guide to the Works of John Dewey* (Carbondale, Ill., 1970), pp. 200–17; Edward Schaub, 'Dewey's Interpretation of Religion', in Paul Arthur Schilpp (ed.), *The Philosophy of John Dewey* (Evanston, Ill., 1939), pp. 393–416; John K. Roth, 'William James, John Dewey and the "Death-of-God"', *Religious Studies*, 7 (1971), pp. 53–61.
31 Cf. chapter 3, pp. 51ff on James and chapter 5, pp. 79ff on Simmel.
32 Thus argues Gouinlock, *John Dewey's Philosophy of Value*, p. 145.
33 In Dewey's neo-Hegelian phase, the concept of self-realization was central to his ethical thought. Cf. John Dewey, 'Self-Realization as the Moral Ideal' (1893), in *Early Works*, vol. 4 (Carbondale, Ill., 1971), pp. 42–53; Robert Roth (*John Dewey and Self-Realization*) plausibly makes the idea of self-realization a leitmotif of his interpretation of Dewey's entire intellectual development.
34 Dewey, *A Common Faith*, p. 19.

35 Ibid., p. 43. Dewey's language, probably influenced by George Santayana, resembles that of Cornelius Castoriadis in his important work *The Imaginary Institution of Society* (Cambridge, 1987).

36 Ibid., p. 18. On Santayana's theory of religion, cf. the pathbreaking study by Henry Levinson, *Santayana, Pragmatism, and the Spiritual Life* (Chapel Hill, NC/London, 1992).

37 John Dewey, *Human Nature and Conduct. An Introduction to Social Psychology* (New York, 1922), p. 263 (also in *Middle Works*, vol. 14 (Carbondale, Ill., 1983), here p. 504).

38 Dewey, *A Common Faith*, p. 48.

39 Ibid., p. 18.

40 Ibid., pp. 14f.

41 Ibid., p. 33. When I use the concepts 'ideals' and 'values' interchangeably in my text, I am following Dewey's example, who likewise does not seem to make any terminological distinction between them.

42 Ibid., p. 19.

43 As Schleiermacher famously defined religion. Cf. ibid., esp. p. 25.

44 Ibid.

45 Steven Rockefeller stresses that Dewey was able to erase the traces of a purely instrumental orientation to nature in his early works through his long stay in Asia and his study of Chinese philosophy, especially Taoism. His philosophy from this point onwards could gain new currency under the influence of new ecological attitudes. Cf. Rockefeller, *John Dewey. Religious Faith and Democratic Humanism*, pp. 499ff.

46 Dewey, p. 19.

47 Ibid.

48 Ibid., p. 20.

49 John Dewey, *Experience and Nature*, pp. 132–61.

50 Ibid., p. 132.

51 Cf. John Dewey, *Psychology* (1887), in *Early Works*, vol. 2 (Carbondale, Ill., 1967), esp. pp. 282–95; for the significance of this motif for our context, see the earlier chapters on Nietzsche and Scheler in this book.

52 See above, chapter 3; I do not see such points of departure in Durkheim. For this reason it remains a mystery to me why Jürgen Habermas in his *Theory of Communicative Action* should describe Durkheim, together with Mead, as the inaugurator of the paradigm shift from 'purposive activity to communicative action'.

53 This was already recognized by Gouinlock, *John Dewey's Philosophy of Value*, p. 93, n. 64. He also criticized the fact that Dewey made use of George Herbert Mead's findings without properly appreciating his contribution.

54 E.g. Dewey, *Experience and Nature*, pp. 144, 159 and elsewhere.

55 Ibid., pp. 144f, 157, 159f.

56 I shall postpone until chapter 10 a more detailed discussion of the relation of this aspect of Dewey's thinking to Jürgen Habermas's and Karl-Otto Apel's discourse ethics, which dominates modern discussions. On the semantics of the concepts of 'community' and 'democracy' in Dewey and

the American tradition of thought in general, as well as the frequent misunderstandings in Germany, cf. Hans Joas, 'Communitarianism. A German Perspective', Indiana University Institute for Advanced Study. Distinguished Lecture Series, vol. 6 (Bloomington, Ind., 1993).

57 John Dewey, 'Experience, Knowledge, and Value: A Rejoinder', here p. 597 (also in *Later Works*, vol. 14, p. 79).

58 John Dewey, 'Christianity and Democracy'.

59 For a biographical portrait and comprehensive interpretation, cf. Rockefeller, *John Dewey. Religious Faith and Democratic Humanism*, and Westbrook, *John Dewey and American Democracy*. Rockefeller must be given credit for including Dewey's lyric poetry in a study of his religious development. These are important documents attesting to Dewey's search during a time in which he published nothing on the subject of religion. Cf. esp. Rockefeller, pp. 312ff.

60 E.g. John Dewey, 'Religion and Our Schools', *Hibbert Journal*, 6 (1908), pp. 796–809 (also in *Middle Works*, vol. 4, pp. 165–77).

61 Cf. Rockefeller, *John Dewey. Religious Faith and Democratic Humanism*, p. 446.

62 Dewey, *A Common Faith*, p. 2.

63 Ibid., p. 9.

64 Ibid., p. 51.

65 Dewey's obviously idiosyncratic attempt to redefine the concept 'God' initiated extensive misunderstandings and debates in the 1930s. Cf. Rockefeller, *John Dewey. Religious Faith and Democratic Humanism*, esp. pp. 512ff.

66 Dewey, *A Common Faith*, p. 87.

67 Ibid., pp. 51f.

68 See e.g. the essays from Weber's *Gesammelte Aufsätze zur Religionssoziologie*, 3 vols (Tübingen, 1920).

69 Willard Arnett, 'Critique of Dewey's Anticlerical Religious Philosophy', *Journal of Religion*, 34 (1954), pp. 256–66. Also, we should not neglect to mention that Dewey's understanding of Catholicism was largely uninformed and stereotyped. For a refutation see Blewett, 'Democracy as Religion: Unity in Human Relations', p. 52.

70 Robert Bellah et al., *Habits of the Heart*, p. 221.

71 Thus George Santayana, 'Reason in Religion', in idem, *Works*, vol. 4 (New York, 1936), pp. 3–206, here p. 4: 'The attempt to speak without speaking any particular language is not more hopeless than the attempt to have a religion that shall be no religion in particular.'

72 It might be argued that, in his theory of religion, Dewey thereby contravenes postulates which he himself put forward in his ethics and political philosophy.

73 Charles Taylor, 'Reply and Re-articulation', in James Tully (ed.), *Philosophy in an Age of Pluralism. The Philosophy of Charles Taylor in Question* (Cambridge, 1994), pp. 213–57, here p. 229. Taylor's answer to Michael Morgan's essay in this volume ('Religion, History and Moral Discourse', pp. 49–66) and Morgan's contribution itself are generally of the greatest interest for the questions I have discussed here with reference to John Dewey.

Chapter 8   Identity and the Good (Charles Taylor)

1 Of course, my account thereby leaves itself open to the charge that I have ignored important contributions. I cannot at present see that the inclusion of obvious candidates – for example, Max Weber, Martin Heidegger or Martin Buber – would alter the present argument from the more narrow point of view of the *genesis* of values. In contrast, I have omitted a discussion of Sigmund Freud because I do not feel competent to discuss the implications of his work.

2 Iris Murdoch, *The Sovereignty of Good* (London, 1970); Harry Frankfurt, 'Freedom of the Will and the Concept of a Person', *Journal of Philosophy*, 67:1 (1971), pp. 5–20; Bernard Williams, *Ethics and the Limits of Philosophy* (London, 1985); Alasdair MacIntyre, *After Virtue: A Study in Moral Theory* (London, 1981). Others could be added to this list.

3 See for example the fragments on ethics in the appendix to his main work and further ethical writings: George Herbert Mead, *Mind, Self and Society* (Chicago, 1938); idem, *Selected Writings* (ed.) Andrew Reck (Indianapolis, 1964).

4 Herbert Blumer, *Symbolic Interactionism* (Englewood Cliffs, NJ, 1969).

5 A more detailed argument concerning this issue will be found in chapter 9, which is specifically devoted to the sociological conception of identity.

6 Cf. Charles Taylor, *The Explanation of Behaviour* (London, 1964); idem, *Philosophical Papers*, 2 vols (Cambridge, 1985). The most exhaustive monograph on Taylor, to which I am indebted for clarifying several points in my argument, is the excellent book by Hartmut Rosa, *Identität und kulturelle Praxis. Politische Philosophie nach Charles Taylor* (Frankfurt am Main, 1998).

7 Charles Taylor, 'Neutrality in Political Science' (1967), in idem, *Philosophical Papers*, vol. 2, pp. 58–90.

8 Isaiah Berlin, *Vico and Herder* (London, 1976); Charles Taylor, 'Action as Expression', in Cora Diamond and Jenny Teichman (eds), *Intention and Intentionality. Essays in Honour of Gertrude E. M. Anscombe* (Brighton, 1979), pp. 73–89, as well as numerous works in his *Philosophical Papers*. For a summary of the expressivist model of action, see Joas, *The Creativity of Action*, pp. 75–85.

9 Charles Taylor, *Hegel* (Cambridge, 1975).

10 Thus Walter Reese-Schäfer, '"Nach innen geht der geheimnisvolle Weg"'. Einige kritische Bermerkungen zu Charles Taylors Ontologie der Moralität und des modernen Selbst', *Deutsche Zeitschrift für Philosophie*, 44 (1996), pp. 621–34, here p. 621.

11 Charles Taylor, *Sources of the Self. The Making of the Modern Identity* (Cambridge, 1989). What I refer to as the systematic part is part I, pp. 3–107.

12 There is an important anthology on Taylor's work, and several review symposia which are well worth reading. Cf. James Tully (ed.), *Philosophy in an Age of Pluralism. The Philosophy of Charles Taylor in Question* (Cam-

bridge, 1994); the symposia can be found, amongst others, in *Inquiry*, 34 (1991), pp. 133–254; *Philosophy and Phenomenological Research*, 54 (1994), pp. 187–213; *Dialogue. Canadian Philosophical Review*, 33 (1994), pp. 101–31; *Deutsche Zeitschrift für Philosophie*, 44 (1996), pp. 621–70. I have incorporated into this chapter passages from my contribution to the latter symposium ('Ein Pragmatist wider Willen?', pp. 661–70).

13 Frankfurt, 'Freedom of the Will and the Concept of a Person', p. 7 (my emphasis).

14 Ibid., p. 15.

15 Ibid., p. 16.

16 According to Rosa (*Identität und kulturelle Praxis*, p. 46), this distinction is first made by Charles Taylor in 'Responsibility for Self', in Amélie Rorty (ed.), *The Identities of Persons* (Berkeley, 1976), pp. 281–99. And in more detail and more momentously in the essay 'What is Human Agency?', in idem, *Philosophical Papers*, vol. 1, pp. 15–44.

17 Taylor, 'What is Human Agency?', p. 16.

18 See above all Taylor, 'Reply and Re-articulation', p. 249. The following writers have made important criticisms of Taylor's theory of strong evaluations: Ernst Tugendhat, 'Korreferat zu Charles Taylor, "What is Human Agency?"', in idem, *Philosophische Aufsätze* (Frankfurt am Main, 1992), pp. 441–52; Owen Flanagan, 'Identity and Strong and Weak Evaluation', in idem and in Amélie Rorty (eds), *Identity, Character, and Morality* (Cambridge, Mass., 1990), pp. 37–65; Joel Anderson, 'Starke Wertungen, Wünsche zweiter Ordnung und intersubjektive Kritik: Überlegungen zum Begriff ethischer Autonomie', *Deutsche Zeitschrift für Philosophie*, 42 (1994), pp. 97–119; Daniel W. Weinstock, 'The Political Theory of Strong Evaluation', in Tully, *Philosophy in an Age of Pluralism*, pp. 171–93. For a discussion of these critiques, see Rosa, *Identität und kulturelle Praxis*, pp. 98–126.

19 Taylor, *Sources*, p. 74.

20 Ibid., pp. 27ff.

21 Ibid., p. 30.

22 Ibid., p. 31.

23 Taylor, 'What is Human Agency?', p. 29.

24 This idea had already been expressed by Talcott Parsons in *The Structure of Social Action* (New York, 1937), p. 64; on this see Joas, *The Creativity of Action*, pp. 11f.

25 Taylor, *Sources*, p. 47.

26 Ibid. This aspect of Taylor's argument owes much to MacIntyre's ideas (in *After Virtue*).

27 What here sounds so simple and clear hints at complex issues in the logic of historiography, as well as in the history of the genre of autobiography. These cannot be discussed in greater detail here.

28 Taylor, *Sources*, p. 36.

29 Ibid.

30 E.g. Charles Taylor, 'Self-Interpreting Animals', in *Philosophical Papers*, vol. 1, pp. 45–76, here p. 69. There is an excellent discussion of this issue in

Rosa, *Identität und kulturelle Praxis*, esp. pp. 89ff. Taylor's dispute with Kenneth Gergen is also particularly instructive for his understanding of interpretation and articulation. Cf. Stanley Messer, Louis Sass and Robert Woolfolk (eds), *Hermeneutics and Psychological Theory. Interpretive Perspectives on Personality, Psychotherapy, and Psychopathology* (New Brunswick, NJ, 1988), pp. 28–61.

31 Taylor, *Sources*, pp. 62f.

32 Here Taylor's conception of articulation stongly resembles the Two-Languages Argument developed by Robert Bellah's group of authors, and which was discussed in chapter 1.

33 Ibid., pp. 71ff. Martin Seel has astutely characterized Taylor's conception as an 'anti-genealogy of morality'. Cf. Martin Seel, 'Die Wiederkehr der Ethik des guten Lebens', *Merkur*, 45 (1991), pp. 42–9, here p. 49.

34 Taylor, *Sources*, pp. 205f.

35 Ibid., pp. 199–207.

36 Taylor is here (ibid., p. 203) referring to, and concurring with, Max Weber's famous postulate. Cf. Max Weber, *Economy and Society*, vol. 1 (Berkeley, 1978), p. 11.

37 The distinction between moral realism and a Platonism of the good can be quite clearly found in his rejoinder to the essays in *Philosophy and Phenomenological Research*, 54 (1994), p. 211.

38 See above, chapter 6.

39 I should point out at this juncture that the way in which Taylor speaks of the good rather than of values in my view encourages the impression that his realism is Platonism. As Rosa (*Identität und kulturelle Praxis*, esp. p. 110) shows, Taylor did not introduce the concept of the good into his terminology until after developing the theory of strong evaluations. I do not follow Taylor in his choice of words.

40 Taylor, *Sources*, p. 57.

41 Taylor, in Messer et al. (eds), *Hermeneutics and Psychological Theory*, p. 56.

42 Taylor, *Sources*, pp. 72ff, as well as idem, 'Explanation and Practical Reason', in idem, *Philosophical Arguments* (Cambridge, Mass., 1995), pp. 34–60.

43 Charles Taylor, 'The Validity of Transcendental Arguments', in idem, *Philosophical Arguments*, pp. 20–33.

44 Axel Honneth and I have determined the possible status of anthropology in this way in our book *Social Action and Human Nature* (Cambridge, 1988).

45 Rosa is excellent on this point; cf. idem, *Identität und kulturelle Praxis*, pp. 116ff.

46 Ibid., pp. 158f.

47 Taylor, 'Reply and Re-articulation', p. 229.

48 Taylor elaborates this himself in his book *The Ethics of Authenticity* (Cambridge, Mass., 1992).

49 For this reason I hold Mario Moussa's argument to be unjustified. See his review essay 'Writing the History of the "We". The Claims of Practice', *Social Theory and Practice*, 18 (1992), pp. 211–29. In contrast, compare the more positive sociological reviews by Alan Wolfe in *Contemporary Soci-*

ology, 19 (1990), pp. 627–8, and Craig Calhoun in *Sociological Theory*, 3 (1991), pp. 232–63.

50 Cf. above all J. B. Schneewind's review of *Sources of the Self* in *Journal of Philosophy*, 88 (1991), pp. 422–6.

51 Cf. the excellent essay by Michael L. Morgan, 'Religion, History and Moral Discourse', in Tully (ed.), *Philosophy in an Age of Pluralism*, pp. 49–66. Taylor's account of the last hundred years in fact changes tack, moving from intellectual to literary history.

52 Thus argues above all Frances S. Adeney in her review of *Sources of the Self* in *Theology Today*, 48 (1991), pp. 204–10.

53 Taylor, *Sources*, p. 233.

54 Ibid., p. 555 n. 43.

55 Ibid., p. 525 n. 12. There he accuses Mead of behaviourism and neglecting the role language plays in the constitution of the self. See my refutation in: 'Ein Pragmatist wider Willen?', p. 666 and idem, *George Herbert Mead: A Contemporary Re-examination of his Thought*. It is almost grotesque that the only other reference to Mead in Taylor's work attributes to him the authorship of the concept of the 'significant other' – and thus of a concept never used by Mead and which, rather, first occurs in the work of Harry Stack Sullivan.

56 Taylor defines 'identity' as the 'ensemble of (largely unarticulated) understandings of what it is to be a human agent' (Taylor, *Sources*, p. ix). This concept refers to a particular historical and cultural constellation. On the other hand, 'self' is understood as the anthropological possibility of such an identity, according to which we attribute to the individual depth and complexity, as well as an orientation to the good. However, Taylor does not seem to be really consistent in deploying this distinction.

57 Cf. chapter 3 of this book. Taylor appeals instead to Kierkegaard and Dostoevsky.

58 Ryan, *John Dewey and the High Tide of American Liberalism*, p. 361. In a reply to Richard Rorty in *Philosophy and Phenomenological Research*, 54 (1994), pp. 211–13, Taylor makes clear why he is not convinced by Dewey's philosophy.

> Why am I not happy to make my peace with Deweyan social-democracy, plus a sense of the importance of expressive creativity? Because I'm not yet satisfied with the Deweyan constitutive goods. Worse, I am not even sure that Dewey saw the issue I'm here trying to delineate about constitutive goods. It seems to me that every anthropocentrism pays a terrible price in impoverishment in this regard. Deep ecologists tend to concur from one point of view, theists from another. And I am driven to this position from both. (ibid., p. 213)

It would of course be completely misleading if he were to extend his reservations about Dewey to James or Peirce.

59 Taylor, *Sources*, p. 84.

60 Cf. Max Scheler's formula of 'good-in-itself-for-*me*' in his *Formalism*, p. 490 (see chapter 6 above).

Chapter 9   The Concept of Self and its Postmodern Challenge

1 Rorty's most important independent contribution to these questions is his book *Contingency, Irony, Solidarity* (Cambridge, 1989). Further relevant works can be found in his collected essays: *Objectivity, Relativism, and Truth* (Cambridge, 1991); *Essays on Heidegger and Others* (Cambridge, 1991). Critical discussions of Taylor can be found for example in *Philosophy and Phenomenological Research*, 54 (1994), pp. 197–201 (with Taylor's reply pp. 211–13), and in Tully (ed.), *Philosophy in an Age of Pluralism*, pp. 20–33 (with Taylor's reply pp. 219–22). Nicholas Smith offers an excellent comparison of Taylor and Rorty in 'Contingency and Self-Identity. Taylor's Hermeneutics vs. Rorty's Postmodernism', *Theory, Culture and Society*, 13 (1996), pp. 105–20.
2 As Rorty puts it in 'Freud and Moral Reflection', in idem, *Essays on Heidegger and Others*, pp. 143–62, here p. 155.
3 Cf. the beginning of chapter 2 in this book.
4 Michel Foucault, 'Nietzsche, Genealogy, History', in idem, *Language, Counter-Meaning, Practice: Selected Essays and Interviews* (Ithaca, NY, 1977), pp. 139–64.
5 Rorty, *Contingency*, p. 65. Cf. my statement in Joas, *The Creativity of Action*, p. 258, and the literature cited there.
6 Rorty, *Contingency*, p. xiv.
7 Ibid.
8 Rorty's extensive political journalism is evidence of this, most recently in a particularly brilliant essay, 'Fraternity Reigns', in *The New York Times Magazine*, 29 September 1996.
9 Rorty, review of Taylor (in *Philosophy and Phenomenological Research* – see n. 1), p. 199. What is surprising here of course is that Rorty seems to betray his own plea for a strict separation of the private and public sphere when he writes: 'Surely utopian social democratic political thought has generated words of power which are neither reductive nor privatized? Why should not the *social* creative imagination be a hypergood? What is wrong with Dewey as an example of how to be both an anti-reductive naturalist and social romantic?'
10 Interestingly, he thereby makes his own that aspect of Dewey's theory of religion which was criticized here (cf. chapter 7 of this book) – and not the theory of action and value which can likewise be found in Dewey.
11 Richard Rorty, *Philosophy and The Mirror of Nature* (Princeton, 1979).
12 In particular, Rorty continually bases his claims on works by Donald Davidson, e.g. Rorty, 'Non-Reductive Physicalism', in idem, *Objectivity, Relativism, and Truth*, pp. 113–25.
13 Rorty, *Contingency*, p. 10.
14 Rorty omits completely a critical discussion of George Herbert Mead, the

most important pragmatist with respect to this question. It is generally the case that Rorty enlists pragmatism for his own purposes in spectacular fashion, but is at the same time often astonishingly unconcerned with the views and intentions of the classic thinkers of this tradition. The critical literature on the issue of the correctness of Rorty's interpretation of Dewey and pragmatism is accordingly very extensive. I have compiled this and commented on it in my *Pragmatism and Social Theory*, pp. 257ff. There are important essays on Rorty, together with his replies, in Herman Saatkamp Jr. (ed.), *Rorty and Pragmatism. The Philosopher Responds to his Critics* (Nashville, Tenn., 1995). An excellent critical discussion has been published by Jürgen Habermas: 'Rortys pragmatische Wende', *Deutsche Zeitschrift für Philosophie*, 44 (1996), pp. 715–41.

15 In what follows I employ arguments originally advanced in my essay 'The Autonomy of the Self. The Meadian Heritage and its Postmodern Challenge', *European Journal of Social Theory*, 1 (1998), pp. 7–18.

16 Hans-Joachim Schubert has published a particularly clear survey of the various attempts to formulate such a conception; see his *Demokratische Identität. Der soziologische Pragmatismus von Charles Horton Cooley* (Frankfurt am Main, 1995), esp. pp. 245–323. Also useful, and incorporating the later history, is Andrew Weigert's 'Identity. Its Emergence within Sociological Psychology', *Symbolic Interaction*, 6 (1983), pp. 183–206. Philip Gleason delivers a conceptual history of 'identity' in 'Identifying Identity: A Semantic History', *Journal of American History*, 69 (1983), pp. 910–27.

17 William James, *The Principles of Psychology* (1890) (Cambridge, Mass., 1981), pp. 219–78.

18 Ibid., pp. 279–379.

19 Cf. George H. Mead, *Mind, Self, and Society* (Chicago, 1934); idem, *Selected Writings*, ed. Andrew Reck (Indianapolis, 1964). On this see Joas, *G.H. Mead: A Contemporary Re-examination of his Thought*.

20 Hans Joas, 'Pragmatism in American Sociology', in idem, *Pragmatism and Social Theory*, pp. 14–51.

21 Cf. Jürgen Straub, 'Identität und Sinnbildung. Ein Beitrag aus der Sicht einer handlungs- und erzähltheoretischen Sozialpsychologie', in *Jahresbericht 1994/5 des Zentrums für interdisziplinäre Forschung* (Bielefeld, 1996), pp. 42–90, here pp. 42f.

22 Erik H. Erikson, *Identity and the Life Cycle* (New York, 1959). Ernst Tugendhat in particular has protested against the use of the concept of identity in sociology and social psychology. Cf. his book *Selbstbewußtsein und Selbstbestimmung* (Frankfurt am Main, 1979), esp. pp. 247 and 282ff.

23 Cf. Jürgen Habermas, 'Stichworte zur Theorie der Sozialisation', in idem, *Kultur und Kritik* (Frankfurt am Main, 1973), pp. 118–94; idem, 'Moralentwicklung und Ich-Identität', in idem, *Zur Rekonstruktion des Historischen Materialismus* (Frankfurt am Main, 1976), pp. 63–91. Lothar Krappmann put forward an extremely influential synthesis of the state of research in his *Soziologische Dimensionen der Identität. Strukturelle Bedingungen für die Teilnahme an Interaktionsprozessen* (Stuttgart, 1971).

24 Harald Wenzel provides a quite excellent overview of the relevant litera-

ture in his 'Gibt es ein postmodernes Selbst? Neuere Theorien und Diagnosen der Identität in fortgeschrittenen Gesellschaften', *Berliner Journal für Soziologie*, 1 (1995), pp. 113–31.

25 Particularly important in this respect is Kenneth Gergen's *The Saturated Self. Dilemmas of Identity in Contemporary Life* (New York, 1991). The concept of 'patchwork identity' stems from the numerous works by Heiner Keupp on this topic, e.g. 'Grundzüge einer reflexiven Sozialpsychologie. Postmoderne Perspektiven', in idem (ed.), *Zugänge zum Subjekt. Perspektiven einer reflexiven Sozialpsychologie* (Frankfurt am Main, 1994), pp. 226–74, here p. 243.

26 From an early point onwards and writing in the classic tradition, Ralph Turner, 'The Real Self: From Institution to Impulse', *American Journal of Sociology*, 81 (1975/6), pp. 989–1016; see also Anthony Giddens, *Modernity and Self-Identity. Self and Society in the Late Modern Age* (Cambridge, 1991). In the present context, I cannot follow up the empirical questions which arise here.

27 Dietmar Kamper is typical; cf. idem, 'Die Auflösung der Ich-Identität', in Friedrich A. Kittler (ed.), *Austreibung des Geistes aus den Geisteswissenschaften* (Paderborn, 1980), pp. 79–86.

28 See chapter 3 of this book for a discussion of his theory of religion.

29 The assumption of an uninterrupted hegemony of the Cartesian idea of self-transparency is more plausible with respect to French intellectual history. In the symbolic interactionist school an interesting controversy is taking place about the question of how much the pragmatist tradition has to learn from postmodern approaches. The spectrum extends from Norman Denzin – who vehemently defends a postmodern pragmatism and introduces the notion of 'post-pragmatism' for this purpose – to David Maines, for whom postmodern thinking represents mostly a weak imitation of elements which have been articulated earlier and much better in the pragmatist-interactionist tradition. See, among others, Norman Denzin, 'Post-Pragmatism. A Review of Hans Joas, *Pragmatism and Social Theory*', *Symbolic Interaction*, 19 (1996), pp. 61–75; David Maines, 'On Postmodernism, Pragmatism, and Plasterers: Some Interactionist Thoughts and Queries', *Symbolic Interaction*, 19 (1996), pp. 323–40 (as well as Denzin's rejoinder: 'Prophetic Pragmatism and the Postmodern: A Comment on Maines', ibid., pp. 341–55, and Maines's reply: 'On Choices and Criticism: A Reply to Denzin', ibid., pp. 357–62). Another illuminating work is Vincent Colapietro's essay 'The Vanishing Subject of Contemporary Discourse: A Pragmatic Response', *Journal of Philosophy*, 87 (1990), pp. 644–55.

30 Dennis Wrong, 'The Oversocialized Conception of Man in Modern Sociology', *American Sociological Review*, 26 (1961), pp. 183–95.

31 Jürgen Habermas, *The Philosophical Discourse of Modernity* (Cambridge, Mass., 1987).

32 Castoriadis, *The Imaginary Institution of Society*, esp. pp. 273–339. For a critical discussion of Castoriadis see my essay 'Institutionalization as a Creative Process', in *Pragmatism and Social Theory*, pp. 154–71.

33 Castoriadis, *The Imaginary Institution of Society*, p. 104.

34 In a critical discussion of Manfred Frank's critique of intersubjectivist thought, Lutz Wingert has made explicit the idea also contained in Habermas's writings of a necessarily 'broken intersubjectivity'; cf. idem, 'Der Grund der Differenz: Subjektivität als ein Moment von Intersubjektivität', in Micha Brumlik and Hauke Brunkhorst (eds), *Gemeinschaft und Gerechtigkeit* (Frankfurt am Main, 1993), pp. 290–305.

35 A famous example is Peter L. Berger and Hansfried Kellner, 'Marriage and the Construction of Reality', in Hans-Peter Dreitzel (ed.), *Recent Sociology No. 2. Patterns of Communicative Behavior* (London, 1970), pp. 49–72.

36 On this, see the section entitled 'Primary Sociality' in Joas, *The Creativity of Action*, pp. 184–95.

37 George Herbert Mead, 'The Psychology of Punitive Justice', *American Journal of Sociology*, 23 (1918), pp. 577–602.

38 George Herbert Mead, 'The Psychological Bases of Internationalism', *Survey*, 33 (1915), pp. 604–7; idem, 'National-Mindedness and International-Mindedness', *International Journal of Ethics*, 39 (1929), pp. 385–407.

39 By taking his inspiration from Hegel and from Mead, Axel Honneth attempts in a very subtle manner to do justice to this interweaving in his theory of the struggle for recognition; cf. idem, *The Struggle for Recognition*.

40 Rorty, *Contingency*, p. 92.

41 Ibid., pp. 89–90.

42 Ibid., p. 178.

43 Ibid., pp. 92f.

44 Starting from this premise, I have attempted, in various studies on violence and its consequences, to clarify somewhat the euphoric effects of experiences of violence and changes in identity after perpetrating or suffering violence. Cf. Hans Joas, 'Sprayed and Betrayed. Gewalterfahrung im Vietnamkrieg und ihre Folgen', in Hans Joas and Wolfgang Knöbl (eds), *Gewalt in den USA* (Frankfurt am Main, 1994), pp. 300–13; idem, 'Handlungstheorie und Gewaltdynamik', in Wolfgang Vogt (ed.), *Gewalt und Konfliktbearbeitung*. In principle, it would be necessary to elaborate the puzzling common features of creativity and destructiveness, of the experience of value commitment and traumatization, yet without erasing their differences. But this would exceed the scope of this book.

45 These thoughts are heading in the direction indicated by Castoriadis. My formulation refers to Axel Honneth, 'Dezentrierte Autonomie. Moralphilosophische Konsequenzen aus der modernen Subjektkritik', in Christoph Menke and Martin Seel (eds), *Zur Verteidigung der Vernunft gegen ihre Liebhaber und Verächter* (Frankfurt am Main, 1993), pp. 149–63. Jürgen Straub's writings aim energetically at the same goal; see e.g. his 'Identitätstheorie im Übergang? Über Identitätsforschung, den Begriff der Identität und die zunehmende Beachtung des Nicht-Identischen in subjekttheoretischen Diskursen', *Sozialwissenschaftliche Literaturrundschau*, 23 (1991), pp. 49–71; idem, 'Geschichte, Identität und Lebensglück. Eine psychologische Lektüre "unzeitgemäßer Betrachtungen"', in Klaus Müller and Jörn Rüssen (eds), *Historische Sinnbildung* (Reinbek, 1997), pp. 165–94. Starting from a pragmatist position, Philip Selznick thinks along similar

lines in a discussion of Buddhism in his *The Moral Commonwealth. Social Theory and the Promise of Community* (Berkeley, 1992), pp. 224f.
46 Taylor, *Sources*, p. 480.
47 Smith, 'Contingency and Self-Identity', p. 116.
48 Taylor, 'Reply to Richard Rorty', *Philosophy and Phenomenological Research*, 54 (1994), p. 212.
49 Cf. Joas, *The Creativity of Action*, p. 257.

Chapter 10   Values and Norms: The Good and the Right

1 Taylor's silence in this regard was discussed in chapter 8. It is nevertheless quite remarkable to what extent younger authors also circumvent the terrain between Nietzsche and the latest Anglo-Saxon philosophy. See, for example, Seel, *Versuch über die Form des Glücks*.
2 For an impressive example, see Orlando Patterson's study of the genesis of the value of 'freedom' in antiquity from the experiences of a social order based on slavery: *Freedom*, vol. 1, *Freedom in the Making of Western Culture* (New York, 1991).
3 Cf. chapter 8, pp. 132ff.
4 Abraham Edel expresses this rather well in his superb overview of the history of this problem: 'The story of the good and the right is not . . . the tale of two isolated concepts sitting for philosophical portraits in a variety of grand poses' ('Right and Good', in Philip Wiener (ed.), *Dictionary of the History of Ideas*, vol. 4 (New York, 1973), pp. 173–87, here p. 173).
5 Dewey and Tufts, *Ethics*. For the question of the relationship between the good and the right in Dewey's ethics, see Welchman, *Dewey's Ethical Thought*, pp. 157ff, and Honneth, 'Between Proceduralism and Teleology'.
6 As, for example, in Charles Taylor, 'The Nature and Scope of Distributive Justice', in idem, *Philosophical Papers*, vol. 2, pp. 289–317.
7 Especially in his quarrel with Habermas, in Charles Taylor, 'Die Motive einer Verfahrensethik', in Wolfgang Kuhlmann (ed.), *Moralität und Sittlichkeit. Das Problem Hegels und die Diskursethik* (Frankfurt am Main, 1986), pp. 101–35; idem, 'Language and Society', in Axel Honneth and Hans Joas (eds), *Communicative Action. Essays on Jürgen Habermas' 'The Theory of Coummunicative Action'* (Cambridge, 1991), pp. 23–35. See also his debate with Rawls: 'Le juste et le bien', *Revue de métaphysique et de morale*, 93 (1988), pp. 33–56. On the whole, Taylor attempts to find a mediatory position in the controversy between liberalism and communitarianism. See Taylor, 'Cross-Purposes: The Liberal-Communitarian Debate', in Nancy Rosenblum (ed.), *Liberalism and the Moral Life* (Cambridge, Mass., 1989), pp. 159–82.
8 Taylor, *Sources*, pp. 59ff and 77ff.
9 Ibid., pp. 87ff.
10 Ibid., pp. 531f, n. 60 and pp. 532f, n. 66. Of great significance for Taylor's argument here is Bernard Williams's work *Ethics and the Limits of Philosophy*, esp. pp. 174ff. Williams summarizes his thought as follows:

Many philosophical mistakes are woven into morality. It misunderstands obligations, not seeing how they form just one type of ethical
considerations. It misunderstands practical necessity, thinking it
peculiar to obligations. Beyond all this, morality makes people think
that, without its very special obligation, there is only inclination;
without its utter voluntariness, there is only force; without its ultimately pure justice, there is no justice. Its philosophical errors are
only the most abstract expressions of a deeply rooted and still
powerful misconception of life. (ibid., p. 196)

Williams also shows to good effect that this kind of moral theory behaves
like a kind of religion, although – unlike the Christian religion – it thinks
it can manage without a concept of mercy and divine love.

11 Taylor, 'Reply to Richard Rorty', p. 213.
12 Cf. Philip Selznick's excellent, contrasting remarks on the question of the
    good in the areas of education, defence, health and environment policy in
    his *The Moral Commonwealth*, pp. 380ff, here p. 384.
13 This cannot, of course, be demonstrated here with respect to individual
    thinkers like Foucault, Lyotard or Derrida. For an excellent discussion of
    the question of the ethical dimensions in the works of these authors, see
    Richard Bernstein, *The New Constellation. The Ethical-Political Horizons of
    Modernity/Postmodernity* (Cambridge, Mass., 1992).
14 The notion of reflective equilibrium has its origin in John Rawls's *A Theory
    of Justice*, but has another meaning there. The concept refers to the
    concretization of the 'original position' that he envisages. See John Rawls,
    A Theory of Justice (Oxford, 1980), p. 17. In the recent debates, Rawls is the
    main reference point for the thesis of the primacy of the right over the
    good. I will not concern myself either with his gradual moderation and
    modification of this thesis within the framework of the liberalism–com-
    munitarianism controversy, or with the relationship between the concep-
    tion presented here and his thought as a whole.
15 Cf. chapter 8 of this book, pp. 142ff. Taylor's thoughts on 'practical
    reasoning', which he develops above all in the essay 'Explanation and
    Practical Reason', fit very well with this attempt at a solution, but are not
    applied by him to the question of the good and the right.
16 I have already brought out these two distinctive features in two studies on
    George Herbert Mead. Cf. my *G. H. Mead: A Contemporary Re-examination
    of his Thought*, pp. 121ff, esp. p. 127; idem, 'The Creativity of Action and
    the Intersubjectivity of Reason – Mead's Pragmatism and Social Theory',
    in idem, *Pragmatism and Social Theory* (Chicago/London, 1993), pp. 238–61.
17 John Dewey, *Human Nature and Conduct*; idem, *Experience and Nature*,
    pp. 166ff; Mead, *Mind, Self, and Society* (Chicago, 1934).
18 Mead, *Mind, Self, and Society*, p. 327.
19 In this respect the pragmatist theory thus resembles the rational choice
    theory and the universal developmental psychology in the Piaget–Kohl-
    berg tradition. For Durkheim's relationship to the notion of a universal co-
    operative morality, cf. Joas, *The Creativity of Action*, pp. 58–61.

20 Joas, *Pragmatism and Social Theory*, pp. 251–5.
21 Mead, 'Fragments on Ethics', in idem, *Mind, Self, and Society*, pp. 379–89.
22 Following Dewey's theory of value, Henry Richardson sees this particularly clearly in 'Beyond Good and Right: Toward a Constructive Ethical Pragmatism', *Philosophy and Public Affairs*, 24 (1995), pp. 108–41, here esp. p. 113.
23 Ibid., p. 132.
24 Cf. Ricoeur, *Oneself as Another* (Chicago/London, 1992), p. 177. I feel the argument I have presented here and developed from a pragmatist point of view is supported and confirmed after the subsequent reading of the ethical chapters of Ricoeur's book (pp. 170–298). Cf. also his *Liebe und Gerechtigkeit* (Tübingen, 1990).
25 Richardson, 'Beyond Good and Right', pp. 127ff.
26 For Mead's understanding of the 'social act' as a complex group activity, cf. Mead, *Mind, Self, and Society*, p. 7 n. 7; for the thesis of a 'primary sociality' of the capacity for action, see Joas, *The Creativity of Action*, pp. 184–95; for the thesis of 'irreducibly social goods', cf. Taylor, *Philosophical Arguments*, pp. 127–45.
27 Ricoeur, *Oneself as Another*, pp. 208ff.
28 The thrust of the Kant critiques of Dewey (*Ethics*, pp. 219–25; *Later Works*, vol. 7) and Mead (*Fragments*), as well as Max Scheler (see chapter 6 of this book) are similar to Ricoeur's interpretation of Kant.
29 Cf. Ricoeur:

> As we have repeatedly affirmed, the conflicts that give weight to the contextualist theses are encountered along the path of actualization rather than along that of justification. It is important to be clear about this difference of site so as not to confuse the arguments that stress the historical character of choices to be made along the second path with the skeptical arguments that are addressed to the foundational enterprise. *Oneself as Another* (pp. 283–4)

30 As Honneth assumes in his study on Dewey's ethics, 'Between Proceduralism and Teleology'.
31 The classic work on this topic is Jean Piaget, *The Moral Judgement of the Child* (Harmondsworth, 1977). For the question of the cultural relativity of morality, cf. Traugott Schöfthaler and Dietrich Goldschmidt (eds), *Soziale Struktur und Vernunft* (Frankfurt am Main, 1984).
32 Cf. chapter 1, pp. 12ff. for a discussion of the inadequacies of Parsons's conception of values. Jeffrey Alexander also makes excellent points in his comparison of Parsons and Touraine. Cf. Jeffrey Alexander, 'Collective Action, Culture and Civil Society: Secularizing, Updating, Inverting, Revising and Displacing the Classical Model of Social Movements', in Jon Clark and Marco Diani (eds), *Alain Touraine* (London, 1996), pp. 205–34, here pp. 217ff.
33 See the following works in particular: Jürgen Habermas, 'Remarks on Discourse Ethics', in idem, *Justification and Application* (Cambridge, 1993),

pp. 19–112; idem, *Between Facts and Norms. Contributions to a Discourse Theory of Law and Democracy* (Cambridge, 1996); idem, *The Inclusion of the Other. Studies in Political Theory* (Cambridge, 1998).

34 Habermas, *The Inclusion of the Other*, pp. 33–4.

35 I omit a critical discussion of the work of Karl-Otto Apel. His reception and magisterial interpretation of the work of Charles Sanders Peirce was decisive for the origins of discourse ethics in Germany. See Karl-Otto Apel, *Charles S. Peirce: From Pragmatism to Pragmaticism* (Amherst, Mass., 1981); idem, *Diskurs und Verantwortung* (Frankfurt am Main, 1988).

36 This is clearly visible in his early book on the public sphere on the one hand and, on the other, in his action-theoretical distinction between 'work' and 'interaction' taken up from Hannah Arendt and George Herbert Mead. See Jürgen Habermas, *The Structural Transformation of the Public Sphere* (Cambridge, 1989); idem, 'Labor and Interaction: Remarks on Hegel's Jena Philosophy of Mind', in idem, *Theory and Practice* (Boston, Mass., 1973), pp. 142–69.

37 Jürgen Habermas, 'Vorbereitende Bemerkungen zu einer Theorie der kommunikativen Kompetenz', in idem and Niklas Luhmann, *Theorie der Gesellschaft oder Sozialtechnologie – Was leistet die Systemforschung?* (Frankfurt am Main, 1971), pp. 101–41, here p. 141.

38 Habermas, *The Theory of Communicative Action*, vol. 2, e.g. pp. 107ff.

39 Ibid., pp. 77ff.

40 Ibid., p. 107.

41 Ibid., p. 77.

42 Cf. chapters 4 and 7 of this book.

43 Richard Bernstein, 'The Retrieval of the Democratic Ethos', *Cardozo Law Review*, 17 (1996), pp. 1127–46.

44 Axel Honneth, 'Diskursethik und implizites Gerechtigkeitskonzept', in Wolfgang Kuhlmann (ed.), *Moralität und Sittlichkeit. Das Problem Hegels und die Diskursethik* (Frankfurt am Main, 1986), pp. 183–93, here p. 191. This characterization of the direction of his thought also applies to his book *The Critique of Power: Reflective Stages in a Critical Social Theory* (Cambridge, Mass./London, 1991). The following sentences by Habermas can perhaps be read as an implicit reply to Honneth: 'The equal distribution of communicative freedoms and the requirement of truthfulness *in* discourse have the status of *argumentative* duties and rights, of *moral* duties and rights. So too, the absence of coercion refers to the process of argumentation itself, not to interpersonal relationships *outside* of this practice' (Habermas, *The Inclusion of the Other*, pp. 44–5).

45 As Honneth has since elaborated in his book *The Struggle for Recognition* and in numerous other studies.

46 Jürgen Habermas, 'Reply to Symposium Participants', *Cardozo Law Review*, 17 (1996), pp. 1477–557, here p. 1481.

47 In Peirce's philosophy of science the discourse theory was, as Habermas well knows, accordingly combined with a logic of abduction, of the creative discovery of hypotheses that are worth testing.

48 Thus Scheler in opposition to Kant. See chapter 6 of this book, p. 87 and

p. 91. With dry English humour, Bernard Williams argues for the evaluation of the mere discussion of a possibility:

> One does not feel easy with the man who in the course of a discussion
> of how to deal with political or business rivals says, 'Of course, we
> could have them killed, but we should lay that aside from the
> beginning.' It is characteristic of morality that it tends to overlook the
> possibility that some concerns are best embodied in this way, in
> deliberative silence. (*Ethics and the Limits of Philosophy*, p. 185)

49 Habermas, *Between Facts and Norms*, p. 163.
50 Habermas, *The Inclusion of the Other*, p. 45.
51 Essentially, we are dealing with only two essays: Jürgen Habermas, ' "To
    Seek to Salvage an Unconditional Meaning without God is a Futile
    Undertaking": Reflections on a Remark of Max Horkheimer', in idem,
    Justification and Application, pp. 133–46 and idem, 'Exkurs: Transzendenz
    von innen, Transzendenz ins Diesseits', in idem, *Texte und Kontexte* (Frank-
    furt am Main, 1991), pp. 127–56, here p. 141. These were recently supple-
    mented by the essay directly concerned with the question of moral
    motivation: Jürgen Habermas, 'A Genealogical Analysis of the Cognitive
    Content of Morality', in idem, *The Inclusion of the Other*, pp. 3–46.
52 See chapter 3 of this book.
53 Habermas, 'Reflections on a Remark', p. 146.
54 Habermas, 'Remarks on Discourse Ethics', pp. 69–76, here p. 75.
55 Habermas, 'Reflections on a Remark', p. 146.
56 Habermas, *Between Facts and Norms*, p. 5. Johannes Weiß had already
    argued along these lines as early as 1983. See idem, 'Verständigungsorien-
    tierung und Kritik', in idem, *Vernunft und Vernichtung. Zur Philosophie und
    Soziologie der Moderne* (Opladen, 1993), pp. 223–37.
57 Thus Habermas in the essay 'A Genealogical Analysis', in which he tackles
    this problem head-on for the first time (p. 274 n. 51).
58 Habermas, *Theory of Communicative Action*, vol. 1, pp. 36ff.
59 Habermas, 'On the Employments of Practical Reason', in idem, *Justification
    and Application*, pp. 1–17.
60 Habermas, *Between Facts and Norms*, pp. 159–61.
61 Habermas, *Justification and Application*, p. vii. In opposition to Habermas,
    Thomas McCarthy emphasizes 'the dialectical interdependence *in practice*
    of these *analytically* distinguishable aspects . . . Thus, *in practice* political
    deliberation is not so much an interweaving of separate discourses as a
    multifaceted communication process that allows for fluid transitions
    among questions and arguments of different sorts.' See McCarthy, 'Legiti-
    macy and Diversity: Dialectical Reflections on Analytical Distinctions',
    Cardozo Law Review, 17 (1996), pp. 1083–125, here p. 1096, and p. 1105.
    Habermas accepts this in a legal-theoretical, but not in a general discourse-
    theoretical regard.
62 Albrecht Wellmer, *Ethik und Dialog. Elemente des moralischen Urteils bei Kant
    und in der Diskursethik* (Frankfurt am Main, 1986); Klaus Günther, *Der Sinn*

für Angemessenheit: Anwendungsdiskurse in Moral und Recht (Frankfurt am Main, 1988).

63 As Axel Honneth, influenced by postmodern reflections on ethics, has energetically demanded. See Honneth, 'The Other of Justice: Habermas and the Ethical Challenge of Postmodernism', in Stephen White (ed.), *Cambridge Companion to Habermas* (Cambridge, 1995), pp. 289–325.

64 Habermas, 'On the Employments of Practical Reason', p. 14.

65 See chapter 7 of this book, p. 117ff.

66 For these definitions, see Habermas, *Between Facts and Norms*, p. 255 and idem, 'On the Employments of Practical Reason', p. 6 (where the quotation is to be found). I shall not deal with two further determinations, the binary versus graduated coding of the validity claim and the different criteria for the coherence of 'systems of norms' or 'constellations of value', since it seems to me that these are only logical properties of the first distinguishing feature.

67 Habermas, though, seems to waver as far as his precise understanding of the concept of value is concerned. Whilst in *Between Facts and Norms* (p. 255) he still defines values along utilitarian lines as 'intersubjectively shared preferences', in *The Inclusion of the Other* (p. 6) he writes: 'What in each instance is valuable or authentic forces itself upon us, so to speak, and differs from mere preferences in its binding character, that is, in the fact that it points beyond needs and preferences.' Here the feeling of captivation inherent in the experience of value, which must be central to a modern theory of value, finds appropriate expression (under Taylor's influence?).

68 Bernstein, 'The Retrieval of the Democratic Ethos', p. 1140.

69 Habermas, *The Inclusion of the Other*, p. 6.

70 Habermas, *Between Facts and Norms*, p. 256.

71 See the chapters on Scheler, Dewey and Taylor in this book.

72 Habermas, 'On the Employments of Practical Reason', p. 2.

73 Taylor explicitly contests this connection in 'Motive einer Verfahrensethik', pp. 104 and 108. The most sophisticated argument can be found in Ricoeur, *Oneself as Another*.

74 I am referring to my criticism of Habermas's *Theory of Communicative Action*. See Hans Joas, 'The Unhappy Marriage of Hermeneutics and Functionalism', in idem, *Pragmatism and Social Theory*, pp. 125–53. I have attempted to elaborate a theory of action inspired by pragmatism in *The Creativity of Action*. Just as Habermas uses the concept 'neo-Aristotelianism' in the area of ethics, so he employs that of the 'philosophy of praxis' in the sphere of action theory, in order to occlude the differences between those who describe themselves as neo-Aristotelians and the philosophy of Taylor, pragmatism and others (see Joas, *The Creativity of Action*, pp. 102ff). I find the use of such terminology misleading and irritating.

75 Habermas, *Between Facts and Norms*, p. 83.

76 Ibid.

77 Habermas, *The Inclusion of the Other*, p. xxxvi (my emphasis, H. J.).

78 Habermas, *Between Facts and Norms*, pp. 73–4.

79 Ibid., p. 445.
80 I should point out, if only briefly, that there have been a number of
interesting attempts in the recent literature to bring together the good and
the right in the sense of a balancing through the actor, as well as to
integrate ethics of prescription and of striving. A critical discussion of
these studies must, however, be omitted here. Besides the studies already
referred to in this context, the following should be mentioned: Seel, *Versuch
über das Glück*; Hans Krämer, *Integrative Ethik* (Frankfurt am Main, 1995);
Wolfgang Schluchter, 'Gesinnungsethik und Verantwortungsethik', in
idem, *Religion und Lebensführung*, vol. 1, pp. 165–338; Christoph Menke,
'Die Vernunft in Widerstreit. Über den richtigen Umgang mit praktischen
Konflikten', in idem and Martin Seel (eds), *Zur Verteidigung der Vernunft
gegen ihre Liebhaber und Verächter* (Frankfurt am Main, 1993), pp. 197–218;
idem, *Tragödie im Sittlichen. Gerechtigkeit und Freiheit nach Hegel* (Frankfurt
am Main, 1996); as well as, of course, all the recent work by John Rawls,
especially his *Political Liberalism* (New York, 1993).
81 Rainer Forst has produced the best overview, although his conclusions do
not by any means always coincide with mine. See his *Kontexte der Gerechtigkeit. Politische Philosophie jenseits von Liberalismus und Kommunitarianismus*
(Frankfurt am Main, 1994).
82 For a critique of 'rights talk' see Mary Ann Glendon, *Rights Talk: The
Impoverishment of Political Discourse* (New York, 1991).
83 I used this formulation for the first time in my article 'Angst vor der
Freiheit?', *Die Zeit*, 11 April 1997. It alludes, of course, to the 'New Golden
Rule' which Amitai Etzioni has placed at the centre of his communitarian
programme: 'Respect and uphold society's moral order as you would have
society respect and uphold your autonomy.' See Amitai Etzioni, *The New
Golden Rule. Community and Morality in a Democratic Society* (New York,
1996), here p. xviii.
84 The merit of Etzioni's book lies, in my opinion, in its creative contributions
to this space.
85 Ricoeur (in *Liebe und Gerechtigkeit*) elaborates this point best of all.
86 This question was developed and pursued for the United States by the
group around Robert Bellah. See especially Robert Bellah et al., *Habits of
the Heart*. For the application of this question in a German context, see my
'Communitarianism, A German Perspective', and especially my 'Was hält
die Bundesrepublik zusammen? Alte und neue Möglichkeiten sozialer
Integration', in Friedhelm Hengsbach and Matthias Möhring-Hesse (eds),
Eure Armut kotzt uns an. Solidarität in der Krise (Frankfurt am Main, 1995),
pp. 69–82.

Bibliography

Adeney, Frances S., 'Review of Taylor, *Sources of the Self*', *Theology Today*, 48 (1991), pp. 204–10.

Alexander, Jeffrey, 'Collective Action, Culture and Civil Society: Secularizing, Updating, Inverting, Revising and Displacing the Classical Model of Social Movements', in Jon Clark and Marco Diani (eds), *Alain Touraine* (London, 1996), pp. 205–34.

Alexander, Jeffrey, 'Theorizing the Good Society: Ethical, Normative and Empirical Discourses', Ms. (Los Angeles, 1996).

Alexander, Jeffrey and Smith, Philip, 'The Discourse of American Civil Society: A New Proposal for Cultural Studies', *Theory and Society*, 22 (1993), pp. 151–208.

Alexander, Thomas, *John Dewey's Theory of Art, Experience and Nature. The Horizon of Feeling* (Albany, NY, 1987).

Anderson, Joel, 'Starke Wertungen, Wünsche zweiter Ordnung und intersubjektive Kritik: Überlegungen zum Begriff ethischer Autonomie', *Deutsche Zeitschrift für Philosophie*, 42 (1994), pp. 97–119.

Antonio, Robert J., 'Nietzsche's Antisociology: Subjectified Culture and the End of History', *American Journal of Sociology*, 101 (1995), pp. 1–43.

Apel, Karl-Otto, *Charles S. Peirce: From Pragmatism to Pragmaticism* (Amherst, Mass., 1981).

Apel, Karl-Otto, *Diskurs und Verantwortung* (Frankfurt am Main, 1988).

Arnett, Willard, 'Critique of Dewey's Anticlerical Religious Philosophy', *Journal of Religion*, 34 (1954), pp. 256–66.

Bauman, Zygmunt, *Postmodern Ethics* (Oxford, 1993).

Baumgarten, Eduard, *Die geistigen Grundlagen des amerikanischen Gemeinwesens*, vol. 2 (Frankfurt am Main, 1938).

Beckert, Jens, *Grenzen des Marktes. Die sozialen Grundlagen wirtschaftlicher Effizienz* (Frankfurt am Main, 1997).

Bellah, Robert, 'The Idea of Practices in 'Habits'. A Response', in Charles H.

Reynolds and Ralph V. Norman (eds), *Community in America. The Challenge of 'Habits of the Heart'* (Berkeley, 1988), pp. 269–88.

Bellah, Robert, et al., *Habits of the Heart: Individualism and Commitment in American Life* (Berkeley/London, 1985).

Berger, Peter L. and Kellner, Hansfried, 'Marriage and the Construction of Reality', in Hans-Peter Dreitzel (ed.), *Recent Sociology No. 2. Patterns of Communicative Behavior* (London, 1970), pp. 49–72.

Berlin, Isaiah, *Vico and Herder* (London, 1976).

Bernstein, Richard, *John Dewey* (New York, 1967).

Bernstein, Richard, *The New Constellation. The Ethical-Political Horizons of Modernity/Postmodernity* (Cambridge, Mass., 1992).

Bernstein, Richard, 'The Retrieval of the Democratic Ethos', *Cardozo Law review*, 17 (1996), pp. 1127–1146.

Bershady, Harold, 'Introduction', in Max Scheler, *On Feeling and Knowing and Valuing* (Chicago, 1992), pp. 1–46.

Blewett, John, S.J., 'Democracy as Religion: Unity in Human Relations', in idem (ed.), *John Dewey: His Thought and Influence* (New York, 1966), pp. 33–58.

Bloch, Werner, 'Der Pragmatismus von Schiller und James', *Zeitschrift für Philosophie und philosophische Kritik*, 152 (1913), pp. 1–41 and 145–214.

Blumer, Herbert, *Symbolic Interactionism* (Englewood Cliffs, NJ, 1969).

Bühl, Walter, 'Max Scheler', in Dirk Käsler (ed.), *Klassiker des soziologischen Denkens*, vol. 2 (Munich, 1978), pp. 178–225.

Caillois, Roger, *L'homme et le sacré* (Paris, 1939).

Calhoun, Craig, 'Review of Charles Taylor, *Sources of the Self*', *Sociological Theory*, 3 (1991), pp. 232–63.

Capps, Donald and Jacobs, Janet (eds), *The Struggle for Life. A Companion to William James's 'The Varieties of Religious Experience'*, Society for the Scientific Study of Religion, Monograph Series, 9 (n.p., 1995).

Castoriadis, Cornelius, *The Imaginary Institution of Society* (Cambridge, 1987).

Cladis, Mark, *A Communitarian Defense of Liberalism. Émile Durkheim and Contemporary Social Theory* (Stanford, 1992).

Colapietro, Vincent, 'The Vanishing Subject of Contemporary Discourse: A Pragmatic Response', *Journal of Philosophy*, 87 (1990), pp. 644–55.

Coleman, James S., *Foundations of Social Theory* (Cambridge, Mass., 1990).

Comte-Sponville, André, *Petit traité des grandes vertus* (Paris, 1995).

Cook, Karen S., et al., 'Exchange Theory: A Blueprint for Structure and Process', in George Ritzer (ed.), *Frontiers of Social Theory. The New Syntheses* (New York, 1990), pp. 158–84.

Cotkin, George, *William James, Public Philosopher* (Urbana, Ill., 1994).

Croce, Paul Jerome, *Science and Religion in the Era of William James. Eclipse of Certainty, 1820–1880* (Chapel Hill, NC, 1995).

Denzin, Norman, 'Post-Pragmatism. A Review of Hans Joas, *Pragmatism and Social Theory*', *Symbolic Interaction*, 19 (1996), pp. 61–75.

Denzin, Norman, 'Prophetic Pragmatism and the Postmodern: A Comment on Maines', *Symbolic Interaction*, 19 (1996), pp. 341–55.

Deploige, Simon, *Le conflit de la morale et de la sociologie* (Paris, 1911).

Dewey, John, *Psychology* (1887), in *Early Works*, vol. 2 (Carbondale, Ill., 1967).

Dewey, John, 'Christianity and Democracy' (1893), in *Early Works*, vol. 4 (Carbondale, Ill., 1971), pp. 3–10.

Dewey, John, 'Self-Realization as the Moral Ideal' (1893), in *Early Works*, vol. 4 (Carbondale, Ill., 1971), pp. 42–53.

Dewey, John, 'Religion and Our Schools', *Hibbert Journal*, 6 (1908), pp. 796–809.

Dewey, John, *Human Nature and Conduct. An Introduction to Social Psychology* (New York, 1922).

Dewey, John, *Experience and Nature* (1929) (London, 1958).

Dewey, John, *A Common Faith* (New Haven, Conn., 1934).

Dewey, John, *Art as Experience* (1934) (New York, 1980).

Dewey, John, 'Experience, Knowledge, and Value: A Rejoinder', in Paul Arthur Schilpp (ed.), *The Philosophy of John Dewey* (Chicago, 1939); pp. 517–608.

Dewey, John, 'Theory of Valuation', in *International Encyclopedia of Unified Science*, vol. II, no. 4 (Chicago, 1939) *Later Works*, vol. 13 (Carbondale, Ill., 1988), pp. 189–251.

Dewey, John, *The Quest for Certainty* (New York, 1980).

Dewey, John, 'From Absolutism to Experimentalism', in *Later Works*, vol. 5 (Carbondale, Ill., 1984), pp. 147–60.

Dewey, John and Tufts, James, *Ethics* (New York, 1908 and 1932).

Diggins, John Patrick, *Mussolini and Fascism. The View from America* (Princeton, 1972).

Dilthey, Wilhelm, 'Das Problem der Religion', in idem, *Gesammelte Schriften*, vol. 6 (Leipzig/Berlin, 1924), pp. 288–305.

Dülmen, Richard van, 'Der deutsche Katholizismus und der Erste Weltkrieg', *Francia*, 2 (1974), pp. 347–76.

Durkheim, Émile, 'Individualism and the Intellectuals' (1898), *Political Studies*, 42 (1969), pp. 14–30.

Durkheim, Émile, 'De la définition des phénomènes religieux' (1899), in idem, *Journal sociologique* (Paris, 1969), pp. 140–65.

Durkheim, Émile, *Suicide: A Study in Sociology* (London, 1952).

Durkheim, Émile, 'The Determination of Moral Facts', in idem, *Sociology and Philosophy* (London, 1952), pp. 80–97.

Durkheim, Émile, 'Value Judgments and Judgments of Reality', in idem, *Sociology and Philosophy* (London, 1952), pp. 35–79.

Durkheim, Émile, *Essays on Morals and Education* (London, 1979).

Durkheim, Émile, *Pragmatism and Sociology* (Cambridge, 1983).

Durkheim, Émile, *The Division of Labour in Society* (Basingstoke, 1984).

Durkheim, Émile, *The Elementary Forms of Religious Life* (New York, 1995).

Durkheim, Émile and Mauss, Marcel, *Primitive Classification* (1903) (Chicago, 1994).

Edel, Abraham, 'Right and Good', in Philip Wiener (ed.), *Dictionary of the History of Ideas*, vol. 4 (New York, 1973), pp. 173–87.

Edel, Abraham, 'The Concept of Value and its Travels in Twentieth-Century America', in Murray G. Murphey and Ivar Berg (eds), *Values and Value Theory in Twentieth-Century America. Essays in Honour of Elizabeth Flower* (Philadelphia, 1988), pp. 12–36.

Edie, James M., *William James and Phenomenology* (Bloomington, Ind., 1987).

Eggenschwyler, Werner, 'War Nietzsche Pragmatist?', *Archiv für Geschichte der Philosophie*, 26 (1913), pp. 37–47.

Eisenstadt, Shmuel, 'Social Structure, Culture, Agency, and Change', in idem, *Power, Trust, and Meaning. Essays in Sociological Theory and Analysis* (Chicago, 1985), pp. 1–40.

Erikson, Erik H., *Identity and the Life Cycle* (New York, 1959).

Ertel, Chr., 'Von der Phänomenologie und jüngeren Lebensphilosophie zur Existentialphilosophie M. Heideggers', *Philosophisches Jahrbuch der Görres-Gesellschaft*, 51 (1938), pp. 1–28.

Etzioni, Amitai, *The Active Society* (New York, 1968).

Etzioni, Amitai, *The New Golden Rule. Community and Morality in a Democratic Society* (New York, 1996).

Etzioni, Amitai (ed.), *The Essential Communitarian Reader* (Lanham, Md., 1998).

Fetscher, Iring, 'Max Schelers Auffassung von Krieg und Frieden', in Paul Good (ed.), *Max Scheler im Gegenwartsgeschehen der Philosophie* (Berne/Munich, 1975), pp. 241–58.

Firsching, Horst, *Moral und Gesellschaft. Zur Soziologisierung des ethischen Diskurses in der Moderne* (Frankfurt am Main, 1994).

Firsching, Horst, 'Émile Durkheims Religionssoziologie – Made in Germany?', in Volkhard Krech and Hartmann Tyrell (eds), *Religionssoziologie um 1900* (Würzburg, 1995), pp. 351–63.

Firsching, Horst, 'Die Sakralisierung der Gesellschaft', in Volkhard Krech and Hartmann Tyrell (eds), *Religionssoziologie um 1900* (Würzburg, 1995), pp. 159–93.

Flanagan, Owen, 'Identity and Strong and Weak Evaluation', in idem and Amélie Rorty (eds), *Identity, Character, and Morality* (Cambridge, Mass., 1990), pp. 37–65.

Forst, Rainer, *Kontexte der Gerechtigkeit. Politische Philosophie jenseits von Liberalismus und Kommunitarinismus* (Frankfurt am Main, 1994).

Foucault, Michel, 'Nietzsche, Genealogy, History', in idem, *Language, Counter-Meaning, Practice: Selected Essays and Interviews* (Ithaca, NY, 1977), pp. 139–64.

Fournier, Marcel, *Marcel Mauss* (Paris, 1994).

Frankfurt, Harry, 'Freedom of the Will and the Concept of a Person', *Journal of Philosophy*, 67:1 (1971), pp. 5–20.

Frankfurt, Harry, 'The Importance of What We Care About', *Synthese*, 53 (1982), pp. 257–72.

Friess, Horace L., 'Dewey's Philosophy of Religion', in Jo Ann Boydston (ed.), *Guide to the Works of John Dewey* (Carbondale, Ill., 1970), pp. 200–17.

Frischeisen-Köhler, Max, 'Georg Simmel', *Kant-Studien*, 24 (1920), pp. 1–51.

Gadamer, Hans-Georg, 'Das ontologische Problem des Wertes', in *Kleine Schriften IV* (Tübingen, 1977), pp. 205–17.

Garfinkel, Harold, *Studies in Ethnomethodology* (Englewood Cliffs, NJ, 1967).

Gassen, Kurt and Landmann, Michael (eds), *Buch des Dankes an Georg Simmel* (Berlin, 1958).

Gebhardt, Jürgen, 'Die Werte. Zum Ursprung eines Schlüsselbegriffs der politisch-sozialen Sprache der Gegenwart in der deutschen Philosophie des späten 19. Jahrhunderts', in Rupert Hoffmann, Jörg Jantzen and Henning Ottmann (eds), *Anodos. Festschrift für Helmut Kuhn* (Weinheim, 1989), pp. 35–54.

Gephardt, Werner, 'Soziologie im Aufbruch. Zur Wechselwirkung von Durkheim, Schäffle, Tönnies und Simmel', *Kölner Zeitschrift für Soziologie und Sozialpsychologie*, 34 (1982), pp. 1–25.

Gergen, Kenneth, 'If Persons are Texts', in Stanley Messer, Louis Sass and Robert Woolfolk (eds), *Hermeneutics and Psychological Theory. Interpretive Perspectives on Personality, Psychotherapy, and Psychopathology* (New Brunswick, NJ, 1988), pp. 28–51.

Gergen, Kenneth, 'Rejoinder to Charles Taylor', in Stanley Messer, Louis Sass and Robert Woolfolk (eds), *Hermeneutics and Psychological Theory. Interpretive Perspectives on Personality, Psychotherapy, and Psychopathology* (New Brunswick, NJ, 1988), pp. 59–61.

Gergen, Kenneth, *The Saturated Self. Dilemmas of Identity in Contemporary Life* (New York, 1991).

Gerhardt, Volker, 'Die Moral des Immoralismus. Nietzsches Beitrag zu einer Grundlegung der Ethik', in Günther Abel und Jörg Salaquarda (eds), *Krisis der Metaphysik* (Berlin/New York, 1989), pp. 411–47.

Gerhardt, Volker, 'Selbstbegründung. Nietzsches Moral der Individualität', *Nietzsche-Studien*, 21 (1992), pp. 28–49.

Gerhardt, Volker, 'Die Tugend des freien Geistes. Nietzsche auf dem Weg zum individuellen Gesetz der Moral', in Simone Dietz et al. (eds), *Sich im Denken orientieren. Für Herbert Schnädelbach* (Frankfurt am Main, 1996), pp. 198–213.

Gerson, Hermann, 'Die Entwicklung der ethischen Anschauungen bei Georg Simmel', unpublished doctoral dissertation (University of Berlin, 1932).

Giddens, Anthony, *Modernity and Self-Identity. Self and Society in the Late Modern Age* (Cambridge, 1991).

Gleason, Philip, 'Identifying Identity: A Semantic History', *Journal of American History*, 69 (1983), pp. 910–27.

Glendon, Mary Ann, *Rights Talk: The Impoverishment of Political Discourse* (New York, 1991).

Good, Paul (ed.), *Max Scheler im Gegenwartsgeschehen der Philosophie* (Berne/Munich, 1975).

Gorevan, Patrick, 'Heidegger and Scheler. A Dialogue', *Journal of the British Society for Phenomenology*, 24 (1993), pp. 276–82.

Gouinlock, James, *John Dewey's Philosophy of Value* (New York, 1972).

Großheim, Michael, *Von Georg Simmel zu Martin Heidegger: Philosophie zwischen Leben und Existenz* (Berlin, 1994).

Günther, Klaus, *Der Sinn für Angemessenheit: Anwendungsdiskurse in Moral und Recht* (Frankfurt am Main, 1988).

Habermas, Jürgen, 'Vorbereitende Bemerkungen zu einer Theorie der kommunikativen Kompetenz', in idem and Niklas Luhmann, *Theorie der Gesellschaft oder Sozialtechnologie – Was leistet die Systemforschung?* (Frankfurt am Main, 1971), pp. 101–41.

Habermas, Jürgen, 'Labor and Interaction: Remarks on Hegel's Jena Philosophy of Mind', in idem, *Theory and Practice* (Boston, Mass., 1973), pp. 142–69.

Habermas, Jürgen, 'Stichworte zur Theorie der Sozialisation', in idem, *Kultur und Kritik* (Frankfurt am Main, 1973), pp. 118–94.

Habermas, Jürgen, 'Moralentwicklung und Ich-Identität', in idem, *Zur Rekonstruktion des Historischen Materialismus* (Frankfurt am Main, 1976), pp. 63–91.

Habermas, Jürgen, *The Philosophical Discourse of Modernity* (Cambridge, Mass., 1987).

Habermas, Jürgen, *The Structural Transformation of the Public Sphere* (Cambridge, 1989).

Habermas, Jürgen, 'Exkurs: Transzendenz von innen, Transzendenz ins Diesseits', in idem, *Texte und Kontexte* (Frankfurt am Main, 1991).

Habermas, Jürgen, 'Remarks on Discourse Ethics', in idem, *Justification and Application* (Cambridge, 1993), pp. 19–112.

Habermas, Jürgen, '"To Seek to Salvage an Unconditional Meaning without God is a Futile Undertaking": Reflections on a Remark of Max Horkheimer', in idem, *Justification and Application* (Cambridge, 1993), pp. 133–46.

Habermas, Jürgen, 'Georg Simmel on Philosophy and Culture: Postscript to a Collection of Essays', *Critical Inquiry*, 22 (1995), pp. 403–14.

Habermas, Jürgen, *Between Facts and Norms. Contributions to a Discourse Theory of Law and Democracy* (Cambridge, 1996).

Habermas, Jürgen, 'Reply to Symposium Participants', *Cardozo Law Review*, 17 (1996), pp. 1477–557.

Habermas, Jürgen, 'Rortys pragmatische Wende', *Deutsche Zeitschrift für Philosophie*, 44 (1996), pp. 715–41.

Habermas, Jürgen, *The Inclusion of the Other. Studies in Political Theory* (Cambridge, 1998).

Hechter, Michael, 'Values Research in the Social and Behavioural Sciences', in Michael Hechter, Lynn Nadel and Richard E. Michod (eds), *The Origin of Values* (New York, 1993), pp. 1–28.

Hechter, Michael, 'The Role of Values in Rational-Choice Theory', *Rationality and Society*, 6 (1994), pp. 318–33.

Heidegger, Martin, *Being and Time* (London, 1962).

Heidegger, Martin, 'Andenken an Max Scheler', in Paul Good (ed.), *Max Scheler im Gegenwartsgeschehen der Philosophie* (Berne/Munich, 1975), p. 9.

Heidegger, Martin, 'The Word of Nietzsche "God is Dead"', in idem, *The*

Question Concerning Technology and Other Essays (New York, 1977), pp. 53–112.

Helle, Horst Jürgen, 'Enleitung', in idem (ed.) *Georg Simmel. Gesammelte Schniften zur Religious soziologie.* (Berlin, 1989), pp. 7–35.

Hennis, Wilhelm, 'The Spiritualist Foundations of Max Weber's "Interpretive sociology": Weber, Troeltsch and William James's "Varieties of Religious Experience"', in *History of Human Sciences*, 11 (1998), pp. 83–101.

Herder, Johann Gottfried, *Abhandlung über den Ursprung der Sprache* (1772), in *Werke*, vol. 2 (Berlin/Weimar, 1982), pp. 89–200.

Honneth, Axel, 'Diskursethik und implizites Gerechtigkeitskonzept', in Wolfgang Kuhlmann (ed.), *Moralität und Sittlichkeit. Das Problem Hegels und die Diskursethik* (Frankfurt am Main, 1986), pp. 183–93.

Honneth, Axel, 'Nachwort', in Charles Taylor, *Negative Freiheit? Zur Kritik des neuzeitlichen Individualismus* (Frankfurt am Main, 1988), pp. 295–314.

Honneth, Axel, *The Critique of Power: Reflective Stages in a Critical Social Theory* (Cambridge, Mass./London, 1991).

Honneth, Axel, 'Dezentrierte Autonomie. Moralphilosophische Konsequenzen aus der modernen Subjektkritik', in Christoph Menke and Martin Seel (eds), *Zur Verteidigung der Vernunft gegen ihre Liebhaber und Verächter* (Frankfurt am Main, 1993), pp. 149–63.

Honneth, Axel, 'The Other of Justice: Habermas and the Ethical Challenge of Postmodernism', in Stephen White (ed.), *Cambridge Companion to Habermas* (Cambridge, 1995), pp. 289–325.

Honneth, Axel, *The Struggle for Recognition* (Cambridge, 1995).

Honneth, Axel, 'Between Proceduralism and Teleology. An Unsolved Conflict in John Dewey's Moral Theory', *Transactions of the Charles Sanders Pierce Society*, 34 (1998), pp. 689–711.

Honneth, Axel (ed.), *Kommunitarismus* (Frankfurt am Main, 1993).

Honneth, Axel and Joas, Hans, *Social Action and Human Nature* (Cambridge, 1988).

Inglehart, Ronald, *The Silent Revolution. Changing Values and Political Styles among Western Publics* (Princeton, 1977).

Inglehart, Ronald, *Cultural Change* (Princeton, 1989).

Isambert, François-André, 'L'élaboration de la notion de sacré dans l'école durkheimienne', *Archives des sciences sociales des religions*, vol. 21, no. 42 (1976), pp. 35–56.

James, Henry (ed.), *The Letters of William James*, 2 vols (Boston, Mass., 1920).

James, William, 'Bain and Renouvier' (1876), in idem, *Essays, Comments and Reviews* (Cambridge, Mass., 1987), pp. 321–4.

James, William, *The Principles of Psychology* (1890), Cambridge, Mass., 1981).

James, William, 'The Moral Philosopher and the Moral Life' (1897), in idem, *The Will to Believe and Other Essays in Popular Philosophy* (Cambridge, Mass., 1979), pp. 141–62.

James, William, 'The Will to Believe' (1897), in idem, *The Will to Believe and Other Essays in Popular Philosophy* (Cambridge, Mass., 1979), pp. 13–33.

James, William, 'A Certain Blindness in Human Beings', in idem, *Talks to*

Teachers on Psychology and to Students on Some of Life's Ideals (1899) (Cambridge, Mass., 1983), pp. 132–49.

James, William, 'The Will', in idem, *Talks to Teachers on Psychology and to Students on Some of Life's Ideals* (1899) (Cambridge, Mass., 1983), pp. 101–14.

James, William, *The Varieties of Religious Experience* (1902) (Cambridge, Mass., 1985).

James, William, *A Pluralistic Universe* (1909) (Cambridge, Mass., 1977).

Joas, Hans, *G. H. Mead: A Contemporary Re-examination of his Thought* (Cambridge, 1985).

Joas, Hans, 'Review of W. S. F. Pickering, *Durkheim's Sociology of Religion*', *American Journal of Sociology*, 92 (1986/7), pp. 740–1.

Joas, Hans, 'The Unhappy Marriage of Hermeneutics and Functionalism', in Axel Honneth and Hans Joas (eds), *Communicative Action* (Cambridge, 1991), pp. 97–118; also in Hans Joas, *Pragmatism and Social Theory* (Chicago/London, 1993), pp. 125–53.

Joas, Hans, *Pragmatism and Social Theory* (Chicago, 1993).

Joas, Hans, 'American Pragmatism and German Thought: A History of Misunderstandings', in Hans Joas, *Pragmatism and Social Theory* (Chicago/London, 1993), pp. 94–121.

Joas, Hans, 'Communitarianism. A German Perspective', Indiana University Institute for Advanced Study. Distinguished Lecture Series, vol. 6 (Bloomington, Ind., 1993).

Joas, Hans, 'Durkheim and Pragmatism: The Psychology of Consciousness and the Social Constitution of Categories', in idem, *Pragmatism and Social Theory* (Chicago/London, 1993), pp. 55–78.

Joas, Hans, 'Institutionalization as a Creative Process', in idem, *Pragmatism and Social Theory* (Chicago/London, 1993), pp. 154–71.

Joas, Hans, 'Pragmatism and American Sociology', in idem, *Pragmatism and Social Theory* (Chicago/London, 1993), pp. 14–51.

Joas, Hans, 'Sprayed and Betrayed. Gewalterfahrung im Vietnamkrieg und ihre Folgen', in Hans Joas and Wolfgang Knöbl (eds), *Gewalt in den USA* (Frankfurt am Main, 1994), pp. 300–13.

Joas, Hans, 'Kriegsideologien. Der Erste Weltkrieg im Spiegel der zeitgenössischen Sozialwissenschaften', *Leviathan*, 23 (1995), pp. 336–50.

Joas, Hans, 'Was hält die Bundesrepublik zusammen? Alte und neue Möglichkeiten sozialer Integration', in Friedrich Hengsbach and Matthias Möhring-Hesse (eds), *Eure Armut kotzt uns an. Solidarität in der Krise* (Frankfurt am Main, 1995), pp. 69–82.

Joas, Hans, *The Creativity of Action* (Cambridge, 1996).

Joas, Hans, 'Economic Action, Social Action, and the Genesis of Values. An Essay on Amitai Etzioni's Contribution to Social Theory', in David Sciulli (ed.), *Macro Socio-Economics. From Theory to Activism* (London/Armonk, NY, 1996), pp. 35–50.

Joas, Hans, 'Ein Pragmatist wider Willen?', *Deutsche Zeitschrift für Philosophie*, 44 (1996), pp. 661–70.

Joas, Hans, 'Angst vor der Freiheit?', *Die Zeit*, 11 April 1997.

Joas, Hans, 'Handlungstheorie und Gewaltdynamik', in Wolfgang Vogt (ed.), *Gewalt und Konfliktbearbeitung* (Baden-Baden, 1997), pp. 67–74.

Joas, Hans, 'The Autonomy of the Self. The Meadian Heritage and its Postmodern Challenge', *European Journal of Social Theory*, 1 (1998), pp. 7–18.

Jones, Robert Alun, 'On Understanding a Sociological Classic', *American Journal of Sociology*, 83 (1977/8), pp. 279–319.

Jones, Robert Alun, 'Robertson Smith, Durkheim and Sacrifice: An Historic Context for "The Elementary Forms of the Religious Life"', *Journal of the History of the Behavioral Sciences*, 17 (1981), pp. 184–205.

Jones, Robert Alun, 'Durkheim, Frazer, and Smith: The Role of Analogies and Exemplars in the Development of Durkheim's Sociology of Religion', *American Journal of Sociology*, 92 (1986/7), pp. 596–627.

Kamper, Dietmar, 'Die Auflösung der Ich-Identität', in Friedrich A. Kittler (ed.), *Austreibung des Geistes aus den Geisteswissenschaften* (Paderborn, 1980), pp. 79–86.

Kant, Immanuel, *Critique of Practical Reason*, in idem, *Practical Philosophy* (Cambridge, 1997), pp. 137–271.

Kaufmann, Walter, *Nietzsche. Philosopher. Psychologist. Antichrist* (Princeton, 1950).

Keupp, Heiner, 'Grundzüge einer reflexiven Sozialpsychologie. Postmoderne Perspektiven', in idem (ed.), *Zugänge zum Subjekt. Perspektiven einer reflexiven Sozialpsychologie* (Frankfurt am Main, 1994), pp. 226–74.

Kluckhohn, Clyde, et al., 'Values and Value-Orientations in the Theory of Action. An Exploration in Definition and Classification', in Talcott Parsons and Edward Shils (eds), *Toward a General Theory of Action* (New York, 1951), pp. 388–433.

Köhnke, Klaus Christian, *Der junge Simmel in Theoriebeziehungen und sozialen Bewegungen* (Frankfurt am Main, 1996).

Krämer, Hans, *Integrative Ethik* (Frankfurt am Main, 1995).

Krappmann, Lothar, *Soziologische Dimensionen der Identität. Strukturelle Bedingungen für die Teilnahme an Interaktionsprozessen* (Stuttgart, 1971).

Krech, Volkhard, 'Religion zwischen Soziologie und Philosophie. Entwicklungslinien und Einheit des Religionsverständnisses Georg Simmels', *Simmel-Newsletter*, 2 (1992), pp. 124–38.

Krech, Volkhard, 'Zwischen Historisierung und Transformation von Religion: Diagnosen zur religiösen Lage um 1900 bei Max Weber, Georg Simmel und Ernst Troeltsch', in Volkhard Krech and Hartmann Tyrell (eds), *Religionssoziologie um 1900* (Würzburg, 1995), pp. 313–49.

Krech, Volkhard and Tyrell, Hartmann, 'Religionssoziologie um die Jahrhundertwende', in idem (eds), *Religionssoziologie um 1900* (Würzburg, 1995), pp. 11–78.

Kuhn, Helmut, 'Werte – eine Urgegebenheit', in Hans-Georg Gadamer and Paul Vogler (eds), *Neue Anthropologie*, vol. 7 (Stuttgart, 1975), pp. 343–73.

Lehman, Edward, 'The Cultural Dimension of the "Active Society"', unpub. MA (New York University, 1995).

Bibliography

Leinberger, Paul and Tucker, Bruce, *The New Individualists. The Generation after the Organization Man* (New York, 1991).

Leuba, James, 'Studies in the Psychology of Religious Phenomena', *American Journal of Psychology*, 7 (1896), pp. 345–7.

Lévi-Strauss, Claude, *Totemism* (London, 1964).

Levinson, Henry Samuel, *The Religious Investigations of William James* (Chapel Hill, NC, 1981).

Levinson, Henry, *Santayana, Pragmatism, and the Spiritual Life* (Chapel Hill, NC/London, 1992).

Lichtblau, Klaus, *Kulturkrise und Soziologie um die Jahrhundertwende. Zur Genese der Kultursoziologie in Deutschland* (Frankfurt am Main, 1996).

Lockwood David, *Solidarity and Schism. The Problem of Disorder in Durkheimian and Marxist Sociology* (Oxford, 1992).

Luhmann, Niklas, *Zweckbegriff und Systemrationalität* (Tübingen, 1968).

Lukes, Steven, *Émile Durkheim. His Life and Work* (London, 1975).

Lyotard, Jean-François, *The Postmodern Condition. A Report on Knowledge* (Manchester, 1984).

McCarthy, Thomas, 'Legitimacy and Diversity: Dialectical Reflections on Analytical Distinctions', *Cardozo Law Review*, 17 (1996), pp. 1083–125.

MacIntyre, Alasdair, *After Virtue: A Study in Moral Theory* (London, 1981).

Maines, David, 'On Choices and Criticism: A Reply to Denzin', *Symbolic Interaction*, 19 (1996), pp. 357–62.

Maines, David, 'On Postmodernism, Pragmatism, and Plasterers: Some Interactionist Thoughts and Queries', *Symbolic Interaction*, 19 (1996), pp. 323–40.

Marty, Martin, *Modern American Religion*, vol. 1, *The Irony of It All, 1893–1919* (Chicago, 1986).

Mauss, Marcel, review of William James, *Varieties of Religious Experience*, in idem, *Oeuvres*, vol. 1 (Paris, 1968), pp. 58–65.

Mead, George Herbert, 'The Psychological Bases of Internationalism', *Survey*, 33 (1915), pp. 604–7.

Mead, George Herbert, 'The Psychology of Punitive Justice', *American Journal of Sociology*, 23 (1918), pp. 577–602.

Mead, George Herbert, 'National-Mindedness and International-Mindedness', *International Journal of Ethics*, 39 (1929), pp. 385–407.

Mead, George Herbert, *Mind, Self and Society* (Chicago, 1934).

Mead, George Herbert, *Selected Writings*, ed. Andrew Reck (Indianapolis, 1964).

Meier, Kurt, 'Gibt es einen "Bruch" in Durkheims früher Religionssoziologie?', in Volkhard Krech and Hartmann Tyrell (eds), *Religionssoziologie um 1900* (Würzburg, 1995), pp. 129–57.

Menand, Louis, 'W. James and the Case of the Epileptic Patient', *New York Review of Books*, 17 December 1998, pp. 81–93.

Menke, Christoph, 'Die Vernunft im Widerstreit. Über den richtigen Umgang mit praktischen Konflikten', in idem and Martin Seel (eds), *Zur Verteidigung der Vernunft gegen ihre Liebhaber und Verächter* (Frankfurt am Main, 1993), pp. 197–218.

Menke, Christoph, *Tragödie im Sittlichen. Gerechtigkeit und Freiheit nach Hegel* (Frankfurt am Main, 1996).

Merleau-Ponty, Maurice, 'Christianisme et ressentiment', *La vie intellectuelle*, 36 (1935), pp. 278–306.

Messer, Stanley, Sass, Louis and Woolfolk, Robert (eds), *Hermeneutics and Psychological Theory. Interpretive Perspectives on Personality, Psychotherapy, and Psychopathology* (New Brunswick, NJ, 1988).

Moosa, Imtiaz, 'A Critical Examination of Scheler's Justification of the Existence of Values', *Journal of Value Inquiry*, 25 (1991), pp. 23–41.

Moosa, Imtiaz, 'Are Values Independent Entities? Scheler's Discussion of the Relation between Values and Persons', *Journal of the British Society for Phenomenology*, 24 (1993), pp. 265–75.

Moosa, Imtiaz, 'Formalism of Kant's A Priori versus Scheler's Material A Priori', *International Studies in Philosophy*, 27 (1995), pp. 33–47.

Morgan, Michael L., 'Religion, History and Moral Discourse', in James Tully (ed.), *Philosophy in an Age of Pluralism. The Philosophy of Charles Taylor in Question* (Cambridge, 1994), pp. 49–66.

Moussa, Mario, 'Writing the History of the "We". The Claims of Practice', *Social Theory and Practice*, 18 (1992), pp. 211–29.

Müller, Horst, *Lebensphilosophie und Religion bei Georg Simmel* (Berlin, 1960).

Müller-Freienfels, Richard, 'Nietzsche und der Pragmatismus', *Archiv für Geschichte der Philosophie*, 26 (1913), pp. 339–58.

Murdoch, Iris, *The Sovereignty of Good* (London, 1970).

Nehamas, Alexander, *Nietzsche. Life as Literature* (Cambridge, Mass., 1985).

Niebuhr, Reinhold, 'A Footnote on Religion', *The Nation*, 139 (1934), pp. 358–9.

Nietzsche, Friedrich, *The Birth of Tragedy and The Case of Wagner* (New York, 1967).

Nietzsche, Friedrich, *Twilight of the Idols and the Antichrist* (Harmondsworth, 1968).

Nietzsche, Friedrich, *Ecce Homo* (Harmondsworth, 1979).

Nietzsche, Friedrich, *On the Genealogy of Morality* (Cambridge, 1994).

Otto, Rudolf, *Das Heilige*, (Breslau, 1918).

Parsons, Talcott, 'The Place of Ultimate Values in Sociological Theory', *International Journal of Ethics*, 45 (1935), pp. 282–316.

Parsons, Talcott, *The Structure of Social Action* (New York, 1937).

Parsons, Talcott, 'On the Concept of Value-Commitments', in idem, *Politics and Social Structure* (New York, 1969), pp. 439–72.

Pascal, Blaise, *Pensées* (London, 1962).

Patterson, Orlando, *Freedom*, vol. 1, *Freedom in the Making of Western Culture* (New York, 1991).

Perry, Ralph Barton, *The Thought and Character of William James*, 2 vols (Boston, Mass., 1935).

Pfleiderer, Georg, *Theologie als Wirklichkeitswissenschaft. Studien zum Religionsbegriff bei Georg Wobbermin, Rudolf Otto, Heinrich Scholz und Max Scheler* (Tübingen, 1992).

Piaget, Jean, *The Moral Judgement of the Child* (Harmondsworth, 1977).

Pickering, W. S. F., *Durkheim's Sociology of Religion* (London, 1984).

Ramsey, Bennett, *Submitting to Freedom* (New York, 1993).

Randall, John Herman, Jr., 'The Religion of Shared Experience', in Horace M. Kallen (ed.), *The Philosopher of the Common Man. Essays in Honour of John Dewey to Celebrate his Eightieth Birthday* (New York, 1940), pp. 106–45.

Ranulf, Svend, 'Scholarly Forerunners of Fascism', *Ethics*, 50 (1939), pp. 16–34.

Rawls, John, *A Theory of Justice* (Oxford, 1980).

Reese-Schäfer, Walter, ' "Nach innen geht der geheimnisvolle Weg". Einige kritische Bermerkungen zu Charles Taylors Ontologie der Moralität und des modernen Selbst', *Deutsche Zeitschrift für Philosophie*, 44 (1996), pp. 621–34.

Reiter, Michael, 'Opferordnung. Philosophisches Unbehagen in der modernen Kultur und Faszination der Gewalt im Ersten Weltkrieg', unpublished doctoral dissertation (Freie Universität Berlin, 1995).

Renouvier, Charles Bernard, *Essais de critique générale* (Paris, 1875).

Richardson, Henry, 'Beyond Good and Right: Toward a Constructive Ethical Pragmatism', *Philosophy and Public Affairs*, 24 (1995), pp. 108–41.

Ricoeur, Paul, *Liebe und Gerechtigkeit* (Tübingen, 1990).

Ricoeur, Paul, *Oneself as Another* (Chicago/London, 1992).

Rockefeller, Steven, *John Dewey. Religious Faith and Democratic Humanism* (New York, 1991).

Rorty, Richard, *Philosophy and The Mirror of Nature* (Princeton, 1979).

Rorty, Richard, *Contingency, Irony, Solidarity* (Cambridge, 1989).

Rorty, Richard, *Essays on Heidegger and Others* (Cambridge, 1991).

Rorty, Richard, 'Freud and Moral Reflection', in idem, *Essays on Heidegger and Others* (Cambridge, 1991), pp. 143–62.

Rorty, Richard, *Objectivity, Relativism, and Truth* (Cambridge, 1991).

Rorty, Richard, 'Non-Reductive Physicalism', in idem, *Objectivity, Relativism, and Truth* (Cambridge, 1991), pp. 113–25.

Rorty, Richard, 'Review of Charles Taylor, *Sources of the Self*', *Philosophy and Phenomenological Research*, 54 (1994), pp. 197–201.

Rorty, Richard, 'Fraternity Reigns', *The New York Times Magazine*, 29 September 1996.

Rosa, Hartmut, *Identität und kulturelle Praxis. Politische Philosophie nach Charles Taylor* (Frankfurt am Main, 1998).

Roth, John K., 'William James, John Dewey and the "Death-of-God", *Religious Studies*, 7 (1971), pp. 53–61.

Roth, Robert, S.J., *John Dewey and Self-Realization* (Englewood Cliffs, NJ, 1962).

Roth, Robert, S.J., *American Religious Philosophy* (New York, 1967).

Ryan, Alan, *John Dewey and the High Tide of American Liberalism* (New York, 1995).

Saatkamp, Herman, Jr. (ed.), *Rorty and Pragmatism. The Philosopher Responds to his Critics* (Nashville, Tenn., 1995).

Santayana, George, 'Reason in Religion', in idem, *Works*, vol. 4 (New York, 1936), pp. 3–206.

Schaub, Edward, 'Dewey's Interpretation of Religion', in Paul Arthur Schilpp (ed.), *The Philosophy of John Dewey* (Evanston, Ill., 1939), pp. 393–416.

Scheler, Max, *Vom Umsturz der Werte. Abhandlungen und Aufsätze*, in idem, *Gesammelte Werke*, vol. 3 (Berne, 1955).

Scheler, Max, *Schriften aus dem Nachlaß*, vol. 1, in idem, *Gesammelte Werke*, vol. 10 (Berne, 1957).

Scheler, Max, *Erkenntnis und Arbeit. Eine Studie über Wert und Grenzen des pragmatischen Motivs in der Erkenntnis der Welt*, in idem, *Gesammelte Werke*, vol. 8 (Berne, 1960), pp. 191–382.

Scheler, Max, *On the Eternal in Man* (London, 1960).

Scheler, Max, *Ressentiment* (New York, 1961).

Scheler, Max, *Schriften zur Soziologie und Weltanschauungslehre*, in idem, *Gesammelte Werke*, vol. 6 (Berne, 1963).

Scheler, Max, *The Nature of Sympathy* (London, 1964).

Scheler, Max, *Formalism in Ethics and Non-Formal Ethics of Value* (Evanston, Ill., 1973).

Scheler, Max, 'Die Stellung des Menschen im Kosmos', in idem, *Späte Schriften*, *Gesammelte Werke*, vol. 9 (Berne, 1976), pp. 7–71.

Scheler, Max, *Politisch-pädagogische Schriften*, in idem, *Gesammelte Werke*, vol. 4 (Berne, 1982).

Schluchter, Wolfgang, *Religion und Lebensführung*, 2 vols (Frankfurt am Main, 1988).

Schluchter, Wolfgang, *Rationalism, Religion and Domination* (Berkeley/Oxford, 1989).

Schmitt, Carl, 'Die Tyrannei der Werte', in *Säkularisation und Utopie. Ebracher Studien. Ernst Forsthoff zum 65. Geburtstag* (Stuttgart, 1967), pp. 37–62.

Schnädelbach, Herbert, *Philosophy in Germany 1831–1933* (Cambridge, 1984).

Schneewind, Jerome, 'Review of Charles Taylor, *Sources of the Self*', *Journal of Philosophy*, 88 (1991), pp. 422–6.

Schöfthaler, Traugott and Goldschmidt, Dietrich (eds), *Soziale Struktur und Vernunft* (Frankfurt am Main, 1984).

Schubert, Hans-Joachim, *Demokratische Identität. Der soziologische Pragmatismus von Charles Horton Cooley* (Frankfurt am Main, 1995).

Schütz, Alfred, 'Max Scheler's Epistemology and Ethics', in idem, *Collected Papers*, vol. 3 (The Hague, 1996), pp. 145–78.

Schütz, Alfred, 'Max Scheler's Philosophy', in idem, *Collected Papers*, vol. 3 (The Hague, 1996), pp. 133–44.

Seel, Martin, 'Die Wiederkehr der Ethik des guten Lebens', *Merkur*, 45 (1991), pp. 42–9.

Seel, Martin, *Versuch über die Form des Glücks. Studien zur Ethik* (Frankfurt am Main, 1995).

Selznick, Philip, *The Moral Commonwealth. Social Theory and the Promise of Community* (Berkeley, 1992).

Shea, William, 'John Dewey: Aesthetic and Religious Experience', in idem, *The Naturalists and the Supernatural. Studies in Horizon and an American Philosophy of Religion* (Macon, Ga., 1984), pp. 117–41.

Simmel, Georg, *Einleitung in die Moralwissenschaft. Eine Kritik der ethischen Grundbegriffe*, 2 vols (Berlin, 1892–3).

Simmel, Georg, *The Philosophy of Money* (1900) (London, 1978).

Simmel, Georg, *Schopenhauer and Nietzsche* (1907) (Amherst, Mass., 1986).

Simmel, Georg, *Der Krieg und die geistigen Entscheidungen* (Munich, 1917).

Simmel, Georg, *Kant und Goethe* (Leipzig, 1918).

Simmel, Georg, *Lebensanschauung* (Munich/Leipzig, 1918 and 1922).

Simmel, Georg, *Das individuelle Gesetz*, ed. Michael Landmann (Frankfurt am Main, 1968).

Simmel, Georg, *Essays on Religion* (New Haven/London, 1997).

Sloterdijk, Peter, 'Chancen im Ungeheuren. Notiz zum Gestaltwandel des Religiösen in der modernen Welt im Anschluß an einige Motive bei William James (Introduction), in William James, *Die Vielfalt der religiösen Erfahrung* (Frankfurt am Main, 1997), pp. 11–34.

Smith, Nicholas, 'Contingency and Self-Identity. Taylor's Hermeneutics vs. Rorty's Postmodernism', *Theory, Culture and Society*, 13 (1996), pp. 105–20.

Squires, Judith (ed.), *Principled Positions. Postmodernism and the Rediscovery of Values* (London, 1993).

Starbuck, Edwin Diller, *Psychology of Religion* (New York, 1899).

Stikkers, Kenneth, 'Introduction', in Max Scheler, *Problems of a Sociology of Knowledge* (London, 1980), pp. 1–30.

Stikkers, Kenneth, 'Technologies of the World, Technologies of the Self: A Schelerian Critique of Dewey and Hickman', *Journal of Speculative Philosophy*, 10 (1996), pp. 62–73.

Straub, Jürgen, 'Identitätstheorie im Übergang? Über Identitätsforschung, den Begriff der Identität und die zunehmende Beachtung des Nicht-Identischen in subjekttheoretischen Diskursen', *Sozialwissenschaftliche Literaturrundschau*, 23 (1991), pp. 49–71.

Straub, Jürgen, 'Identität und Sinnbildung. Ein Beitrag aus der Sicht einer handlungs- und erzähltheoretischen Sozialpsychologie', in *Jahresbericht 1994/5 des Zentrums für interdisziplinäre Forschung* (Bielefeld, 1996), pp. 42–90.

Straub, Jürgen, 'Geschichte, Identität und Lebensglück. Eine psychologische Lektüre "unzeitgemäßer Betrachtungen" ', in Klaus Müller and Jörn Rüssen (eds), *Historische Sinnbildung* (Reinbek, 1997), pp. 165–94.

Strauß, Botho, 'Anschwellender Bocksgesang', in Heimo Schwilk and Ulrich Schacht (eds), *Die selbstbewußte Nation* (Berlin, 1994), pp. 19–40.

Suckiel, Ellen Kappy, *Heaven's Champion. William James's Philosophy of Religion* (Notre Dame, Ind., 1996).

Swidler, Ann, 'Culture in Action', *American Sociological Review*, 51 (1986), pp. 273–86.

Taylor, Charles, *The Explanation of Behaviour* (London, 1964).

Taylor, Charles, 'Neutrality in Political Science' (1967), in idem, *Philosophical Papers*, 2 vols (Cambridge, 1985), vol. 2, pp. 58–90.

Taylor, Charles, *Hegel* (Cambridge, 1975).

Taylor, Charles, 'Responsibility for Self', in Amélie Rorty (ed.), *The Identities of Persons* (Berkeley, 1976), pp. 281–99.
Taylor, Charles, 'Action as Expression', in Cora Diamond and Jenny Teichman (eds), *Intention and Intentionality. Essays in Honour of Gertrude E. M. Anscombe* (Brighton, 1979), pp. 73–89.
Taylor, Charles, *Philosophical Papers*, 2 vols (Cambridge, 1985).
Taylor, Charles, 'The Nature and Scope of Distributive Justice', in idem, *Philosophical Papers*, 2 vols (Cambridge, 1985), vol. 2, pp. 289–317.
Taylor, Charles, 'Self-Interpreting Animals', in idem, *Philosophical Papers*, 2 vols (Cambridge, 1985), vol. 1, pp. 45–76.
Taylor, Charles, 'Die Motive einer Verfahrensethik', in Wolfgang Kuhlmann (ed.), *Moralität und Sittlichkeit. Das Problem Hegels und die Diskursethik* (Frankfurt am Main, 1986), pp. 101–35.
Taylor, Charles, 'Le juste et le bien', *Revue de métaphysique et de morale*, 93 (1988), pp. 33–56.
Taylor, Charles, 'Cross-Purposes: The Liberal-Communitarian Debate', in Nancy Rosenblum (ed.), *Liberalism and the Moral Life* (Cambridge, Mass., 1989), pp. 139–82.
Taylor, Charles, *Sources of the Self. The Making of the Modern Identity* (Cambridge, 1989).
Taylor, Charles, 'Language and Society', in Axel Honneth and Hans Joas (eds), *Communicative Action. Essays on Jürgen Habermas' 'The Theory of Communicative Action'* (Cambridge, 1991), pp. 23–35.
Taylor, Charles, *The Ethics of Authenticity* (Cambridge, Mass., 1992).
Taylor, Charles, 'Reply to Richard Rorty', *Philosophy and Phenomenological Research*, 54 (1994), pp. 211–13.
Taylor, Charles, 'Reply and Re-articulation', in James Tully (ed.), *Philosophy in an Age of Pluralism. The Philosophy of Charles Taylor in Question* (Cambridge, 1994), pp. 213–57.
Taylor, Charles, 'Explanation and Practical Reason', in idem, *Philosophical Arguments* (Cambridge, Mass., 1995), pp. 34–60.
Taylor, Charles, 'The Validity of Transcendental Arguments', in idem, *Philosophical Arguments* (Cambridge, Mass., 1995), pp. 20–33.
Theunissen, Michael, 'Wettersturm und Stille. Über die Weltdeutung Schelers und ihr Verhältnis zum Seinsdenken', in Paul Good (ed.), *Max Scheler im Gegenwartsgeschehen der Philosophie* (Berne/Munich, 1975), pp. 91–110.
Thome, Helmut, *Wertewandel in der Politik? Eine Auseinandersetzung mit Ingleharts Thesen zum Postmaterialismus* (Berlin, 1985).
Tiryakian, Edward, 'Durkheim, Mathiez, and the French Revolution. The Political Context of a Sociological Classic', *Archives européennes de sociologie*, 29 (1988), pp. 373–96.
Tönnies, Ferdinand, *Der Nietzsche-Kultus. Eine Kritik* (Leipzig, 1897).
Touraine, Alain, *Production de la société* (Paris, 1964).
Troeltsch, Ernst, Review of William James, *The Varieties of Religious Experience*, *Deutsche Literaturzeitung*, 25 (1904), pp. 3021–7.
Troeltsch, Ernst, 'Empirismus und Platonismus in der Religionsphilosophie.

Zur Erinnerung an William James', in idem, *Gesammelte Schriften*, vol. 2 (Tübingen, 1913), pp. 364–85.

Troeltsch, Ernst, *Der Historismus und seine Probleme*, in idem, *Gesammelte Schriften*, vol. 3 (Tübingen, 1922).

Tugendhat, Ernst, *Selbstbewußtsein und Selbstbestimmung* (Frankfurt am Main, 1979).

Tugendhat, Ernst, 'Korreferat zu Charles Taylor, "What is Human Agency?"', in idem, *Philosophische Aufsätze* (Frankfurt am Main, 1992), pp. 441–52.

Tully, James (ed.), *Philosophy in an Age of Pluralism. The Philosophy of Charles Taylor in Question* (Cambridge, 1994).

Turner, Ralph, 'The Real Self: From Institution to Impulse', *American Journal of Sociology*, 81 (1975/6), pp. 989–1016.

Turner, Victor, *The Ritual Process: Structure and Anti-Structure* (Harmondsworth, 1974).

Tyrell, Hartmann, '"Das Religiöse" in Max Webers Religionssoziologie', *Saeculum*, 43 (1992), pp. 172–230.

Ullmann-Margalit, Edna, *The Emergence of Norms* (Oxford, 1977).

Ullrich, Peter-Otto, *Immanente Transzendenz. Georg Simmels Entwurf einer nachchristlichen Religionsphilosophie* (Frankfurt am Main, 1981).

Wallwork, Ernest, 'Durkheim's Early Sociology of Religion', *Sociological Analysis*, 46 (1985), pp. 201–18.

Wattenberg, Ben, *Values Matter Most: How Republicans or Democrats or a Third Party Can Win and Renew the American Way of Life* (New York, 1995).

Weber, Max, 'The Social Psychology of the World Religions', in H. H. Gerth and C. W. Mills (eds), *From Max Weber* (London, 1947), pp. 267–301.

Weber, Max, *Ancient Judaism* (Glencoe, Ill., 1952).

Weber, Max, *Economy and Society*, 3 vols (New York, 1968).

Weigert, Andrew, 'Identity. Its Emergence within Sociological Psychology', *Symbolic Interaction*, 6 (1983), pp. 183–206.

Weinstock, Daniel W., 'The Political Theory of Strong Evaluation', in James Tully (ed.), *Philosophy in an Age of Pluralism. The Philosophy of Charles Taylor in Question* (Cambridge, 1994), pp. 171–93.

Weiß, Johannes, 'Verständigungsorientierung und Kritik', in idem, *Vernunft und Vernichtung. Zur Philosophie und Soziologie der Moderne* (Opladen, 1993), pp. 223–37.

Welchman, Jennifer, *Dewey's Ethical Thought* (Ithaca, NY, 1995).

Wellmer, Albrecht, *Ethik und Dialog. Elemente des moralischen Urteils bei Kant und in der Diskursethik* (Frankfurt am Main, 1986).

Wenzel, Harald, *Die Ordnung des Handelns. Talcott Parsons' Theorie des allgemeinen Handlungssystems* (Frankfurt am Main, 1991).

Wenzel, Harald, 'Gibt es ein postmodernes Selbst? Neuere Theorien und Diagnosen der Identität in fortgeschrittenen Gesellschaften', *Berliner Journal für Soziologie*, 1 (1995), pp. 113–31.

Westbrook, Robert, *John Dewey and American Democracy* (Ithaca, NY, 1991).

Whyte, William H., Jr., *The Organization Man* (Harmondsworth, 1963).

Wickert, Ulrich, *Der Ehrliche ist der Dumme. Über den Verlust der Werte* (Hamburg, 1994).

Williams, Bernard, *Ethics and the Limits of Philosophy* (London, 1985).

Wingert, Lutz, 'Der Grund der Differenz: Subjektivität als ein Moment von Intersubjektivität', in Micha Brumlik and Hauke Brunkhorst (eds), *Gemeinschaft und Gerechtigkeit* (Frankfurt am Main, 1993), pp. 290–305.

Wischke, Mirko, 'Der "Kampf der Moral mit den Grundinstinkten des Lebens". Über die Ambivalenz im Perspektivismus Friedrich Nietzsches', *Synthesis Philosophica*, 21 (1996), pp. 39–48.

Wolfe, Alan, 'Review of Charles Taylor, *Sources of the Self*', *Contemporary Sociology*, 19 (1990), pp. 627–8.

Wrong, Dennis, 'The Oversocialized Conception of Man in Modern Sociology', *American Sociological Review*, 26 (1961), pp. 183–95.

Yack, Bernard, *The Longing for Total Revolution. Philosophic Sources of Social Discontent from Rousseau to Marx and Nietzsche* (Princeton, 1986).

Index